The TALENT DEVELOPMENT PLANNING Handbook

The TALENT DEVELOPMENT PLANNING Handbook

Designing Inclusive Gifted Programs

Donald J. Treffinger • Grover C. Young
Carole A. Nassab • Edwin C. Selby • Carol V. Wittig

CORWIN PRESS
A SAGE Company
Thousand Oaks, CA 91320

For information:

Corwin Press
A SAGE Company
2455 Teller Road
Thousand Oaks, California 91320
www.corwinpress.com

SAGE India Pvt. Ltd.
B 1/I 1 Mohan Cooperative
    Industrial Area
Mathura Road, New Delhi 110 044
India

SAGE Ltd.
1 Oliver's Yard
55 City Road
London EC1Y 1SP
United Kingdom

SAGE Asia-Pacific Pte. Ltd.
33 Pekin Street #02-01
Far East Square
Singapore 048763

Printed in the United States of America

Library of Congress Cataloging-in-Publication Data

The talent development planning handbook: designing inclusive gifted programs/Donald J. Treffinger . . . [et al.].
        p. cm.
Includes bibliographical references and index.
ISBN 978-1-4129-5979-7 (cloth)
ISBN 978-1-4129-5980-3 (paper w/cd)
    1. Gifted children—Education—United States. 2. Gifted children—Education—United States—Curricula—Handbooks, manuals, etc. I. Treffinger, Donald J. II. Title.

LC3993.9.T35 2008
371.95—dc22   2007043277

This book is printed on acid-free paper.

08   09   10   11   12   10 9 8 7 6 5 4 3 2 1

Acquisitions Editor:	David Chao
Editorial Assistant:	Mary Dang
Production Editor:	Libby Larson
Copy Editor:	Rachel Keith
Typesetter:	C&M Digitals (P) Ltd.
Proofreader:	Sally Jaskold
Indexer:	Rick Hurd
Cover Designer:	Monique Hahn

Contents

Acknowledgements   **xi**

About the Authors   **xiii**

SECTION I: OVERVIEW   **1**

1. Introduction and Overview   **3**

Four Generations of Gifted Education   4

   Generation One: The Early 1970s   4

   Generation Two: The Late 1970s   4

   Generation Three: The 1980s Into the Early 1990s   5

   Generation Four: From the Mid-1990s to Today   6

Overview of the Handbook's Contents   10

   Section I. Overview   10

      Chapter 1. Introduction and Overview   10

      Chapter 2. The Six-Stage Systematic Planning Model   10

   Section II. Stage One—Prepare   10

      Chapter 3. Foundations for

         Contemporary Programming   10

      Chapter 4. Innovation and Change   10

      Chapter 5. Planning Logistics   10

   Section III. Stage Two—Clarify Where You Are Now   11

      Chapter 6. Needs Assessment   11

      Chapter 7. Checking the Climate   11

      Chapter 8. Programming Positives and Wish Lists   11

   Section IV. Stage Three—Decide Where to Go Next   11

      Chapter 9. Setting Goals for Your Desired Future   11

      Chapter 10. Constructing the Master Plan   11

      Chapter 11. Constructing the Building Action Plan   11

   Section V. Stage Four—Carry Out Programming   12

      Chapter 12. Implementing

         Contemporary Programming   12

   Section VI. Stage Five—Seek Talents and Strengths   12

      Chapter 13. Identification in

         Contemporary Talent Development   12

   Section VII. Stage Six—Ensure Quality,

     Innovation, and Continuous Improvement   12

      Chapter 14. Quality, Innovation,

        and Continuous Improvement   12

2. The Six-Stage Systematic Planning Model   **13**

  Benefits of Effective Planning   13

    Determine Goals and Objectives for Programming   13

    Focus on Priorities   13

    Facilitate Sharing of Responsibility   14

    Promote Effective Communication   14

    Build Ownership   14

    Stimulate Active Participation   14

    Establish a Foundation for Subsequent Decisions   14

    Avoid Premature Closure   14

    Reduce Dependency on Unilateral
      or Charismatic Leadership   14

  The Six-Stage Systematic Planning Model   15

    Prepare   16

    Clarify Where You Are Now   16

    Decide Where to Go Next   16

    Carry Out Programming   16

    Seek Talents and Strengths   17

    Ensure Quality, Innovation, and
      Continuous Improvement   17

SECTION II: STAGE ONE—PREPARE   **19**

3. Foundations for Contemporary Programming   **21**

  The Nature of Giftedness and Talent   21

    Broadening Conceptions   22

    Understanding a Contemporary View of Talent   22

    Implications for Contemporary Programming   25

      Seven Key Questions   25

      Strengths and Talents Can Be Nurtured   25

      Focus on Creative Productivity   26

      Stronger and Weaker Views of Giftedness   26

      New Challenges and Directions for Identification   27

      A Dual Challenge for Programming   28

  Rationale and Goals for Talent Development   28

  Fundamental Tenets and Beliefs   31

  Identifying the Important Goals and Outcomes for Students   33

  Deciding to Implement a Contemporary, Inclusive Approach   34

  Doing Your Homework   35

4. Innovation and Change   **37**

  The Challenges of Innovation and Change   37

  Responding to Innovation and Change   38

  New Approaches to Teaching and Learning   42

  The School Improvement Challenge   44

    Linking School Improvement and Talent Development   46

5. Planning Logistics   **49**

  Forming a Planning Committee   49

    School Board Participation   49

Community and Parent Participation................................50
Student Participation................................50
Other Human Factors to Consider................................50
Size of the Committee................................51
Fostering Effective Communication Channels................................52
Philosophy and Values of the Committee Members................................52
Developmental Conception of Leadership................................52
Planning for an Effective Group................................55
Getting Acquainted................................55
Group Behavior Guidelines................................56
Understanding and Applying Tools
for Generating and Focusing Ideas................................56
Generating Tools................................58
Focusing Tools................................59
An Informed, Progressive Outlook................................59
Establishing a Working Community
for Contemporary Programming................................60
State Your Goals at the Very Beginning................................60
Establish a Time Line................................60
Establish a Positive Group Climate................................60
Balancing Continuity and Coordination With Autonomy................................63
Take Your Time................................64
Write It All Down!................................64

**SECTION III: STAGE TWO—
CLARIFY WHERE YOU ARE NOW**................................**67**

6. Needs Assessment................................**69**
Interpretation of Needs Assessment Results................................79
Providing Feedback and Discussing Results................................79
Implications for Staff Development and Training................................81
Strengths................................81
Opportunities................................82
Neutral................................82
Challenges................................82
Major Concerns................................82
Additional Sources of Data................................82

7. Checking the Climate................................**87**
Assessing the School Context for Excellence................................88
Ready: Climate and History................................89
Willing: Strategic Priority of Task Development................................90
Able: Setting and Resource Commitments................................91
The Climate Survey for Contemporary Programming................................91
Linking the Inventory Results for
"Ready" With Nine Climate Dimensions................................91

8. Programming Positives and Wish Lists................................**97**
Your Programming Positives................................97
Some Tips for Identifying Programming Positives................................98

Your Wish List   101
Suggestions for Searching Successfully for
     Programming Positives and Wishes   101

**SECTION IV: STAGE THREE—DECIDE
WHERE TO GO NEXT   105**

9. Setting Goals for Your Desired Future   107

10. Constructing the Master Plan   119
The Master Plan   119
     Specific Components of the Master Plan   120
         Philosophy and Vision Statement   120
         Definitions   122
         Goals and Objectives   122
         Identification Policies and Procedures   124
         Programming Commitments   125
         Implementation Guidelines   125
         The Time Line   126
         Resource Considerations   126
         Coordination and Staffing   129
         Professional Development   130
         Evaluation   130
     The Master Plan: Uses and Format   130

11. Constructing the Building Action Plan   133
The Building Action Plan   133
Components of the Building Action Plan   134
     Rationale and Benefits   134
     Establish Your Philosophy and Definitions   135
     Stating Goals and Objectives   136
     Identify Your School's Uniqueness   136
     Assessing Students' Characteristics and Needs   137
     Examining the Regular School Program's Strengths   137
     Extending, Enhancing, or Expanding the Regular Program   138
     Identifying Active Participants and Leaders   138
     Staff Development   138
     Resource and Budget Implications   139
     The Implementation Time Line   139
     Links With Other Initiatives   139
     Evaluation Plan   139
Moving Forward   140

SECTION V: STAGE FOUR—CARRY OUT PROGRAMMING   141

12. Implementing Contemporary Programming   143
The Four Levels of Service   144
     Level I: Programming for All Students   144
     Level II: Programming for Many Students   144

Level III: Programming for Some Students	146
Level IV: Programming for a Few Students	147
Dimensions of Effectiveness and	
Criteria for Healthy School Programming	150
Effective Implementation of Programming	153
A Professional Partnership	157

SECTION VI: STAGE FIVE—SEEK TALENTS AND STRENGTHS — **161**

13. Identification in Contemporary Talent Development	**163**
Changing Views of Identification	163
Exploring New Opportunities and Directions	167
From Identification to Student Action Planning	167
Deliberate Search	168
Constructive Design	171
Monitor and Manage	174
Student Action Planning as a	
Collaborative Problem Solving Process	176
Summary	176

SECTION VII: STAGE SIX—ENSURE QUALITY, INNOVATION, AND CONTINUOUS IMPROVEMENT — **179**

14. Quality, Innovation, and Continuous Improvement	**181**
Elements of Effective Evaluation	183
Indicators of Quality in Programming	193
Innovation and Change	196
Continuous Improvement	196
The Role of the Planning Committee	197
Preparation for Implementation	198
Promoting and Supporting Building Efforts	198
Sharing, Discussing, and	
Updating the Building Action Plans	198
Resource Development and Allocation	198
Stimulating Staff Development Opportunities	199
Implementation and Management	199
Diagnostic Assessment of Student	
Characteristics and Needs	199
Sustaining Programming Positives	200
Extending Enrichment	
Opportunities for Many Students	200
Solving Problems and Stimulating Innovation	200
Monitoring and Coordinating Implementation	201
Continuing Evaluation and Long-Range Planning	201
Designing Regular Updates or Revisions	201
Continuing Evaluation Efforts	201
Long-Range Planning	201
Communication and School-Community Relations	202

Answering Questions   202

Disseminating Program Accomplishments
      and Promoting Good Public Relations   202

Conclusion: Planning Contemporary,
      Inclusive Programming for Talent Development   203

Appendix A: Constructing the Master Plan   **205**

Appendix B: Constructing the Building Action Plan   **215**

References   **223**

Index   **226**

Acknowledgments

Corwin Press would like to acknowledge the following for their contributions to the book:

Cheryl Brockman
Teacher of the Gifted
Jonathan Alder Local School District
Plain City, OH

Mary Beth Cary
Teacher of the Gifted
Worthy County Primary School
Sylvester, GA

Annette Dake
Teacher, Gifted K–5
Bridge Creek Elementary School
Blanchard, OK

Susan D'Angelo
Teacher, Grade 5 and Gifted
Adjunct Professor
Pineview School of the Gifted
University of South Florida
Nokomis, FL

Tara McGuigan
Teacher, Gifted and Talented Education Resource
Madison High School
San Diego City Schools
San Diego, CA

About the Authors

 **Donald J. Treffinger, PhD,** president of the Center for Creative Learning, Inc., in Sarasota, Florida, is an internationally known researcher, writer, teacher, and presenter in the areas of creativity, gifted education, and talent development. He has authored or coauthored more than 60 books and monographs, including *Creative Problem Solving: An Introduction* and *Enhancing and Expanding Gifted Programs: The Levels of Service Approach*, and more than 300 articles. Dr. Treffinger has served as a member of the faculty of several colleges and universities. He has been the recipient of the National Association for Gifted Children's Distinguished Service Award and the E. Paul Torrance Creativity Award. In 2005, Dr. Treffinger received the Risorgimento Award from Destination ImagiNation, Inc., and the International Creativity Award from the World Council for Gifted and Talented Children. Dr. Treffinger has served as editor of *Gifted Child Quarterly*, the research journal of the National Association for Gifted Children (NAGC), and as editor in chief of *Parenting for High Potential*, NAGC's quarterly magazine for parents.

 **Grover C. Young, MA,** of Sarasota, Florida, is an experienced teacher, school administrator, and coordinator of gifted programming and staff development. He has worked with schools and businesses in the areas of creative productive thinking, talent identification and development, and performance-based learning and assessment. Mr. Young has also been actively involved in research and writing on creativity characteristics and on talent development among youth orchestra members. He has worked closely with schools and school districts in planning, implementing, and evaluating talent development programming. Mr. Young is coauthor of *Building Creative Excellence*, *Thinking With Standards*, *The CPS Kit*, and *Enhancing and Expanding Gifted Programs: The Levels of Service Approach*, and has authored or coauthored more than 50 articles and chapters on creativity and talent development.

Carole A. Nassab, MA, MEd, of Sarasota, Florida, is an associate of the Center for Creative Learning. She earned graduate degrees at Harvard University and Lesley College and has been a middle school teacher, guidance counselor, principal, pupil personnel director, adjunct professor, and school board member. Ms. Nassab has authored or coauthored several publications for school and community use, including *Thinking Tools Lessons, Thinking With Standards, The CPS Kit,* and *Enhancing and Expanding Gifted Programs: The Levels of Service Approach.* She has conducted programs on thinking tools and Creative Problem Solving (CPS) for educators, substitute teachers, and teacher educators.

Edwin C. Selby, PhD, of Newton, New Jersey, serves as an associate and member of the board of directors of the Center for Creative Learning in Sarasota, Florida, and as an adjunct professor with Fordham University's Graduate School of Education. Dr. Selby served for many years as a public school music and drama teacher and as a board of education member and officer. He has authored or coauthored a number of articles and books on creativity, problem solving style, and instruction for creative learning and Creative Problem Solving, including *Thinking With Standards, The CPS Kit, VIEW: An Assessment of Problem-Solving Style,* and *An Introduction to Problem-Solving Style.* Dr. Selby has served as a trainer and evaluator for several projects on creativity, problem solving style, and talent development for state education agencies and international educational organizations, including Destination ImagiNation, Inc., and the Future Problem Solving Program.

Carol V. Wittig, MS, of Buffalo, New York, an associate and member of the board of directors of the Center for Creative Learning, is an experienced elementary classroom teacher and gifted programming specialist in public elementary and middle schools. She has been a lead contributor to curriculum development in language arts, math, and social studies for her school district and has also coauthored several publications on creativity and talent development, including *Thinking With Standards, The CPS Kit,* and *Enhancing and Expanding Gifted Programs: The Levels of Service Approach.* Ms. Wittig earned a master's in creative studies from the State University College at Buffalo and has presented many workshops on creativity, Creative Problem Solving, CPS facilitation, learning styles, and talent development both in the U.S. and abroad.

Section I

Overview

Introduction and Overview 1

This handbook concerns the planning and implementing of a contemporary, inclusive approach to programming for talent development. Its main purpose is to guide you in redesigning and revitalizing an existing program, or in designing a new program. It is *not* intended as a "basic textbook" or explanation of gifted education or gifted programs.

Let us begin by addressing some fundamental terminology. We use the phrase *programming for talent development* to refer to all of the efforts made by the home, school, and community to recognize and nurture the many and varied strengths, talents, and sustained interests of many students. We view programming for talent development as a commitment by a school or a school district, its parents, and its community to create, support, and sustain many services through which educators, parents, and community leaders collaborate to seek, bring out, and nurture the strengths, talents, sustained interests, and best potentials of their students. The goals and purposes of programming are broader and more powerful than the mere assigning of a single, fixed group of students to a single, fixed program. This handbook, therefore, does not merely concern "having a gifted program" in your school or school district. It deals with the dynamic and ongoing process of challenging many students to become aware of their best potentials, and to reach those potentials as fully as possible through the opportunities and services offered throughout the school program, the home, and the community.

By "contemporary, inclusive programming," then, our intent is to emphasize an approach to program development that highlights innovation, improvement, growth, and change. Our goal is to enable educators to build constructively on an effective foundation of theory, research, and field experience, rather than to be critical of "traditional" approaches. If your school or district is already involved in gifted education, this handbook may affirm many of your present commitments and practices while also providing stimulation and direction for future growth. If your school or school district is *not* presently involved in gifted programming, this handbook will offer you constructive direction and incentives for beginning such efforts.

This chapter offers a brief historical background of efforts to support gifted education and programming of talent development, presents a rationale for our contemporary approach, and, finally, describes the structure and organization of this handbook.

FOUR GENERATIONS OF GIFTED EDUCATION

Four generations of efforts to support gifted education in the schools might be traced during the period from 1971 to the present. We chose the generation metaphor deliberately, since we identified several distinct time periods in relation to program planning, each with its own unique emphasis, strengths, and limitations.

Generation One: The Early 1970s

Although gifted programs, in one form or another, can be traced back to the early and middle decades of the twentieth century, the early 1970s serves as a commonly accepted marker of the modern era. The federal government's Marland report (1971) inspired a wave of optimism about gifted programs as well as a number of efforts to stimulate program planning and implementation. Interest in giftedness in that era was influenced by a number of factors. These included advances in the psychology of intelligence, a climate receptive to individual differences, an attitude of openness to innovation and change, the promise of imminent federal support for new initiatives, and the fact that there was no active "brightness bashing"—there was a widespread readiness to accept the need for "the best and the brightest" to be encouraged to study and solve many important social problems.

In this generation, training and planning resources in education for the gifted and talented were designed primarily to stimulate awareness of the existence of strengths, talents, or outstanding abilities among students. For example, the early efforts in the 1970s emphasized the importance of recognizing and developing gifts and talents and the potential harm to individuals and society of the failure to do so. Great emphasis was placed on giftedness and talent as an important national resource which should not be wasted in school and society. These efforts focused on stimulating recognition and acceptance, which was an important contribution, but they seldom offered more than admonition or general principles ("Respond to individual differences!") in relation to program planning or implementation.

Generation Two: The Late 1970s

The second generation of resources for trainers followed soon after the first, and was stimulated by several support programs from the U.S. Office of Education's Bureau on the Gifted and Talented, through Public Law 93-380 and subsequent legislation at the federal level. The creation of the National/State Leadership Training Institute on the Gifted/Talented, for example, provided a significant step beyond awareness efforts. As a result of their extensive efforts throughout the country, many states and local school districts began to work on the development of explicit program plans for gifted/talented education. Resources for planning were also developed and distributed by several organizations that grew considerably in the 1970s, such as the National Association for Gifted Children (NAGC) and the Association for the Gifted (TAG) division of the Council for Exceptional Children (CEC).

In a relatively short span of time (1971–1978), gifted programs were planned—at least on paper—in nearly every state in the United States, and in many local districts within each state. There were two major limitations in this generation of training and planning. The first was its reliance on a prescriptively structured design (often referred to as a "cookbook" approach) in which each "plan" often seemed to be an identical copy of everyone else's except for the names and addresses. The second was its tendency to employ a very general set of definitions and principles, often chosen to be broadly acceptable, rather than to design programs on the basis of careful, detailed analyses and applications of research and theory.

Generation Three: The 1980s Into the Early 1990s

In the early 1980s, a third generation of planning approaches emerged. These responded directly to the limitations of the cookbook approach. They emphasized the need to construct a program framework on the basis of a deliberately selected approach or model, and they recognized that, although any program plan might include common components or themes, each school or district's specific plan needed to be unique in many important ways.

In this generation, books and training programs alike emphasized "teaching models," curriculum models, or planning approaches. For example, many programs were planned following Renzulli's (1981) Enrichment Triad Model, Treffinger's (1981) Individualized Program Planning Model (IPPM), Betts's (1985) Autonomous Learner Model, or Feldhusen's Purdue Three-Stage Model (e.g., Feldhusen & Kolloff, 1986, 1988). In this generation, a great many models emerged (some differing from each other in theory or in practice, and others very similar in their basic approach). The strengths of this generation's efforts arose from insistence that programs should take into account a deliberate or systematic structure based coherently and consistently on theory and research, and from their growing recognition of some of the unique considerations of each setting in which a model was adopted. Theory building often ran ahead of research, however, and pressures to "get started now" too often led to school plans that *named* models but did not necessarily represent or implement them very effectively.

The promise of the previous decades was, in many ways, unfulfilled in this generation. Several factors operating in general education influenced the lack of fulfillment for this generation's hopes (while illuminating directions for which programming might continue to evolve). These factors included:

- A shift of focus from the "best and brightest" to the balancing of excellence and equity for all
- A widespread crisis orientation (evidenced by national reports with titles such as "A Nation at Risk" and "The Crisis in American Education")

- The No Child Left Behind (NCLB) legislation, with its strong focus on content standards and testing, often with an emphasis on testing for "minimum competencies" (which can then become "maximum expectancies")
- Financial pressures (in which education has often been viewed as an expense rather than as an investment)
- Unrest or uncertainty concerning how to deal with diversity
- Educators who retreated from individualization in favor of undifferentiated whole group instruction or various "good for everyone" strategies too often perceived as panaceas

But it is also very important to note that the lack of fulfillment of those early promises was not only the result of influences *outside* gifted education. Many of the common decisions and frequent practices within the field also contributed to the problem (or, as the cartoon character Pogo once said, "We have met the enemy, and it is us . . ."). Some of the ways in which gifted education contributed to its own difficulties were:

- Its alienation from school reform and school improvement movements
- Its persistence in holding outdated conceptions of ability and giftedness
- Its clinging to the "measles model" in identification of students (i.e., giftedness is a condition and you either have it or you don't)
- Its limiting itself through programs that seemed to assume that a single program can meet the needs of all high-ability students

Generation Four: From the Mid-1990s to Today

From the mid-1990s until the present, the field has become increasingly diverse and dynamic in response to the pressures (noted above) from within and without gifted education. Today, there are many strongly held, often widely diverging viewpoints. This handbook focuses on the emerging fourth generation of talent development programming. The new generation builds upon new understandings, evidence, and beliefs (through research, theory, and practical experience) initiated in previous generations. It also extends beyond the efforts of previous generations. In part, the need for a new generation arises from our belief that there exists today a much more extensive base of knowledge on which programming must be constructed if it is to have substance and integrity in its own right. The need for a new generation of programming for talent development is not merely a response to political or pragmatic pressures or an exercise in expedience or "jumping onto the latest bandwagon." We need a new generation of programming in order to do what we know today is the right thing to do.

But the need for a new approach also acknowledges an obvious practical reality: it's a new and different world in today's schools, and it is continuing to change rapidly even as we participate in it. Efforts to plan and carry out gifted programming in today's schools must be linked closely to many other new initiatives: site-based management or participative decision making, school restructuring, and school improvement planning.

These educational changes, paralleled in the corporate business world, for example, by total quality and continuous improvement priorities, are not just fads or passing fancies. They are fundamental changes in the ways in which we design, organize, and carry out educational programs at all levels. They have a substantial impact on the decisions that will be made about all aspects of curriculum, instruction, administration, and day-to-day management and operation of the schools, and they have important consequences for and effects on every component of the school program.

These new and powerful changes in education require that we look beyond the previous approaches to planning for gifted programming in at least the following four ways:

1. *Understanding that awareness is not enough.* It is not adequate to conduct "awareness" level programs for staff and administrators. It is essential to provide the skills and support that educators need to be able to plan, implement, and evaluate programming effectively and to guide them in integrating concern for talent development with other contemporary demands and pressures.

2. *Recognizing that today's environment demands more than cookbooks.* The complexity of today's schools, and the variety of changes and challenges faced by educators, are far greater and more diverse than they have ever been before. This indicates without doubt that a simple, prepackaged or "cookbook" approach to planning for programming for gifted education (or any other specific program area) will not be effective. There are simply too many other considerations, all interacting with each other in a variety of ways, that must be studied and coordinated. Every school today must deal with so many curricular, instructional, and programmatic concerns and demands that no one dimension can be considered independent of the others.

3. *Looking beyond "the model."* The notion of adopting a model also seems dated and inadequate for two principal reasons. First, contemporary understandings of talents and abilities, assessment, and instructional strategies are complex and multidimensional. No single gifted program model can reasonably be expected to take into account all of the major dimensions of these areas that must be integrated into the school's work. Second, successful implementation of new directions in education today clearly requires deliberate efforts to recognize and respond to the individual climate of the school, its staff and students, and its surrounding context (district, community, state, nation, and increasingly even its global context).

4. *Dealing with innovative thinking and approaches.* Finally, the new generation builds upon a growing body of evidence, within gifted education and from many allied fields of study, about the nature of human abilities and talents, their distribution among people, their recognition, and the ways they can be nurtured. In addition, in the decades since the Marland report, research and development have expanded regarding student characteristics and styles, the nature and nurture of effective thinking, models and methods of learning and instruction, and our understanding of the nature and implementation of many programming models for recognizing and nurturing students' gifts and talents.

We refer to the emerging fourth generation presented in this handbook as the generation of contemporary, inclusive programming, since it builds on these foundations. In this contemporary generation, we recognize that it is not possible to treat gifted programs as separate entities, isolated from and independent of all of the other issues, concerns, and priorities confronting the modern school. We must deal effectively, and usually simultaneously, with many different challenges. Each of these is complex in and of itself, and collectively, they become even more challenging in their combined and interactive effects. Some aspects that our task might include are:

- Understanding the complex dynamics of leadership and facilitation for change
- Seeking ways to link gifted programming or talent development with the broader concern for school improvement
- Dealing with new views of teaching and learning
- Dealing with new and constantly changing personal, interpersonal, and societal dynamics
- Knowing and being able to use complex, multi-stage models for planning, development, implementation, and evaluation

As it emerges, the new generation of approaches is diverse and does not represent a consensus approach. It is reflected in the work of many individuals and groups. Feldhusen's (1992) *Talent Identification and Development in Education (TIDE)* approach involves talent profiles and growth plans for students with strengths in one or more specific talent domains, emphasizing multiple services at the elementary, middle, and secondary levels. Renzulli and his associates address talent development, school improvement, and schoolwide enrichment in a variety of publications, including *Schools for Talent Development* (Renzulli, 1994), *The Schoolwide Enrichment Model* (Renzulli & Reis, 1997), *Total Talent Portfolio* (Purcell & Renzulli, 1998), *The Multiple Menu Model* (Renzulli, Leppien, & Hays, 2000), and *Enrichment Clusters* (Renzulli, Gentry, & Reis, 2003). Our work on the Levels of Service (LoS) approach (Treffinger, 1998; Treffinger, Young, Nassab, & Wittig, 2004b) involves planning, organizing, and implementing programming within schools or districtwide that spans four levels: services for all, many, some, and few students. Many modern approaches to programming have moved away from a single, fixed program, delivered to a single set of students, and emphasize instead the importance of recognizing and responding to a variety of strengths, talents, and sustained interests among students through diverse and varied services or learning experiences.

Thus, another major influence contributing to the emerging new generation of programming involves revitalizing and expanding a focus on responsiveness to the individual characteristics and strengths of each learner. Today's efforts extend significantly beyond the "individualized instruction" models of the 1970s and challenge educators to design appropriate and challenging learning opportunities based on data- or assessment-driven profiles of student characteristics and needs. Rogers's work on "matching the program to the child" in Re-forming Gifted Education (2002) represents one such effort. Others have drawn on learning styles theory and research (e.g., Dunn, Dunn, & Treffinger, 1992); many have also been influenced by work on differentiation of curriculum and instruction (e.g., Gregory & Chapman, 2006; Heacox, 2001; Tomlinson, 2001, 2004).

Success in programming for talent development (as well as for any systematic school innovation or improvement initiative) will not come from knowledge of any *one* challenge. If we expect schools to be successful in establishing and maintaining a new generation of programming, today's professionals must bring to their tasks high levels of competence, confidence, and commitment in all of these important areas,

This handbook provides a collection of practical resources to help you chart your course more accurately, efficiently, and effectively. You might use the resources in this handbook in a deliberate way to plan programming (or to redesign existing programs). You might also be selective in choosing and applying only certain resources that will help you to address a specific need or question in your setting. The handbook is not intended to prescribe a single, fixed method or pathway that all schools or districts should apply in a fixed, inflexible manner. Using the resources in this handbook *can*:

- Help you to identify major areas in which decisions should be made
- Help you to describe significant dimensions of the foundation for effective programming
- Challenge you to reexamine existing procedures and practice in the light of contemporary theory and research
- Encourage you to conceptualize and define programming constructively
- Highlight possible areas of concern or omission in local planning efforts
- Help you to identify important questions that must be addressed and potentially valuable resources for dealing with those questions
- Inspire you to investigate challenging new directions and opportunities
- Stimulate and encourage innovation and progress
- Encourage and support comprehensive planning for school improvement
- Offer a foundation for continuity and comparability of general practices from one school to another

The activities in the handbook *do not*:

- Mandate specific actions, decisions, or models
- Impose on any school a specific set of methods or materials
- Require the use of specific identification instruments or procedures
- Limit or constrain the services that can be offered or the students for whom such services can be provided by individual schools

While the intent of the handbook is to provide assistance and resources to facilitate planning and implementation of a contemporary, inclusive approach to talent development, it will not take the place of careful study of the literature, nor is it intended to eliminate the need for the services of trained professionals at the local level.

OVERVIEW OF THE HANDBOOK'S CONTENTS

The handbook is organized into seven major sections and 14 chapters. Section I includes an introduction and overview. Sections II through VII follow our Systematic Planning Model's six stages. Each chapter also includes resources that you can reproduce as transparencies and/or handouts as part of your planning and preparation for programming. The handbook also contains a CD on which you will find a number of reproducible resources, presentations, and templates for a number of forms from the handbook.

Section I. Overview

This introductory section includes two chapters: this chapter and Chapter 2, which presents an overview of our planning framework.

Chapter 1. Introduction and Overview. This introduction and overview chapter provide an orientation to the handbook and an overview of its structure and contents.

Chapter 2. The Six-Stage Systematic Planning Model. This chapter presents a brief rationale for engaging in a deliberate, carefully designed planning process, then presents our six-stage planning model, the purpose of which is to guide your planning process and identify specific procedures for organizing and carrying out that process at the district and school levels.

Section II. Stage One—Prepare

In preparing for the implementation of contemporary programming, you will complete several key "advance" tasks and create and maintain the best possible communication channels between the school and the public. Preparation involves gathering data, identifying resources, stimulating awareness, promoting understanding, and building informed commitment to contemporary programming (on paper and in practice).

Chapter 3. Foundations for Contemporary Programming. Chapter 3 presents current thinking about the nature of giftedness and talent. This chapter also provides information about the rationale, goals, and philosophy of the contemporary approaches to talent development.

Chapter 4. Innovation and Change. This chapter examines the challenges of recognizing and dealing with change in today's school context and gives a brief discussion of problem solving styles and the role of the change agent. The chapter also discusses the new demands and definitions of "workplace basics" (skills that will be required for future personal and career success), their impact on broader school improvement challenges, and their implications for teaching and learning in general education as well as for talent development.

Chapter 5. Planning Logistics. This chapter offers practical guidance about forming planning committees, leadership, and guiding the planning process effectively.

Section III. Stage Two—Clarify Where You Are Now

The second major planning responsibility is a thorough self-study that involves an open acknowledgment of your present context, commitment, and activities. The steps in accomplishing this self-study include (a) conducting a systematic needs assessment, (b) checking the context for excellence and assessing the climate supporting programming in your setting, and (c) clarifying your current program's positives and your wish list for the future. Section III consists of three chapters.

Chapter 6. Needs Assessment. Conducting a careful and focused needs assessment is an important step in clarifying your current status. This chapter provides practical needs assessment tools and suggests additional sources of data that might be considered.

Chapter 7. Checking the Climate. This chapter provides resources for assessing your climate for adopting, supporting, and implementing contemporary, inclusive programming with a specific Programming Climate Survey. It includes information about being "ready, willing, and able" to move forward with contemporary programming.

Chapter 8. Programming Positives and Wish Lists. In this chapter, we present specific resources to assist you in defining and describing your current programming positives and in constructing a general wish list for future programming efforts. This chapter includes a number of specific tips for searching effectively for your programming strengths and wishes.

Section IV. Stage Three—Decide Where to Go Next

The third major planning step involves looking at the future, setting your goals for programming, and creating a district Master Plan and/or Building Action Plans.

Chapter 9. Setting Goals for Your Desired Future. This chapter provides resources to guide you in looking closely at your current reality, as defined in Section III, and your "desired future" for implementation of contemporary programming. These resources will guide the process of establishing goals for your programming efforts.

Chapter 10. Constructing the Master Plan. The Master Plan provides a general umbrella or an overall set of parameters that will guide and support subsequent building level efforts. It establishes a framework within which each building can clarify key issues regarding support and resources.

Chapter 11. Constructing the Building Action Plan. The next major activity in this stage involves creating and implementing Building Action Plans. Working within general parameters of the Master Plan, each building should be charged with creating its own plan of action. The tasks in this stage can be initiated simultaneously with ongoing planning at the district level and will certainly contribute to the discussions and work that take place at that level.

Section V. Stage Four—Carry Out Programming

Chapter 12. Implementing Contemporary Programming. This chapter presents a brief summary of several key topics to guide you in designing and delivering programming activities and services. As an example of a contemporary, inclusive approach, the chapter includes an overview of four "Levels of Service" that we addressed in greater detail in our book *Enhancing and Expanding Gifted Programs: The Levels of Service Approach* (Treffinger, Young, Nassab, & Wittig, 2004b).

Section VI: Stage Five—Seek Talents and Strengths

Chapter 13. Identification in Contemporary Talent Development. This chapter presents a brief summary of a number of emerging issues and opportunities for the challenges of identification. Although many school programs must operate within the confines of specific local or state mandates, most contemporary approaches to programming today challenge us to look at (and for) students' interests, strengths, and characteristics in new ways. We expect continuing work in the field of gifted/talented education to yield significant advances and new perspectives in this area.

Section VII. Stage Six—Ensure Quality, Innovation, and Continuous Improvement

In order to accomplish the necessary balance between stability and change in a program, your plan should include specific provisions for evaluation data to be gathered, analyzed, and used in the decision making process. From the initial planning stages, consider the kinds of evaluation data that will be helpful and necessary and the ways in which those data will be obtained, reviewed, and their results applied.

Chapter 14. Quality, Innovation, and Continuous Improvement. The final chapter presents specific practical suggestions to guide program evaluation and documentation. These involve designing and conducting systematic evaluation, using evaluation data to monitor and document programming, using evaluation data to promote innovation, and using evaluation to guide continuous improvement.

The Six-Stage Systematic Planning Model 2

Six major stages provide the foundation for the planning process recommended in this handbook. The following sections and chapters of the handbook provide detailed discussions of each of the six planning stages as well as resources to help you carry out those stages effectively. This chapter explains the importance of a deliberate planning process and presents an overview, or "advance organizer," of the six stages of the Six-Stage Systematic Planning Model.

BENEFITS OF EFFECTIVE PLANNING

Good planning is beneficial for almost any project: a new business, an ice cream social conducted by a civic or church group, a student's independent study project . . . or a school's approach to programming for talent development. The benefits are numerous, and a few are highlighted here.

Determine Goals and Objectives for Programming

According to common wisdom, "if you don't know where you are going, you might wind up somewhere else." While many people may initially agree that programming is important or desirable for a school, an effective planning process will challenge them to look beyond superficial statements as they seek clarification and consensus regarding specific goals and objectives.

Focus on Priorities

It will be important to keep your attention and effort focused on the directions and tasks that represent your true priorities so as not to support the drain of energies that results when committee members drift aimlessly from one task to another. Lack of focus on priorities causes unnecessary dissent in a group, inhibits progress, and results in loss of interest and nonparticipation by those involved in creating programs or conducting projects.

Facilitate Sharing of Responsibility

Through a well-designed and implemented planning process, responsibility for the outcomes and results is spread among many colleagues rather than merely assigned to a limited number of individuals.

Promote Effective Communication

The planning process involves seeking input, ideas, questions, and concerns from a variety of sources. It creates opportunities for two-way communication, offering checks and balances for better decisions and grassroots support and reducing the likelihood of overlooking important issues or concerns that are essential to success.

Build Ownership

In all new programming efforts, commitment and support are much greater when people participate in creating the program rather than have it handed to or imposed upon them from higher sources of authority. Individuals will make greater investment of their time and energy to programs that they have helped to create and justify, and there will be significantly stronger commitment to the success of the plan.

Stimulate Active Participation

Many individuals bring unique talents, perspectives, and skills to the creation of effective programming; without a systematic planning process, many of these may go unrecognized and untapped.

Establish a Foundation for Subsequent Decisions

Throughout our country's history, we have had to turn repeatedly to our Constitution for guidance in judicial decisions and for vital checks and balances in monitoring executive and legislative actions and their consequences. In the same way, a carefully crafted planning document can provide a valuable reference point for future decisions.

Avoid Premature Closure

Effective planning encourages you to carefully examine the pluses and minuses of many approaches or models, employing criteria for weighing their implications and suitability in relation to your school's unique character and needs, rather than to adopt a particular model or viewpoint on the basis of recent exposure, emotional appeal, power bargaining among key individuals, or expedience.

Reduce Dependency on Unilateral or Charismatic Leadership

Planning helps to ensure that the success of programming will not be determined merely by the energy, enthusiasm, or credibility of an individual who single-handedly takes charge of decisions and implementation. Programs that result from a single charismatic leader's actions may find life and support only as long as that person's "stock" remains high—or until she or he becomes interested in something else, or departs entirely from the school. Effective planning leads to services that outlive the tenure and actions of the individuals who first proposed them.

THE SIX-STAGE SYSTEMATIC PLANNING MODEL

Our planning framework includes six major stages in the planning process. These stages are (1) Prepare, (2) Clarify Where You Are Now, (3) Decide Where to Go Next, (4) Carry Out Programming, (5) Seek Talents and Strengths, and (6) Ensure Quality, Innovation, and Continuous Improvement. Figure 2.1 presents a graphic representation of the model, and the major tasks of the six

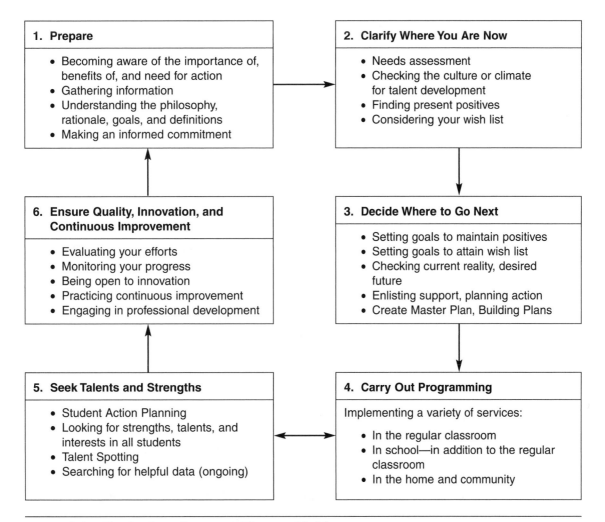

Figure 2.1 The Six-Stage Systematic Planning Model

planning process stages are described below. (The accompanying CD includes a PowerPoint presentation on the Six-Stage Systematic Planning Model.)

Prepare

In preparing for talent development programming, you will complete four steps:

a. Building awareness of the importance of, benefits of, and need for action; establishing a foundation of information and awareness

b. Gathering information about the nature of giftedness and talent

c. Understanding the philosophy, rationale, and goals of a contemporary, inclusive approach

d. Making an informed commitment to implement programming

Clarify Where You Are Now

The second major planning responsibility is a thorough self-study that involves an open acknowledgment of your present context, commitment, and activities. Steps to accomplish this self-study are:

a. Conducting a careful needs assessment

b. Checking the culture or climate for talent development

c. Identifying your present positives in talent development programming

d. Constructing your wish list

Decide Where to Go Next

The third major planning step involves looking at the future. To help you create a plan for designing the future, we recommend following these steps:

a. Setting goals for maintaining your current programming positives

b. Setting goals for attaining your wish list

c. Checking your current reality and your desired future

d. Enlisting support and planning for action

e. Creating your Master Plan and/or Building Action Plan(s)

Carry Out Programming

This stage involves preparation for taking the initial steps to implement programming. The steps in this stage are:

a. Implementing programming in the regular classroom setting

b. Implementing programming in school that extends beyond the regular classroom

c. Encouraging activities that take place outside the school (home, community)

d. Ensuring that programming involves careful consideration of multiple levels of service

Seek Talents and Strengths

This stage involves initiating deliberate efforts to locate or recognize students' strengths, talents, and sustained interests. The steps for this stage include:

a. Active, deliberate Talent Spotting efforts

b. Looking for strengths, talents, and interests in all students

c. Constructing and monitoring records of Student Action Planning data

d. Creating, supporting, applying, and documenting in an ongoing way your search for data regarding students' strengths, talents, and interests

Ensure Quality, Innovation, and Continuous Improvement

In order to accomplish the necessary balance between stability and change in a program, your plan should include specific provisions for evaluation data to be gathered, analyzed, and used in the decision making process. From the initial planning stages, consider the kinds of evaluation data that will be helpful and necessary and the ways in which you will obtain those data, review them, and apply the results. The steps include:

a. Designing and conducting systematic evaluation of your efforts

b. Using evaluation data to monitor and document programming

c. Using evaluation data to promote innovation and manage change

d. Refocusing: continuous improvement

e. Supporting and conducting professional development.

To assist you in monitoring your progress as you undertake these six major stages, use the summary checklist in Figure 2.2 to record the dates and decisions made by your planning committee in relation to each stage of the planning process. (The accompanying CD includes this checklist as a Word document for your convenience.) Provide all members of the planning committee with copies of this checklist so that they can participate in monitoring the decision making process and have a realistic perspective on the committee's progress through the planning process.

Planning Stage/Actions:	Who:	Dates:
Prepare		
Clarify		
Decide		
Carry Out		
Seek Strengths		
Evaluate and Document		

Figure 2.2   Planning activities checklist

Section II

Stage One— Prepare

Section II deals with "Prepare," the first stage of the Systematic Planning Model. Preparing involves the initial steps that will enable you to carry out your planning for a contemporary, inclusive approach in an effective and efficient way. The key tasks in this stage are:

- Be clear about the nature of giftedness and talents, as well as the importance and benefits of your approach to programming for talent development, and of the value of taking action in your setting to move toward effective implementation.
- Understand, and be able to share, specific information regarding the rationale, philosophy, definitions, and goals that provide the foundation of a contemporary approach.
- Gather information that will be helpful to share with others as you enlist their support and active involvement. Be ready to explain the important linkages between talent development and other school change and school improvement goals and initiatives.
- Identify and apply tools and strategies relating to the logistics of, and leadership for, effective planning for programming.
- Invite your school's staff and parents, district personnel, and community leaders to make an informed commitment to implementing your programming approach.

You will probably enter this stage when you are anticipating taking your initial steps in program planning, or possibly when you are preparing to redesign or restructure an existing program. When you exit this stage, you will have made an informed decision about considering your approach, and you will have an initial team or task force ready to begin in-depth planning at the school or school district level. The three chapters in Section II provide information and resources to help you as you carry out these tasks.

Foundations for Contemporary Programming 3

This chapter provides an overview of the basic foundations for a contemporary, inclusive approach to programming—the emerging "fourth generation" of programming described in Chapter 1. We begin by examining our changing and broadening understanding of the nature and definition of giftedness and talent. The chapter also considers the rationale and goals for contemporary approaches to talent development.

THE NATURE OF GIFTEDNESS AND TALENT

One of the most complex problems encountered by many educators and educational planning committees is dealing effectively with definitions. It is complex because words such as *gifted*, *giftedness*, *bright*, *capable*, *talented*, *precocious*, and *genius* (and many others you could generate easily!) mean so many different things to different people. This is true in everyday conversation, in the media, and even in professional use. Many efforts at planning gifted programs have floundered over the issue of finding a mutually agreeable definition.

The breadth and diversity of understandings of the term *intelligence* can also be observed by examining many informal definitions. Consider, for example, some of the responses offered by educators, parents, and students who were asked to complete the statement, "Intelligence is when a person is able to . . ." Common responses included:

- Perform complex tasks well and consistently
- React to people and situations with good common sense
- Gather, organize, use, and apply information
- Deal with new, unusual, and changing situations
- Find and know the areas in which he or she is able to excel and go beyond others

- Form, organize, maintain, and access a rich storehouse of knowledge and experience (and put it to use)
- Be curious, continuing to ask questions and seek meaningful answers
- Deal with different types of people constructively, or with "diplomacy"
- Be persuasive; bring others around to a point of view
- Learn from previous mistakes (their own and others)
- Maintain an open and inquiring mind
- Go beyond the information given
- Perform operations and processes efficiently and effectively (and not rely on trial and error)
- Filter incoming stimuli and information: judge its value, correctness, and usefulness, see its potentials, and act accordingly
- Judge or weigh options and make good decisions
- Engage in abstract thinking, planning, and "taking the long view"
- Define and solve complex, difficult problems and assignments

Broadening Conceptions

Just as there are many and varied understandings of intelligence in informal uses of the terms *intelligence*, *ability*, *aptitude*, and *talent*, there are also diverse views among professionals. It is unlikely that any single definition will meet with universal acceptance. It is clear, however, that most conceptions of human talents and abilities have broadened considerably in the last three decades. Major theorists and researchers in intelligence and human behavior have stimulated today's practitioners to expand their understanding or definition of giftedness. Bloom (1985), for example, studied giftedness through talent development; Gardner (1983) formulated a view of multiple intelligences; Sternberg (1986) proposed the Triarchic Theory to describe intelligence; Torrance (1962, 1987) researched creative abilities; Guilford (1959, 1967) proposed the multifaceted Structure of the Intellect, and so on. These studies are illustrated in Figure 3.1 and referenced at the end of this handbook. Through the work of many scholars, from a variety of perspectives and disciplines, we have come to the unambiguous and no longer avoidable conclusion that giftedness cannot be defined in relation to a single score or simple quantitative index or cutoff point.

Renzulli (1978) defined giftedness as the interaction among ability, creativity, and task commitment. Amabile (1983) and Torrance (1989) emphasized that creative productivity arises from a synthesis of abilities, skills, and motivation. Treffinger (1991) proposed that giftedness is represented through achievement and creative productivity, over a sustained period of time (perhaps years or even decades), in a domain that matters to the person.

Understanding a Contemporary View of Talent

The following principles regarding the nature and definition of giftedness and talent are essential for any school or school district examining gifted programming today to consider.

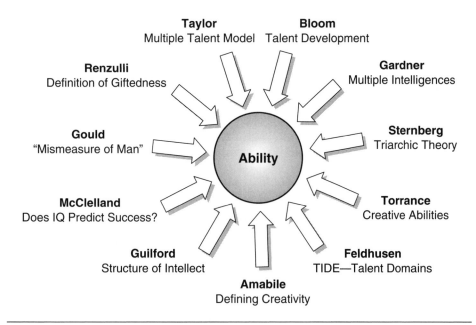

Figure 3.1   Our broadening view of human talents and abilities

1. Intelligence and talent (I/T) can be improved or strengthened with training and instruction.

2. There are multiple types; I/T is not a single unitary construct.

3. Intellectual development is a lifelong challenge; it begins at an early age and continues into adulthood.

4. High performance in one area is possible and desirable (intelligence is not an all-or-none phenomenon).

5. I/T is a combination of nature and nurture. There are genetic contributions, but environment has a powerful impact and role.

6. The ability to apply and use I/T in practical real-world settings is highly significant.

7. Traditional psychometric views and instruments (e.g., IQ) are neither sufficient nor adequate for an understanding of I/T.

8. There are alternative methods of assessment. We should be open to using many and varied resources and instruments.

9. To the extent that tests can be developed and used, they must be valid and reliable and must be used appropriately.

10. Staff development is essential so that all staff share essential knowledge of I/T, to promote "buy in" and to enhance school practice. We *know* more than we *do* in schools today.

11. No one has yet told the whole story; we must remain open to growth, change, and progress (but that should not prevent us from moving forward in practice).

12. I/T involves "higher level" thinking (including creative and critical thinking, problem solving, and decision making).

13. I/T can be expressed and applied in many media or content domains.

14. We need continuing research to validate theories and examine "best practices."

15. Knowledge acquisition, organization, and access are positive dimensions of I/T, but their importance arises from meaningful application.

16. Looking at an I/T profile that emphasizes a person's particular strengths and interests is more powerful than asking where the person's test scores fall in a statistical distribution.

17. We value individual strengths and differences. Differences are not deficits.

18. All people have worthwhile I/T, although each person may differ in degree and development of any of its dimensions.

19. People need to be informed, aware, and open to new approaches to I/T, and to be ready to implement multiple I/T approaches.

20. Students learn in varied ways through their I/T and need a variety of activities and varied physical facilities (and resources) to do that.

21. Teaching for I/T development also involves varied methods, approaches, and resources.

22. Individuals should be aware of their own I/T strengths and needs, and of how to apply and use them effectively.

Our working definition of talent is: Talent can be viewed as potential for significant contributions or productivity (in original or creative ways) in any domain of inquiry, expression, or action over an extended period of time. Talent emerges from aptitudes and/or from sustained involvement in areas of strong interest or passion. It is not simply a natural endowment or a "gift." The chart below summarizes the key elements of our view of talent.

Talent Refers To . . .

Strengths and sustained interests to be nurtured

Strengths that are assessed in qualitative as well as quantitative ways

Inferences drawn from a person's accomplishments over a sustained period of time (may well be years)

Behavior that is manifest in diverse and varied ways or styles

Productivity and a strong sense of involvement or investment, passion, disciplined work, and self-initiated learning

Metaphor: "collage" rather than "snapshot"

Implications for Contemporary Programming

Given the extensive body of theory and research that supports an expanded conception of giftedness and talent, what practical implications are there for contemporary approaches to programming? Let us examine several key implications.

Seven Key Questions

Whatever definition you adopt or create (and it very well may be one which draws upon and synthesizes several viewpoints), you should consider the following seven important questions:

- Does the definition reflect contemporary knowledge of the nature and diversity of human talents and abilities?
- Does the definition take into account the importance of environmental impact and developmental differences?
- Does the definition describe people's strengths and talents in relation to meaningful, well-documented personal characteristics and style preferences?
- Does the definition reflect appropriately the variability in human performance over time and in various situations?
- Does the definition consider strengths, talents, and sustained interests that recognize and respect diversity and cultural differences?
- Does the definition take into account the possibility of expanding human talents or abilities through effective instructional interventions? (That is, does it recognize that many—perhaps all—important components of giftedness might be nurtured?)
- Does the definition provide a clear and effective foundation for practical instructional planning, rather than merely lead to categorical inclusion or exclusion decisions?

Strengths and Talents Can Be Nurtured

Contemporary conceptions of giftedness and talent involve characteristics that can be nurtured or enhanced through appropriate instruction and experiences. When expressed and focused in a particular area or direction, and when recognized and nurtured through appropriate instruction and guidance, these skills and abilities provide the foundation for creative, productive behavior.

Although each set of characteristics includes factors that may be naturally present and even readily observable at an early age in some individuals, they are not simply "you have it or you don't" dimensions of human ability and talent. It is evident that these factors can be developed through instruction, and may be stronger or more active at different times and for different durations, under varying circumstances, among many people. Therefore, do not view giftedness as a single, fixed trait that any given individual permanently possesses or lacks; rather, view talent as a construct involving four important elements: characteristics, context, operations, and content. These are illustrated in Figure 3.2.

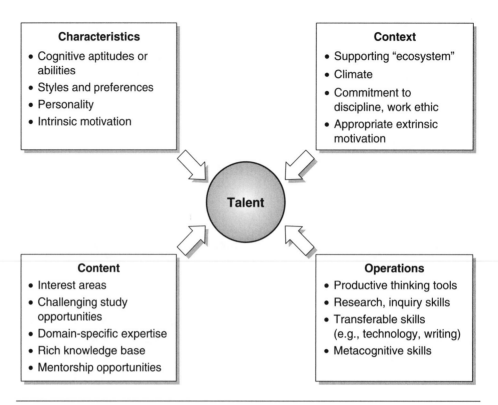

Characteristics
- Cognitive aptitudes or abilities
- Styles and preferences
- Personality
- Intrinsic motivation

Context
- Supporting "ecosystem"
- Climate
- Commitment to discipline, work ethic
- Appropriate extrinsic motivation

Talent

Content
- Interest areas
- Challenging study opportunities
- Domain-specific expertise
- Rich knowledge base
- Mentorship opportunities

Operations
- Productive thinking tools
- Research, inquiry skills
- Transferable skills (e.g., technology, writing)
- Metacognitive skills

Figure 3.2   Components of talent

Source: From the Center for Creative Learning, Inc.

Focus on Creative Productivity

Giftedness involves what people are able to do with what they know, and how they make new and valued contributions to any area in which they work. It is more than good memory, an impressive array of trivial information, or merely "knowing about" something. When we speak of someone as gifted, it is most appropriately a statement of the individual's track record or history of productivity and accomplishments over an extended period of time.

Stronger and Weaker Views of Giftedness

We also distinguish between "strong" and "weak" views of giftedness, as illustrated in the chart on page 27. A strong view is closely linked to the real world and a person's actual accomplishments and productivity over an extended period of time. It is closely linked to action, and to events or products that capture our attention, challenge us, synthesize ideas, transform work or events, or improve the quality or appreciation of life. By contrast, a weak view focuses only on high scores on a test, or uses the designation "gifted" as a label or categorical placement based on a fixed set of data about a person's knowledge or status in a statistical distribution. The stronger view of giftedness has greater influence than the weaker view on contemporary, inclusive approaches to programming.

What Makes the Definition of Giftedness Strong or Weak?

A strong definition takes into account . . .	A weak definition is based on . . .
Creative accomplishments (creative productivity)	High scores on a test or paper-and-pencil instrument
Performance over a sustained period of time	One-time or "one-shot" static classification
Action and attainments that are powerful, dynamic	A person's status or a categorical label, which puts the person in a box
Important contributions to human life—actions, events, or products that capture our attention, challenge us, synthesize ideas, transform work or events, improve life quality	An individual's grasp or knowledge of "information"; no necessary sense of action, application, impact, or contribution
Sources within an individual and their contributions to others, touching many people	Whether or not a person is "in the category," as if giftedness is within and for the individual completely
Observable, evident actions and outcomes in the real world	No necessary relationship or linkage to any real-world actions or outcomes

New Challenges and Directions for Identification

A new focus on talent identification and development is not simply a cosmetic change or new terminology for "gifted education"; it is, indeed, a fundamentally new orientation to the nature, scope, and practice of our field. Talent development spans the lifetime, reminding us to seek ways to recognize, nurture, and apply many and varied talents among children, adolescents, and adults.

It also involves our growing recognition of the contextualization of talents and aptitudes as we move beyond a conception of giftedness focused only on abilities or "gifts" presumed to exist entirely within the head of the individual. Talents arise from, and talented performances over time are influenced by, many social, cultural, and circumstantial (or climatic) factors outside a person's internal, testable cognitive abilities. Many factors influence the definition, development, and expression of talents in profoundly important ways, leading researchers and practitioners toward new views of identification that focus on profiling talents and responding in varied ways, and away from traditional selection models (gifted or not gifted; in or out).

A Dual Challenge for Programming

In addition to stimulating new dialogue about the nature and breadth of talents and the nature and focus of identification, talent development also challenges educators to explore innovative and varied approaches to programming. It involves a dual task: responding appropriately (and flexibly) to the needs of students who already demonstrate very high levels of accomplishment in any talent area, *and* initiating deliberate actions to seek and nurture the talents of all students. Talent development challenges educators to respond in more varied and effective ways to the strengths, talents, and sustained interests of all students in ways that are commensurate with each person's characteristics and needs.

Contemporary understandings of giftedness and talent also challenge educators to take a "long view" of talent development: to consider what students can become as well as what might be observed about them today. Expressing and developing strengths and talents can involve an extended process and set of experiences that may unfold or blossom over a period of many years. Strengths and talents may emerge and be expressed early in life, or through a process of gradual development over years or even decades. An important implication of this reality is that it reminds us that what we see in any snapshot of a person is not necessarily what we might observe in the future, nor is it a limitation or boundary on what might emerge and thrive in that person through continuing learning and growth. (One person captured this point by saying, "Lack of evidence is not evidence of lack.") In an important sense, then, when someone asks, "Is this student gifted?" the most honest answer is "Time will tell." Our most important challenge in effective programming may well be to provide appropriate, challenging, and developmental learning opportunities and experiences for our students, with an emphasis on bringing out the best in every learner.

RATIONALE AND GOALS FOR TALENT DEVELOPMENT

Modern educators recognize that the expectations and demands made of today's schools are greater and more important than ever before in our history. As the complexity of our world increases, as the rate of change with which we must cope increases constantly, and as our children and youth face more and more difficult personal, career, and social challenges than any previous generation, the demands on education also increase. We realize today, more than ever, that not only knowledge, but talent, imagination, problem solving, and judgment are qualities far too important in the world of the present and the future to be wasted or unfulfilled. We recognize that talented accomplishments in many areas will be essential to progress, to our quality of life, and perhaps to survival, and we recognize that schools share in the responsibility for nurturing many and varied dimensions of giftedness and talent, including, for example:

- Science, medicine, technology, and engineering (to find solutions to problems of hunger, disease, and the destruction of our living environment)
- Leadership, social and behavioral sciences, and organizations (to solve the problems of justice, equality, diversity, and governance)

- Arts, culture, and entertainment (to bring us new opportunities and to enhance and celebrate creative expressions that add joy and meaning to life)
- Ethical and moral principles and philosophical analysis (to guide individuals and groups in understanding and dealing effectively with the most complex concepts and challenges of human existence)
- Personal fulfillment (enabling individuals to live in greater mental, emotional, and physical health and to celebrate their own talents as well as those of others)

We may not be confident in our ability to assess and select those young people who display the greatest potential for significant accomplishments in these areas, or in any other specific talent dimensions. In truth, these accomplishments often unfold over many years in an individual's life. They are the products of many complex factors over and beyond one's specific experiences in school. Educators today are rightfully called upon to make every possible effort to discern students' special needs, interests, and potentials, and to provide educational opportunities for their nurture. Increasingly we must deal with the responsibility of serving as important "guardians of the future." To achieve our goals for a contemporary approach to talent development, we need to:

- Promote deliberate and systematic efforts in schools to seek, recognize, respond to, and enhance the development of the strengths, talents, and sustained interests of students and staff
- Support schools' efforts to establish and maintain a culture that values, promotes, and rewards excellence in many areas
- Guide schools in their efforts to create, support, and enhance a climate conducive to innovation and the recognition and development of talents among their students and staff
- Stimulate and support ongoing efforts by schools to recognize individuality and to promote higher levels of thinking, learning, and productivity among students and staff, as well as to encourage independent, responsible self-direction
- Foster ongoing professional development to enable educators to expand their ability to recognize and nurture students' strengths and talents
- Support and enhance effective use of community resources to expand learning opportunities and enrichment for all students
- Encourage all staff members to be aware of the academic, personal, social, and emotional characteristics and needs associated with giftedness and talent, and to support their efforts to respond positively and effectively to such needs when observed among any of their students
- Encourage ongoing dialogue and actions in schools that will lead to ambitious visions of their goals and mission and promote their attainment

The checklist in Figure 3.3 (which is also on the accompanying CD) may be a useful tool for examining and discussing the extent to which your school's (or school district's) personnel support these general goals for programming.

Programming for Talent Development: An Initial Assessment

Use this form to offer individuals, teams, or larger groups the opportunity to do a preliminary self-assessment of their own current commitments and activities to support and carry out programming for talent development. In the first column, the respondent rates his or her personal effectiveness in meeting the goals of talent development. In the second column, the respondent rates his or her perception of the overall effectiveness of the organization in meeting the goals for talent development programming (i.e., the effectiveness of your school or your district, depending on the level you are assessing).

	My Own Effectiveness	Our Group's Effectiveness
1. I (We) keep student success and productivity in the forefront of my (our) policies, procedures, and actions.	(low) 1—2—3—4—5 (high)	(low) 1—2—3—4—5 (high)
2. I (We) make deliberate efforts to seek, recognize, respond to, and enhance the development of students' strengths, talents, and interests.	(low) 1—2—3—4—5 (high)	(low) 1—2—3—4—5 (high)
3. I (We) offer appropriate and challenging learning opportunities and experiences for all students.	(low) 1—2—3—4—5 (high)	(low) 1—2—3—4—5 (high)
4. I (We) create, maintain, and support a culture for teaching and learning that values, promotes, and rewards excellence.	(low) 1—2—3—4—5 (high)	(low) 1—2—3—4—5 (high)
5. I (We) create, support, and enhance an environment or climate conducive to developing, recognizing, and celebrating individuals' talents.	(low) 1—2—3—4—5 (high)	(low) 1—2—3—4—5 (high)
6. I (We) recognize and honor individuality, helping all students to be aware of their learning styles and preferences and providing opportunities for them to study, explore, learn, and perform in their best ways.	(low) 1—2—3—4—5 (high)	(low) 1—2—3—4—5 (high)
7. I (We) incorporate creative thinking, critical thinking, problem solving, and decision making on a daily basis.	(low) 1—2—3—4—5 (high)	(low) 1—2—3—4—5 (high)
8. I (We) encourage independent, responsible self-direction and teach the skills required for independent, self-directed learning.	(low) 1—2—3—4—5 (high)	(low) 1—2—3—4—5 (high)
9. I (We) inspire individuals to become aware of, and to make optimum use of, their own strengths, talents, and interests, for their own benefit and for the benefit of others.	(low) 1—2—3—4—5 (high)	(low) 1—2—3—4—5 (high)
10. I (We) use many and varied resources [people, places, and materials] to expand learning opportunities and enrichment for all learners.	(low) 1—2—3—4—5 (high)	(low) 1—2—3—4—5 (high)
11. I am (We are) talent spotter(s) on a daily basis, always alert for signs of strengths, talents, and interests in every person.	(low) 1—2—3—4—5 (high)	(low) 1—2—3—4—5 (high)
12. I (We) engage in ongoing dialogue, learning, and communication to sustain commitments to innovation and continuous improvement.	(low) 1—2—3—4—5 (high)	(low) 1—2—3—4—5 (high)

Figure 3.3   Initial Assessment

FUNDAMENTAL TENETS AND BELIEFS

In creating this handbook, we drew on many insights from theory and research as well as from our years of experience in working with gifted and talented programs at both the local and state levels. We have been influenced by a number of underlying principles and beliefs from several areas of study, including gifted education, cognitive and developmental psychology, educational administration, curriculum and instruction, and others. These principles provide a foundation on which effective school practice can, and should, be based. Exemplary programming for talent development is the result of careful planning and ongoing review and analysis. It does not come about by chance. Our approach to contemporary programming builds on 22 fundamental tenets and belief statements (which you can also download in PDF format from the Center for Creative Learning's Web site at www.creativelearning.com by going to the Talent Development page and then clicking on the link to the "Fundamental Tenets and Beliefs" PDF file). They are:

1. All students have worthwhile potentials and interests. Appropriate and challenging instruction can lead to significant achievement and satisfaction in at least one (and often more than one) talent area for many students. Talents exist and may be expressed and developed in many important and worthwhile domains.

2. Some students show advanced levels of talent and accomplishment very early in their lives. With sustained effort, encouragement, and support, many students will continue to pursue the development and expression of their strengths and talents and thus may eventually attain a very high level of excellence and accomplishment.

3. Talent development is lifelong and fundamental to personal growth and healthy development. As children mature, previously unrecognized strengths and talents ("hidden potentials") often emerge, and talents may also become more specific, focused, and sustained.

4. New opportunities enable talents and interests to change, grow, or emerge over time. We can affirm talent when we see it, but we should not declare that it does not exist if, at any single instance, we do not see it. ("Lack of evidence *now* is not necessarily evidence of lack *forever.*")

5. Creative productivity, which occurs through both individual and group efforts, is commonly manifested by quality products that are shared with appropriate audiences.

6. Moving toward creative productivity in any domain involves a constant struggle for balance between *playfulness* (openness to experience, a sense of curiosity and exploration, risk taking, and toying with possibilities) and *rigor* (disciplined inquiry, hard work, and extended effort).

7. A person's learning style provides powerful information about how her or his strengths and talents can best be expressed and used and also provides a basis for appropriate and challenging instruction.

8. Nurturing talent potential is far more important for educators than simply categorizing, labeling, or sorting.

9. Talent development occurs in an ecosystem of development. Appropriate and challenging programming occurs in settings or through agencies outside the school and requires the commitment and support of the home and community as well as the school.

10. Home, school, and community all contribute to deliberate efforts to recognize students' emerging strengths, talents, and sustained interests. We must be talent spotters in order to become talent developers.

11. Participation in activities or experiences in which various talents can be expressed and used can be effective starting points for talent recognition and development.

12. Talent development requires significant personal ownership and investment, sustained effort, discipline, commitment, and work ethic on the part of the individual, as well as resources, support, and encouragement from others.

13. Effective programming for talent development involves many and varied resources and levels of service. These support, extend, expand, or enhance, rather than supplant, the daily school program.

14. Appropriate and challenging educational experiences are fundamental responsibilities of the school, not "privileges" or special activities.

15. Programming activities include six areas (differentiated basics, appropriate enrichment, effective acceleration, independence and self-direction, personal growth and social development, and career preparation with a futuristic outlook); appropriate and challenging services in any of these areas often cross traditional subject or grade level designations.

16. Talent development in the school setting requires the commitment and support of a broad cross section of staff, adequate professional time for deliberate and explicit planning, and recognition of the need for and importance of gradual implementation over several years.

17. Recognizing and documenting all students' strengths, talents, and sustained interests is a flexible, ongoing, and inclusive process, not a one-time event.

18. Placing our concern for appropriate and challenging programming in the forefront of our work (e.g., Treffinger, 1998) leads us to move away from the traditional questions associated with "identification" (Is the student gifted or not? What criteria qualify the student for designation or selection?) and opens the door for a more powerful and dynamic process of identifying ways to respond to students' strengths, talents, and interests.

19. Talent Spotting emphasizes searching for and documenting students' unique characteristics and their related instructional needs, enabling us to focus on bringing out the best in all students.

20. Profiling is a useful process for clarifying and describing all students' strengths and talents in relation to *action planning for talent development.* It uses

formal and informal sources (e.g., test data, rating scales, observations and performance tasks, portfolios, and self-report data) to guide planning for talent development.

21. Helping students to recognize and understand their own emerging talents and then to use their self-knowledge in personal goal setting and career planning are also important outcomes of profiling and action planning.

22. Commitments to continuous improvement and innovation require ongoing professional development for all staff members, consistent with the principles of adult learning and effective leadership.

IDENTIFYING THE IMPORTANT GOALS AND OUTCOMES FOR STUDENTS

What goals and outcomes for students are at the heart of contemporary, inclusive approaches to talent development? When we ask groups, "Why should there be gifted or talented programming in your schools?" some of the most common responses emphasize the importance of providing learning opportunities that are appropriate and challenging for students, commensurate with their strengths and talents, and that will enable students to reach or fulfill their high potential. We are less concerned with determining "exactly" who is or is not gifted (and, in fact, we doubt that such precise categorizations are actually possible!) than with nurturing students' strengths, talents, and sustained interests and providing learning opportunities that contribute to important goals and outcomes in three main areas: (1) Healthy, Effective Person, (2) Independent Learner, and (3) Creatively Productive Person. The chart below summarizes these three areas and the goals they include. Your commitment to programming for talent development involves the challenge of guiding and empowering students to attain these goals.

Desired Student Outcomes of Programming for Talent Development

Healthy, Effective Person

- Competent—demonstrates mastery of basic skills
- Aware of personal styles or preferences and their implications for effective learning and productivity
- Personally and socially effective
- Thinks and reasons soundly and fairly
- Functions effectively in team or group settings
- Identifies and carries out effective leadership practices
- Confident in own abilities, commitments, and judgments
- Committed to lifelong learning and talent development

(Continued)

(Continued)

Independent Learner

- Sets goals and defines task or project outcomes
- Identifies methods and resources for meeting goals
- Carries out appropriate actions and activities
- Pursues projects and products with passion and vigor
- Monitors, manages, and modifies actions as needed
- Uses a variety of tools and technologies to design, produce, and share products
- Evaluates accomplishments and plans new directions

Creatively Productive Person

- Sees many possibilities or connections
- Looks at problems in varied and original ways
- Sustains and enhances existing strengths
- Innovates—formulates new possibilities and directions
- Communicates ideas and shares products with others
- Expresses and acts on principles, values, and convictions
- Committed to improving the quality of life for self and others
- Confident and courageous in pursuing goals and purposes despite obstacles

DECIDING TO IMPLEMENT A CONTEMPORARY, INCLUSIVE APPROACH

Successful implementation of a contemporary approach to talent development programming is both demanding and rewarding. It will require time, commitment, effort, and the willingness to challenge assumptions and practices, to take risks, and to acknowledge and solve problems. It is not a quick and easy method. The chart below summarizes why (and why not) a school or school district might make the decision to implement a contemporary approach to programming.

Why Support a Contemporary Approach?

1. It is consistent with research on human abilities, thinking skills, and learning styles.

2. It helps us manage change by integrating our efforts and priorities.

3. It recognizes and celebrates present positives while promoting continuous improvement.

4. It stimulates innovation to help us raise our vision of the future to new levels.

5. It reminds us where to keep the compass set: what's important for students?

6. It is consistent with contemporary views of curriculum and instruction.

7. It supports effective instructional practices for all students.

8. It challenges school staff, students, and community to reach for excellence.

Why *Not* Adopt a Contemporary Approach to Gifted Programming?

1. It's hard work.

2. It takes a long time (perhaps four to six years, and then ongoing efforts to sustain and improve!).

3. It requires cooperation and teamwork.

4. It redefines traditional roles (requiring broad-based involvement of administrators, staff, and community in planning, decision making, and problem solving).

5. It is not a high-profile program.

6. It demands creativity and initiative (there is no one right way to do it and no "cookbook" to follow).

7. It requires complex planning, forecasting, and risk taking.

8. It reminds us of the need to invest in professional development.

DOING YOUR HOMEWORK

Finally, we note that preparation for contemporary programming will also involve a deliberate effort to learn about the field and about the essential components of effective programming; there will be plenty of "homework" for everyone who will be involved in the process. This homework may include books, journal articles, Web-based resources, presentations by experts in the field, coursework (if it is available), or site visits to other schools or districts implementing contemporary approaches in order to observe and learn from their experiences.

The Staff Book Study: A Case Example of Preparation

In our ongoing work with several school districts in Indiana on planning for and implementation of the Levels of Service (LoS) approach to programming (Treffinger, Young, Nassab, & Wittig, 2004b), we learned that several schools began the task of studying contemporary programming in an innovative and collaborative way. The districts' leaders (administrators or gifted education coordinators) initiated, in some cases even prior to their involvement in the

(Continued)

(Continued)

statewide project, a staff book study program. They obtained multiple copies of the LoS book, distributed them to all staff members to read, and conducted a series of discussions in staff meetings. This gave the staff an opportunity to share their positive reactions, concerns, and questions and to begin establishing a foundation for program planning before any formal commitments were made to pursue such an initiative. The discussions provided opportunities for everyone's voice to be heard and helped to build ownership and support for subsequent efforts.

Innovation and Change 4

"It was the best of times and the worst of times . . ."

—Charles Dickens, *A Tale of Two Cities*

In this chapter we review some important principles and issues concerning innovation and change. Everyone involved in education today must deal with these issues. To be effective in planning any new educational programming, we must be aware of these forces and must be able to deal with them effectively. These challenges influence contemporary talent development programming as well as the schools' broader concerns for school improvement.

THE CHALLENGES OF INNOVATION AND CHANGE

American life changed in many ways in every decade of the twentieth century, and it continues to change rapidly in the twenty-first century. Every day we experience innovation and change in a variety of ways: new products, new vocabulary, new questions and issues, new organizations, new opportunities, and new problems and challenges. Children today accept as ordinary or commonplace many products, experiences, and living conditions that were unheard of, and often beyond the imagination of, their grandparents or even their parents. Today's children take for granted such things as color television, computers, cell phones, and the Internet—things that not so very long ago were topics only for science fiction.

Whether these changes are "good" or "bad" for our country as a whole, or for any groups or individuals, may be debatable. But the fact that change has taken place, and continues to occur, is not debatable. Rapid change is an inescapable reality of our time.

These changes influence every human institution—the family, the political system, the work place, the health care system—and, very dramatically, the schools. It is very easy to see that "the winds of change are blowing" in schools today. Some of the ways in which rapid change can easily be seen in schools today include:

- Drug and substance abuse, neglect, and child abuse
- Increasing numbers of latchkey children

- Increasing numbers of students from homes with one parent or caregiver
- Pressures to expand the curriculum with more information about more and more varied subjects
- Legislation that leads to increasing pressure to measure learning and school effectiveness based on high-stakes tests and standards
- Pressures to deal in school with many challenges that were previously handled in other settings
- Expanding social, cultural, geographic, and economic diversity among our students
- Heightened attention on individual differences and learning styles
- Pressures to incorporate technology and related skills
- Growing emphasis on new and expanding instructional strategies and technologies

In schools everywhere, teachers and administrators can be heard, as if in a common refrain: "Everyone wants us to do more and more. Things are always being added to our platter, but no one ever seems to remove anything from it!" All too often, the sheer number of new concerns, and the rate at which they appear before us, create fear and frustration. There always seems to be too much to do and not enough time or support to do it, even under the best of circumstances.

The impact of change on schools and schooling has been so extensive for several reasons. First, schools themselves must deal directly with changes, such as in technology. Student materials have been affected by technological changes, as we have moved from the "ditto" or spirit master to photocopies to today's Web-based resource distribution. Advances in information and communications technology have taken us from reliance on reels of film or slides to today's video programming, satellite dishes, and laser videodiscs, or from video-cassettes to CDs to DVDs. Computational resources have moved from the slide rule to the programmable calculator and the personal computer. Computer technology is now an everyday component of the school environment, and the use of networking and communications resources (e.g., fax machines, modems, the Internet, text messaging, podcasting) is commonplace.

Changes occurring in other social institutions also have other kinds of impact, extending directly into schools in very powerful ways. Changes in the home and family structure and in the workplace have had many influences on what children bring with them into the school experience, on what is expected of schools today, on the outcomes or results that are defined for education, and on how teaching and learning should take place, day in and day out.

RESPONDING TO INNOVATION AND CHANGE

Not everyone is enthusiastic about the rapid change and innovation we have experienced. Some people are confused or bewildered by change, while others may be rigid in their opposition or resistance to accepting change or doing anything in a new or different way. Many factors can prevent change, including fear, lack of information and skills, lack of confidence, and lack of resources and support. Even among people who are not strongly resistant to change, research has shown that individuals differ, as a matter of style or personal preference, in the way in which they deal with or respond to change. How do people and organizations tend to deal with innovation and change? How do we deal with those who seem to be committed to maintaining the status quo? Try to involve them, of course. But it is equally important to make sure they don't sink a ship that is sailing in the right direction! The chart below summarizes (in a light-hearted way) several different ways in which people often respond to change. Do you recognize some of them?

Responding to Change

Some people are basically satisfied with the way things are now.

And if their attitude is: *We might describe them as:*

Improvement Motivated   **Growing!** ("Things are okay now, but they could always be better.")

Maintain the Status Quo   **Glowing!** ("Since things are okay now, we should leave them alone.")

Over the Hill   **Slowing!** ("Things are okay; maybe there is room for improvement, but I'll be retiring soon . . . it will be someone else's challenge.")

Other people feel dissatisfied with the way things are now.

And if their attitude is: *We might describe them as:*

Improvement Motivated   **Itching!** ("This system is a mess, but I can fix it . . .")

Maintain the Status Quo   **Complaining!** [Isn't that the word you had in mind?] ("It's a mess, and no one can make it any better.")

Over the Hill   **Ditching!** ("It's a mess, but I'll be out of here soon anyway.")

Research indicates that people use a variety of different styles for solving problems, managing change, and dealing with new ideas. Treffinger, Selby, Isaksen, and Crumel (2007) identified three important dimensions of problem solving style: Orientation to Change, Manner of Processing, and Ways of Deciding. (You can obtain more information about problem solving style by visiting www.ViewStyle.net.)

To illustrate the importance of style and its relevance to the challenges of managing change in education today, let us consider the Orientation to Change dimension of problem solving style, in which there are two contrasting styles:

the explorer and the developer. The chart below presents several of the principal ways in which people differ in relation to their preference for one or the other of these styles.

Orientation to Change: Two Differing Styles

Explorers . . .	*Developers . . .*
Break away from the existing system or ways of operating	Stay within existing paradigm or system
Challenge problem definitions	Accept problem definitions
Are often seen as undisciplined	Are often seen as steady, disciplined
Are unique, visionary, ingenious	Are precise, reliable, dependable
Emphasize doing things differently	Emphasize doing things better
Like extensive change, action NOW	Like gradual, incremental change
Know the newest trends and exciting possibilities	Know how to get ideas through the system, gain support
Question or disregard means	Make goals of means
Find structure, authority confining, limiting	Find structure, authority enabling, guiding
Seek high levels of novelty	Seek "just enough" novelty to get the job done

Source: Based on Selby, Treffinger, & Isaksen, 2002

What are the implications of style preferences in dealing with change for education today?

• *Balance is important.* Both styles "bring value to the party." There isn't just one right way to deal with new ideas or change. An effective team learns to value both continuity and originality, and to recognize and value the differing strengths and preferences of all of its members.

• *Developers must work to be open to new possibilities.* If we hold too tightly to the way things are now, or the way they used to be, growth can be stifled and a program can become stagnant and ineffective. It is important to be able to consider new ideas.

• *Explorers must work toward successful implementation.* Just as those with a "developer" preference must work to be open to new ideas, those with an "explorer" preference must also learn to seek and value the strengths of the current reality, and to know when and how to work for growth within a system.

In summary, *being aware of change* and *managing change effectively* will be very important considerations in your planning efforts for talent development *and* for school improvement. The chart below summarizes a number of important research-based suggestions regarding constructive ways of dealing with change.

> ## Dealing With Change
>
> - Know what you want to accomplish before you begin trying to attain it.
> - Recognize the impact of problem solving styles and leadership styles.
> - Remember that change is an ongoing process, not a one-time event.
> - Change is better when we create it (are proactive) than when it just happens (are reactive).
> - Both "top-down" and "bottom-up" change can work.
> - Change is inevitable (but growth is optional).

Keep in mind, of course, that dealing with change requires a commitment of time and energy, deliberate planning and assessment of needs, the inevitable need to deal with obstacles and setbacks along the way, constant reshaping and refining of your goals, the ability to think creatively and critically and solve problems, the recognition and rewarding of progress along the way, and ongoing efforts to establish and maintain a supportive climate. It is often said that people resist change, but our experience indicates that this is not always true, especially when change efforts are carefully designed and attend to these important factors. Factors that may lead people to be resistant to or hesitant about change may include:

- Lack of clarity about ownership, authority, responsibilities, control, or competence
- Failure to address existing personal commitments
- Permitting coalitions to "line up" or take sides early
- Introducing changes into an environment that is already turbulent for other reasons
- Inadequate attention to and discussion of legitimate concerns about an innovation or change
- Badly managed implementation

You must be aware of these potential sources of resistance and be willing and able to acknowledge them when they occur. Respond to them in an open, problem-solving approach (rather than in an argumentative or defensive manner), and work constructively and collaboratively to help overcome potential obstacles and to address legitimate issues and concerns thoroughly. Any change agent (a person, team, or group working to effect change) will always find it necessary to balance several opposing pressures or concerns. These paradoxical challenges are illustrated in Figure 4.1.

The role of the change agent can be complex, demanding, and at times very frustrating. If you are aware of these tensions and challenges, you will be better prepared to deal with them in a constructive way. However, if you attempt to ignore or deny them, they will persist and grow, and may have negative consequences for you and for the goals you are attempting to promote! The qualities of an effective change agent include:

- Knowledge of change processes and an effective sense of their dynamics and operation

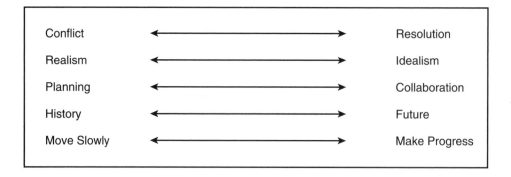

Figure 4.1   Paradoxes for change agents

- Strong guiding value system
- Strong interaction and communication skills
- High level of energy and commitment
- Style assessment, debriefing, and application skills
- Working grasp of creative and critical thinking and problem-solving tools and their effective facilitation
- Commitment to a collaborative orientation

NEW APPROACHES TO TEACHING AND LEARNING

Contemporary advances in education, psychology and cognitive science, management and organizational behavior, and other related fields offer today's schools a wealth of information and opportunities for improvement and innovation—opportunities to extend, expand, and enhance our efforts to recognize and nurture strengths and talents in all students. These include:

1. *Different ways that students learn.* Major advances have been made in identifying students' unique learning styles and using those data in instructional planning. While teachers have always been admonished to "recognize and respond to individual differences," progress in this area has enabled educators today to translate the admonition into practice effectively.

2. *Different ways that students think.* There have been many advances in our ability to define and translate into instructional practice specific skills relating to creative thinking, critical thinking, decision making, and problem solving. These advances enable all teachers to be more effective in challenging students' thinking beyond recall and recognition.

3. *Expanding views of human talents and abilities.* As noted in Chapter 3, research on the nature, variety, and development of human intelligences and talents has challenged educators to expand their views far beyond the traditional reliance on IQ and related constructs. Research clearly documents that human intelligence and talent potentials are considerably richer, more diverse, and more amenable to nurture than has previously been envisioned.

4. *Varying dimensions of the learning environment.* Extensive progress has been made in the last decade in research and development on group dynamics, characteristics of effective teams, organizational climate, leadership, and collaborative or cooperative skills. These efforts have provided significant new insights into classroom organization and structure, instructional delivery, and classroom management.

5. *Students' strengths, talents, and sustained interests (not just their weaknesses and deficiencies).* New approaches to teaching and learning actively search for, use, and develop students' "positive needs" or talents. Our conception of needs does not focus on deficiencies or weaknesses. Instead, we emphasize students' *best* potentials. They involve students' *strengths, sustained interests, and talents.* Some writers have referred to these as abilities or aptitudes (e.g., Guilford, 1977), or even as intelligences (e.g., Gardner, 1983). We prefer the term *talents* (e.g., Feldhusen, 1992).

6. *Many and varied settings or environments and instructional resources.* Advances in technology and learning resources, and an expanding concept of where and how worthwhile learning takes place, have also had major impacts on the emergence of new paradigms in education. New technologies bring powerful new learning opportunities into any classroom. In addition, however, increasing focus on school-business partnerships, mentoring, community resources, and other resource-based approaches to teaching and learning have challenged educators to expand their views beyond textbooks and classrooms. Today, it is essential to consider the ecosystem of teaching and learning, or a complex network that includes the school, the home, and the community (as illustrated in Figure 4.2).

7. *Deliberate efforts to promote transfer, including dealing with real problems and challenges.* Educators today are increasingly aware that transfer does not occur automatically, and that if we expect students to be able to apply and use their knowledge, we must provide for both instruction and assessment that is similar to the experiences and challenges students will encounter in real-life situations outside school.

8. *The new basics.* America's view of education has changed in many ways, and no approach to long-range school improvement or effective, contemporary talent development programming can proceed without considering those changes. In the late 1980s, many national reports from governmental agencies, educational organizations, and the private sector began identifying new conceptions of "basic skills," or new views of the skills that would be essential for personal and vocational success in the 1990s and beyond. There is a relatively high degree of consistency and agreement among these reports as to the nature of these "new basics," as illustrated in Figure 4.3. An interesting concern, of course, is the resistance that these directions have met, primarily in the political arena, across more than two decades. While it is clear that a large number of educators and employers value these new basics, and while new calls for them have been issued in every decade, political leaders have yet to embrace them. In time, this may change; in the meantime, we urge educators to continue to be advocates for these basics as elements of best practice.

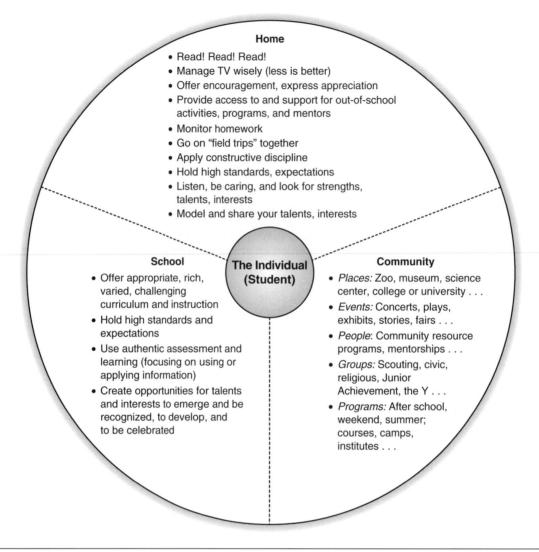

Figure 4.2 The ecosystem for talent development

Source: From the Center for Creative Learning, Inc.

THE SCHOOL IMPROVEMENT CHALLENGE

What are the major challenges and issues that must be considered in a well-designed, effectively implemented school improvement or long-range planning process? New directions in education have caused many professionals and community members to look very closely at school improvement and long-range planning challenges.

Some school improvement initiatives have focused primarily on bringing all students to a certain minimum level of achievement. In relation to seeking a rich, comprehensive view of school improvement, such a focus is not adequate. If "school improvement" means primarily (or only) focusing on minimum competencies, often leading them to become "maximum expectancies," all learners may be insufficiently challenged and the school may fall short in its responsibility to seek and nurture the strengths and talents of its students.

**SCANS Report—Thinking Skills
(United States Department of Labor, 1991)**

- Creative thinking
  (generating new ideas)

- Decision making
  (specifying goals and constraints,
  generating alternatives, considering
  risks, and evaluating and choosing best
  alternatives)

- Problem solving
  (recognizing problems and devising and
  implementing plan of action)

- Seeing things in the mind's eye
  (organizing and processing symbols,
  pictures, graphs . . .)

- Knowing how to learn
  (using efficient learning techniques to
  acquire and apply new knowledge and
  skills)

- Reasoning
  (discovering a rule or principle . . . and
  applying it when solving a problem)

**The Basics of Tomorrow . . .
(Gisi & Forbes, 1982)**

- Evaluation and analysis skills

- Critical thinking

- Problem solving strategies

- Organization and reference skills

- Synthesis

- Application

- Creativity

- Decision making, given
  incomplete information

- Communication skills, through a
  variety of modes

**"Workplace Basics"
(Carnevale, Gainer, & Meltzer, 1991)**

- The foundation
  (Knowing how to learn)

- Competence
  (Reading, writing, and computation)

- Communication
  (Listening and oral communication)

- Adaptability
  (Creative thinking and problem solving)

- Personal management
  (Self-esteem, goal setting, motivation,
  personal and career development)

- Group effectiveness
  (Interpersonal skills, negotiation,
  teamwork)

- Influence
  (Organizational effectiveness,
  leadership)

Figure 4.3   The new basics

In contrast, more constructive, comprehensive approaches to school improvement share many goals and purposes with contemporary approaches to talent development programming. A major goal of significant school improvement initiatives is to improve learning for all students and to create schools that provide stimulating teaching and learning environments. Many school improvement plans address goals for all students that were, in the early generations of gifted education, proposed as goals for gifted programs. These include, for example, engagement in higher-order thinking, involvement in individual and group projects, the development of research and inquiry skills, and the application of presentation skills. School improvement plans often involve continuous progress in basic skill areas, through the use of leveled approaches to reading and mathematics instruction, providing all students with educationally sound programs based on their characteristics and needs. Restructuring or school improvement efforts often require consistent and coherent policies across curriculum, assessment, professional development, teacher and administrator development, and accountability systems. They require the support of the broader community, including business and industry, as well as the entire education community.

Linking School Improvement and Talent Development

In many schools, school improvement planning and gifted/talented education have been treated as independent, unrelated, or even competing priorities. It has been common for each to proceed within a school district as a separate, independent activity, with little or no effort to identify common goals or concerns, or to seek ways in which one might support or enhance the other.

In the emerging new generation of contemporary talent development programming, seeking and articulating common goals and concerns can be a collaborative and mutually supportive venture. School improvement planning contributes to the goals and priorities of talent development programming in many ways, including:

- Building bridges with the total school program
- Recognizing and sustaining existing program strengths
- Providing an effective starting point for locating and making the best use of many people and materials, for the benefit of all students
- Enriching education by expanding, extending, and enhancing learning opportunities for all students

By the same token, new views of talent development can also make significant contributions to the school improvement process, by, for example:

- Supporting a focus on students' strengths, talents, and interests that prevents us from becoming paralyzed with weaknesses and deficiencies

- Stimulating the search for ways to bring out the best among our students, our staff, our parents, and our community
- Providing resources and people to expand and support the school's efforts to promote higher-level thinking skills, independence and self-direction, and other areas traditionally associated with gifted education that can be incorporated into the total school program in meaningful ways

Several of the new and emerging trends and issues, and the evolving ways of describing our tasks, that emerge from our efforts to link school improvement and contemporary talent development programming are summarized in Figures 4.4 and 4.5.

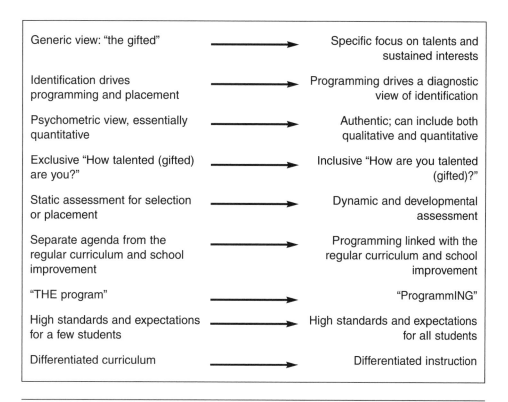

Figure 4.4   New and emerging trends and issues

The challenges of improvement, innovation, and change that have been part of the landscape of education for several decades remain important concerns for all educators, and that is likely to be a continuing reality in the foreseeable future. These factors have significant impact on all educational planning and decision making, and are also essential considerations in planning and carrying out contemporary approaches to talent development programming.

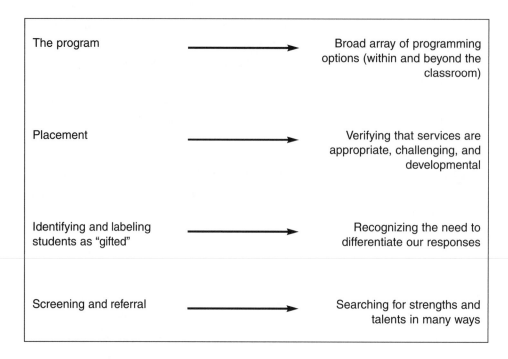

The program   ⟶   Broad array of programming options (within and beyond the classroom)

Placement   ⟶   Verifying that services are appropriate, challenging, and developmental

Identifying and labeling students as "gifted"   ⟶   Recognizing the need to differentiate our responses

Screening and referral   ⟶   Searching for strengths and talents in many ways

Figure 4.5   Evolving ways of viewing and describing our tasks

Planning Logistics 5

This chapter examines the organizational and "start-up" tasks necessary for effective planning. These include (a) forming a planning committee, (b) considering a developmental conception of leadership, (c) planning for an effective group, and (d) establishing a working community for contemporary programming.

FORMING A PLANNING COMMITTEE

Although the makeup of the planning committee may vary from one setting to another, and from the school to the districtwide level, several common threads run through the majority of successful planning committees. The fundamental principle for selecting participants for a planning committee is to seek breadth of participation. Your planning committee should represent a cross section of your staff. More specifically, those who should ordinarily be represented on a planning committee include:

- Administrator(s)
- Library or media specialist
- Counselor(s)
- School psychologist
- Teachers at each unit involved (elementary, middle, senior high)
- Gifted education specialist
- Curriculum specialist(s)

Other stakeholder groups to consider include school board members, parent and community representatives, and students. The appropriateness of their participation is a matter for local decisions, based on the unique situation, experience, and judgment of each school or district.

School Board Participation

The participation of school board members on a districtwide planning committee is a matter on which there are differences of opinion. Since we know of no research that has addressed this question specifically, we consider it entirely a *local option*. In some local settings, board members seek involvement in planning committees and participate actively. The benefits of board participation can include better consideration of resource and policy issues, improved communication between the board and staff, greater mutual understanding of needs and concerns, and the opportunity for board members to bring more complete and accurate information to the board during its planning and decision making.

Community and Parent Participation

Although many of the issues to be addressed by the planning committee are professional in nature, and the general community would not be expected to have the technical background or expertise necessary to make such decisions, it is advisable for the planning committee to include parent and community participation. An informed community is more likely to be committed to supporting new programming, and parents are greatly concerned about the quality, effectiveness, and impact of school programs on students because the lives and futures of their children are involved.

The committee can also benefit from the professional and technical expertise in other related fields (e.g., financial or budgeting skills, knowledge of community history and resources, technology, publicity and public relations) that community members can bring to the committee. Help parent representatives to think of their role on the committee in relation to program planning on a broad level, not merely as advocacy for the immediate perceived needs of their own children.

Student Participation

In our experience, it is not yet the usual strategy in planning school programs to include students, although it is not unheard of for them to be included in at least some aspects of the planning process. Students can provide unique perspectives regarding their school experiences, interests, and needs—and educators may gain valuable insights from their participation.

Other Human Factors to Consider

It will also be beneficial to ensure that the committee:

Includes productive members. It is helpful to know something about the personalities and track record of individuals being considered for the committee. Who will really produce? Who will not lose interest quickly and drop by the wayside? Who has a foundation of knowledge and skills to offer special expertise to the committee? Who will not use the committee to grind the same old axes? Strive to include on the committee those people who will make good faith efforts to contribute and work together, even though there may be honest disagreements or varying points of view among them, and who will be willing to put the success of the group ahead of their personal goals and agendas.

Includes people who have credibility or the respect of their peers. To promote ownership and acceptance of the group's efforts, ensure that the committee members are individuals who have earned the professional regard of their colleagues.

Has clout. The committee must either (preferably) include people who have authority or responsibility for follow-up and decision making, or have a charge in which it is clear that their efforts will lead to action rather than just be set aside or tabled at higher levels.

Devotes time and effort that will be needed for group process and team building. There is no perfect group, but people can learn to work together in productive and supportive ways. The committee should allow time to examine and understand the learning and thinking styles of individual members, and to establish guidelines and procedures for effective group management and decision making.

The planning committee does not have to be a new and separately created committee; many schools and districts are already at or nearing "committee overload." If you have already established a school improvement or long-range planning committee, for example, it may be wise to incorporate the principles and tasks described in this handbook into its work. The planning committee will continue to function throughout the planning stages described in this handbook. It will also guide future planning and development in a continuing role.

SIZE OF THE COMMITTEE

The committee should be either small enough to be manageable or large enough to develop effective, working subcommittees. There is no magic number, but our experience suggests that 8 to 12 members is a reasonable range for effective communication and workable scheduling. Several factors may also influence decisions about the committee's size in specific situations, including, for example, history of past practices, ordinary or customary local policies, and the total number of schools or communities that must be represented for districtwide planning.

If the committee is too small, there is a greater risk that it will not effectively represent the interests and concerns of the many stakeholders. It will also be likely to create too much work for everyone, and individuals may easily become bogged down, discouraged, or unproductive. Finally, others may too easily perceive a small committee as an "in" group that serves only the needs and special interests of its own members. On the other hand, if the committee becomes too large, effective communication may become very difficult, both during meetings and for follow-through between meetings. Also, it will be difficult to schedule meetings because of conflicting schedules and the time pressures on individual members. It is likely to be difficult to make decisions or reach consensus on difficult issues, and splinter groups or factions may develop easily.

FOSTERING EFFECTIVE COMMUNICATION CHANNELS

Since planning at the district level generally involves a group with a broad-based and diverse structure, enabling the major educational stakeholders (e.g., teachers, parents, administrators, community members) to exchange ideas and suggestions, maintaining effective communication can be a logistical challenge. Be certain, early in the planning process, to provide opportunities for the group to receive information about the planning committee's makeup and the various roles its members represent. Figure 5.1 provides a form to help ensure that the committee members know each others' names and roles and are able to contact each other. (This form is also on the accompanying CD.)

PHILOSOPHY AND VALUES OF THE COMMITTEE MEMBERS

The members of the committee should each have their own copy of appropriate study resources. The participants should understand and agree that all committee members will read and study the materials they receive in preparation for their work together. All committee members should have an opportunity to share their general attitudes, values, and commitments as educators; the committee will be strengthened by an explicit commitment to making deliberate efforts to improve the quality of learning and instruction for students. The committee should not overlook the basic question ("Will this benefit students?") or let it drop out of sight. It should be a clear and unequivocal statement of the vision that drives the planning process. There are three key questions that should remain constantly prominent in our talent development programming efforts:

- Will this benefit students?
- Will this enhance our ability to "stretch" their talents and interests?
- Will this challenge students, and help us to bring out the best they can be and do?

DEVELOPMENTAL CONCEPTION OF LEADERSHIP

Proper planning requires effective leadership, to be sure. However, it is very important to recognize that contemporary approaches to leadership emphasize that it is both situational and developmental.

The work of Hersey and Blanchard and their associates (e.g., Blanchard, 1987, 2006; Hersey, Blanchard, & Johnson, 2000), for example, emphasizes different kinds of leadership behavior or "styles" that will be appropriate and necessary, depending upon:

- The nature of the task, and the group's knowledge and skills with respect to the tasks the group is expected to complete

PLANNING COMMITTEE

School or District: _____   Date: _____

Name	Representing	E-mail Address	Phone
Chair:			

INITIAL MEETING SCHEDULE: _____
(Date, Time, Place)   _____

Figure 5.1 Planning committee members form

Source: Copyright © The Center for Creative Learning, Inc.

- The willingness of the group to carry out the task
- The amount of personal and interpersonal support required by group members
- The group's commitment to and enthusiasm for carrying out the tasks

Effective leadership implies that leadership behaviors or strategies must be selected on the basis of knowledge of these factors and their interrelationships. No single style or approach will be equally effective across all tasks, for all participants, or for the same participants, as tasks vary throughout a project. It is widely recognized today that effective leadership involves careful analysis of tasks, interpersonal relationships, and the developmental level (competence and commitment) of the group members.

Research on leadership reveals that "leadership is not the private reserve of a few charismatic men and women. It is a process ordinary people use when they are bringing forth the best from themselves and others" (Kouzes & Posner, 2002, p. xxiii). Kouzes and Posner (2002, p. 22) have identified five practices and 10 commitments of leadership; these are:

- Model the way

    1. Find your voice by clarifying your personal values.

    2. Set the example by aligning actions with shared values.

- Inspire a shared vision

    3. Envision the future by imagining exciting and ennobling possibilities.

    4. Enlist others in a common vision by appealing to shared aspirations.

- Challenge the process

    5. Search for opportunities by seeking innovative ways to change, grow, and improve.

    6. Experiment and take risks by constantly generating small wins and learning from mistakes.

- Enable others to act

    7. Foster collaboration by promoting cooperative goals and building trust.

    8. Strengthen others by sharing power and discretion.

- Encourage the heart

    9. Recognize contributions by showing appreciation for individual excellence.

    10. Celebrate the values and victories by creating a spirit of community.

Through these contemporary models, leadership is best understood in relation to:

- Varied styles and strategies
- Active participation by all group members

- Shared responsibility among group members for decision making and impact

Rather than viewing leadership as individual heroics, then, we now recognize the importance and value of bringing out the creativity and productivity of others in ways that recognize and build upon their strengths and talents. Successful leadership enables or empowers followers rather than permitting or allowing them to carry out the leader's directives. The actions toward which leaders direct their efforts may vary in relation to the nature of the change they are attempting to promote and the level of impact they seek to attain.

Isaksen and Tidd (2006) presented evidence to support the conclusion that contemporary views of leadership styles and practices contribute positively and significantly to creating and maintaining a supportive climate in many different organizational settings and contexts. A developmental approach to leadership, considered in concert with efforts to assess and improve climate (which we address specifically in Chapter 7), will contribute in powerful ways to planning and implementing contemporary, inclusive approaches to talent development.

PLANNING FOR AN EFFECTIVE GROUP

A number of additional factors will help you to establish an effective climate or setting for a productive planning committee. These include (a) getting acquainted, (b) group behavior guidelines, (c) understanding and applying generating and focusing tools, and (d) having an informed, progressive outlook.

Getting Acquainted

Begin group building by making sure everyone is introduced to each of the others. It is not enough to know one another's names. In larger districts with several buildings, there may very well be people who know each other only as a face. Select and use an exercise to break the ice and help people get to know one another; this creates a positive tone for future interactions.

Understanding each member, and their various working styles, is important in establishing a productive context for the committee. It will be helpful for the group to engage in some self-assessment of the members' preferred learning and working styles. For example, taking and discussing together instruments such as the VIEW assessment (Selby, Treffinger, & Isaksen, 2002), the Myers-Briggs Type Indicator (Myers, McCaulley, Quenk, & Hammer, 1998), or the Building Excellence Survey (Rundle & Dunn, 2005) can help members of the group to understand better their own preferences and needs as well as the way other group members may differ. Although some instruments require trained personnel to administer, score, and interpret, you may have access to qualified people in your area. Alternatively, there are many informal inventories and self-description checklists that might be useful to help the group examine and discuss their preferences. In many areas, state school board associations and similar groups may offer facilitation resources to support team building efforts.

Group Behavior Guidelines

Establish some general guidelines for the group's behavior. Effective group facilitators understand that it is wise to separate generating ideas from judging them, and to allow time and opportunity for both processes. They also follow several general guidelines to ensure group productivity; these are summarized in the box below.

Guidelines for Generating and Focusing Options

When generating options:

- Defer judgment
- Seek quantity
- Encourage freewheeling
- Look for combinations

When focusing options:

- Use affirmative judgment
- Be deliberate
- Search for novelty
- Stay on course

Source: From Treffinger, Isaksen, & Stead-Dorval, 2006.

Your group would be wise, for example, to follow the "affirmative judgment" guideline (Treffinger, Isaksen, & Stead-Dorval, 2006). In an all-too-typical group situation, new ideas are often greeted with criticism or ridicule: "That won't work because . . ." or "We've already [or never] tried that before" or any of a number of familiar idea killers (see Figure 5.2). The goal of affirmative judgment is to treat new ideas with more sensitivity, to give them a better opportunity to be examined and studied. Instead of saying, "Yes, *but* . . . ," we say, "Yes, *and* . . ."

Understanding and Applying Tools for Generating and Focusing Ideas

Many planning groups flounder because they get trapped in endless rounds of discussion or argument without ever being able to reach closure. The consequences are often very unpleasant for all concerned. Although such problems are sometimes described primarily as personality clashes, lack of leadership, or group dynamics problems, effective groups deal with them by knowing and using deliberate tools to generate options as well as to focus their thinking and make decisions (Isaksen, Dorval, & Treffinger, 1998, 2000; Treffinger, Isaksen, & Stead-Dorval, 2006; Treffinger & Nassab, 2005; Treffinger, Nassab, Schoonover, Selby, Shepardson, Wittig, & Young, 2006). Knowing and using

The Handy Dandy Checklist Or . . . How to Kill Ideas!

1. That idea is silly or ridiculous.

2. We've tried it before.

3. We've never tried it before.

4. It will cost too much.

5. It's not in our area of responsibility.

6. It's too radical a change.

7. We don't have the time.

8. It will make other things obsolete.

9. We're too small to do that.

10. It's not practical in our situation.

11. The community will be upset.

12. Let's get back to reality.

13. That's not our problem!

14. The old way has always worked well enough.

15. You're several years ahead of your time.

16. We're not ready for it.

17. It isn't in the budget.

18. You can't teach old dogs new tricks.

19. The Board (Administration . . . Management . . .) won't go for it.

20. We'll look foolish if it fails.

21. We've done OK without it.

22. Let's think about it for a while.

23. Let's form a committee to study it.

24. Has it worked for anyone else?

25. It won't work at our level (or in our area).

Figure 5.2   Idea killers

Source: From the Center for Creative Learning, Inc.

these tools can help groups to use their creativity and imagination in thinking of new possibilities, and to reduce arbitrary, emotionally stressed decision making. It's important to be able to manage both idea generation and idea evaluation skillfully and deliberately.

Generating Tools

Brainstorming is probably the most widely known and used (and often abused) tool for generating ideas. Other practical tools to help a group generate many, varied, unusual, and detailed options include Brainstorming with Post-It Notes, Brainwriting, Attribute Listing, SCAMPER and other idea checklists, Force-Fitting, and the Morphological Matrix (see sources cited in the previous paragraph).

Figure 5.3 presents an example of an application of a generating tool other than brainstorming (in this case, the Morphological Matrix tool) that might be used in thinking about many, varied, and unusual programming activities. By considering a number of possible people, places, processes, and products that might be involved in nurturing students' strengths and talents and then exploring many possible combinations, a group's understanding of "multiple programming options" might expand considerably! Not all the 10,000 possible combinations (or more) would necessarily represent workable options, but even if only one percent were promising, 100 new possible ways to recognize and nurture strengths and talents might emerge.

Programming for Talent Development: 10,000 Possibilities			
People	**Places**	**Processes**	**Products**
Physician	Shopping Mall	Problem Solving	Written Report
Lawyer	Zoo	Knowledge	Multimedia
Architect	Classroom	Analyzing	Drama/Play
Truck Driver	Playground	Evaluating	Painting
Engineer	Museum	Listening	Software
Musician	Restaurant	Hypothesizing	Video
Custodian	Theater	Interviewing	Music or Song
Inventor	Swimming Pool	Deducing	Legislation
Farmer	Sports Arena	Forecasting	Poem
Retailer	Hospital	Experimenting	Sculpture

Figure 5.3   The Morphological Matrix

Note: By adding just five more entries to each of the four columns, the number of possibilities increases from 10,000 to more than 50,000. Consider the exciting possibilities for building the strengths and talents of many students in many ways!

Focusing Tools

Just as there are specific, deliberate tools to assist groups in generating options, tools also exist to support groups in the tasks of analyzing, refining, strengthening, and choosing and making decisions; we refer to these as "focusing tools." From the sources cited above, some specific focusing tools include ALoU, Hits and Hot Spots, Paired Comparison Analysis (PCA) for ranking or prioritizing alternatives, the Evaluation Matrix for evaluating options using a variety of specific criteria, and Sequencing S–M–L for ordering or arranging selected options.

Instead of killing an idea or suggestion by finding all its faults and weaknesses, for example, try using a constructive focusing tool, such as ALoU. Begin by giving *advantages*, or positive responses to the idea. Next, express *limitations* or concerns by asking, "How might we . . . ?" rather than by saying, "We can't because . . ." Consider how to *overcome* the limitations. Devote some time to stating the *unique features*—the distinctive elements—of the idea. This tool, and the affirmative judgment principle on which it is based, ensures that people will feel comfortable sharing their ideas even when those ideas are not set in stone. Applying this principle and tool helps to prevent the quick and rigid fixation on a particular idea or strategy that often occurs when people make decisions without an open mind. Affirmative judgment (with the ALoU tool) helps to set a positive atmosphere, a constructive mindset, in which people can explore ideas for the mutual benefit of all.

An Informed, Progressive Outlook

It will help your group to make deliberate efforts to remain focused and aware of your tasks. Avoid the pressure for premature closure, making certain that many constructive ideas and questions can be heard. Help people within the group to avoid locking in on slogans or overly emotional appeals. Find a nice way to let people know that blanket statements of "must" or "must not" seldom move the group forward. Encourage an atmosphere of mutual discovery and exploration. Some sentence starters that encourage an open attitude include:

"I wonder how we might . . . ?"

"In what ways might we . . . ?"

"Wouldn't it be interesting if . . . ?"

"See what other ideas you can add to this one."

"Let's play around with the idea of . . . "

Use and encourage all group members to use statements such as "That's really interesting, and . . . ," or "Could you say more about that idea? It sounds intriguing." If people understand that planning is a process of mutual exploration, with the constant goal of setting the best possible course of action for our students and our schools, then such dialogue will follow easily.

Finally, make sure that everyone understands that this is a working group that will succeed only if everyone cooperates and does his or her part. It would be better to have fewer people working diligently than to have meetings come to a screeching halt because the person who has been given the essential charge is too busy to get around to doing what he or she has agreed to do.

The sample meeting agenda form (Figure 5.4) and the sample meeting outcomes record (Figure 5.5) may be useful to you in maintaining clarity and commitment regarding tasks and responsibilities. The accompanying CD also includes these forms.

ESTABLISHING A WORKING COMMUNITY FOR CONTEMPORARY PROGRAMMING

Even before you begin to gather any specific data regarding programming goals, activities, or services, take some time to establish shared working attitudes and norms to help ensure that meetings run smoothly and result in a high level of productivity. We feel certain that everyone reading this has sat through at least one unproductive meeting that left you feeling frustrated, angry, and unenthusiastic. We hope that you will be able to avoid those feelings in your meetings by establishing a context of enthusiasm and commitment to work toward a shared goal. These suggestions may help you to establish a comfortable and productive atmosphere that might be characterized as a "working community."

State Your Goals at the Very Beginning

At your very first meeting, present and discuss a set of initial goals to help everyone establish a shared understanding of the committee's "charge" or overall task. An appropriate statement to make might be: "We have been charged with exploring programming for talent development. Our initial goals should be to establish a working definition and philosophy based on our unique qualities and strengths, and then to gather data about options that fit in with our definition and philosophy."

Establish a Time Line

Work to determine, at least tentatively, a time line for carrying out the committee's work, and for moving from planning to implementation. An initial statement, for example, might be: "The board would like an interim report in three months, and it seems that we will need a definition and philosophy—at least in rough draft—to show them." We will address a long-term time line, and provide additional resources to guide the committee's overall planning, in Chapter 10.

Establish a Positive Group Climate

After laying out the purposes of the group, it is time to focus on the group itself. The group has a mission, and they may have "met" each other, but they may have little or no experience in working with each other, nor do they (in all

---

Planning Committee Meeting Agenda

Meeting Date: _____ Place: _____ Time: _____

The major topics we expect to address at this meeting are:

1. _____

2. _____

3. _____

Specific Agenda   **Expected Time Required**

Opening and Announcements   _____ minutes

Review of Previous Meeting—Minutes   _____ minutes

OLD BUSINESS AND REPORTS   _____ minutes

_____

_____

_____

_____

NEW BUSINESS

Topic   Anticipated Action   Estimated Time

_____

_____

_____

_____

Figure 5.4   Planning committee meeting agenda form

Source: Copyright © The Center for Creative Learning, Inc.

Planning Committee Meeting Outcomes

Meeting Date: _____Start Time: _____ End Time: _____

Members Present:

Members Absent:

Summary of Major Tasks Addressed at This Meeting.

1. _____

2. _____

3. _____

4. _____

Actions to Take	Who's Responsible?	Target Date	Completed

Figure 5.5   Planning committee meeting outcomes record

Source: Copyright © The Center for Creative Learning, Inc.

likelihood) have a good feeling about how to get from goal to glory! We call this aspect of planning "group building," and it is a critical step in creating effective planning meetings. Without this step, your group may bog down in personality conflicts, political wrangling, or grandstanding on the part of people who need lots of airtime. Many published collections of icebreaker activities are available (e.g., Ukens, 1996; West, 1999).

Balancing Continuity and Coordination With Autonomy

In planning for contemporary programming at the districtwide level, it is always a complex challenge to create and maintain the proper balance between centralized, districtwide decision making and site-based decision making by individual schools. On the one hand, there are a number of valid and important concerns that can probably best be considered district level matters. These lead to consistency among units of the district, continuity over time, coherence of overall philosophy and outlook, and fairness in resource allocation, management, and evaluation. There would probably be general agreement that the school district must accept the responsibility of setting general parameters for program design, development, and implementation and for monitoring individual schools' efforts systematically.

On the other hand, there are also significant dimensions of program planning that may well be unique to each school, and thus for which the planning may be best delegated to the individual building level. Make the individual school or building the focal point for decisions in areas that involve:

- The specific culture, history, traditions, and commitments of the school
- Variability in administrative styles
- Diversity of interests and talents among staff members
- Demographic factors (parent and community makeup, geographic setting)
- Availability or proximity of specialized resources
- The nature of the school's organization and structure, with emphasis on day-to-day instructional transactions between teachers and students

The fundamental challenge, therefore, is to balance a centralized need for continuity and coordination with the individual school's need for autonomy and the opportunity to reflect its specific priorities and personality. Contemporary programming involves two levels of planning. At the *macro* level, the district should develop an overall plan or structure to guide each of its individual schools and to promote comparability and continuity among individual school programs. At the *micro* level, there are specific considerations for individual schools, representing the individual character of each school. This is not to say that an individual school cannot embark on implementing programming on its own. Indeed, we can envision some instances in which an individual school, with district sanction, might implement a contemporary approach as a pilot project or in an effort to respond to unique circumstances that differ from those of the district as a whole.

Take Your Time

Allow ample time for program development; poorly planned programs won't thrive in the long run. *The initial planning stages in a school or district will generally require at least six months, and more likely one year.* Creating written plans at the school and district levels are the beginning steps in accomplishing successful programming. Implementation, staff development and participation, community awareness and support, and modifications as the plans are translated into practice involve more extended time and effort. In many important ways, these are *ongoing* concerns in all high-quality programs. Successful programming requires care and feeding, which will extend beyond the initial planning year, perhaps by *three to five years.* Keep in mind, too, that planning for effective programming is an ongoing process, not a one-time event.

Write It All Down!

Your goals, decisions, and intended procedures should be presented in a specific, detailed, written plan. We provide detailed guidelines and resources for written plans at the district and school levels in subsequent chapters of this handbook. Creating an explicit written plan will help to ensure that:

1. Everyone will know what decisions have been made. No one will truthfully be able to say, "I didn't know that decision had been made."

2. The program plan will exist beyond the initial energies and enthusiasm of its original proponents. Without written guidelines, programming may exist only in the minds of the original champions, or survive only as long as those champions are present and involved.

3. A written plan provides a basis for ongoing study, review, and modification, without the need to reinvent the wheel.

As you proceed through the entire Six-Stage Systematic Planning process, several different kinds of documents or written products may result. Following is a list of five, with a short description of each.

1. *Comprehensive Master Plan.* A complete and detailed Master Plan, the content of which will be addressed in detail in Chapter 10.

2. *Executive summary.* A concise summary of the Master Plan's major features, and their implications for policy and fiscal resources, for those who wish to acquaint themselves with the Plan's general content.

3. *Marketing plan.* A separate document describing the committee's plans for presenting and reviewing the Master Plan with various important "constituencies" within the district or school community: the board, the administration, the staff, other community members, and perhaps the students.

4. *Time line.* A concise summary outlining the major stages in program development for approximately three to five years. It can be used to establish a broad framework for program development extending beyond the initial planning year.

5. *Building Action Plans.* For each building or school, there will also be a specific, written Action Plan, as provided by the Master Plan. The content and development of the Action Plan will be discussed in Chapter 11.

The box below provides a summary checklist of start-up questions to guide your initial work with your committee.

---

1. Is there administrative authorization and support for a planning committee and its work?

2. Have you established among the staff the need for and importance of such a committee?

3. Has a responsible, effective person accepted the responsibility for organizing and convening the committee?

4. Have you determined the size and structure of the committee?

5. Has there been an opportunity for prospective committee members to identify themselves, and have specific committee members been determined?

6. Have you collected and shared information to provide committee members with appropriate background information about contemporary programming?

7. Has there been any preliminary gathering of data to provide initial input for the committee?

8. Have decisions been made, and appropriate resources or materials been obtained, for the necessary group building and organizational tasks of the initial committee meeting?

9. Have you established an appropriate date, time, and place for meetings?

Section III

Stage Two— Clarify Where You Are Now

Section III deals with "Clarify Where You Are Now," the second stage of the Six-Stage Systematic Planning model. Clarifying involves identifying your present "state of the art" or your "current reality" in relation to gifted education or talent development programming. This stage guides you in laying an effective foundation for contemporary programming.

The key tasks in this stage are:

- Assessing your needs in six important programming areas (in both your present gifted/talented programming and in other aspects of your total school program)
- Assessing the climate of your school or school district to determine whether you are ready, willing, and able to implement programming (or to identify the areas that need work to help you to move in that direction)
- Identifying your current "programming positives"—the activities and services that are now in place and working effectively
- Identifying your wish list for programming—activities and services you might do, do more, do better, or do differently to strengthen your talent development programming

You will enter this stage with the goal of closely examining your pathway for implementing a contemporary approach, and you will exit this stage with a clearer understanding of your school or district's current strengths and needs. The three chapters in Section III provide information and resources to help you in carrying out these tasks effectively and efficiently.

Needs 6
Assessment

This chapter addresses needs assessment, an essential dimension of the "Clarify Where You Are Now" stage in the Six-Stage Systematic Planning Model. National statistics about schools (and especially about what's wrong or what needs improvement) cannot be applied directly to any individual district or school. Furthermore, good planning does not begin with stereotypes or vague assertions about what is, or might be, the case in your setting. Thus, begin your efforts by finding out where you really are.

In practice, there are important benefits of "acknowledging the present" and establishing your current reality in relation to gifted and talented programming. First, you will get people talking together, focusing their attention on the challenges of improvement and innovation. Second, you will very likely discover many positive dimensions of your current reality. Becoming aware of these helps to reduce defensiveness about improvement efforts and offsets some stresses and tensions produced by the constant bombardment of what's wrong with our schools. Third, you will identify some present efforts that are consistent with the goals of a contemporary, inclusive approach to programming. You will discover that a contemporary approach is not new and strange, and that you are already doing it in a number of important ways. This will provide a comfortable entry point for others as they consider additional opportunities and challenges.

This chapter describes our structured Needs Assessment Inventory, a practical tool you can use to take stock of your current status in relation to six programming areas. (The inventory and scoring key are presented in Figure 6.1; they are also on the CD accompanying this handbook.)

The six programming areas included in the Needs Assessment Inventory are:

- Differentiated Basics
- Appropriate Enrichment
- Effective Acceleration
- Independence and Self-Direction
- Personal Growth and Social Development
- Career Perspectives and Futuristic Orientation

(*Text continues on page 79*)

Needs Assessment Inventory

NAME/IDENTIFICATION _____   POSITION _____

SCHOOL _____   DATE _____

Introduction and Purposes

The purposes of this inventory are to help your school determine the activities and services you presently provide for talent development, to identify areas for possible improvement, and to identify promising directions for new activities and services. Talent development refers to your school's efforts to recognize students' strengths and sustained interests and to nurture those strengths and interests through a variety of appropriate, challenging, and developmental opportunities. This inventory addresses six important areas of programming for talent development. These are:

- **Differentiated Basics.** Programming that takes into account students' unique characteristics, talents, interests, abilities, skills, and learning style preferences as the basis for providing individualized and varied learning opportunities.

- **Appropriate Enrichment.** Programming that expands, extends, or enhances students' learning experiences above and beyond minimum expectations, integrating process and content skills with an emphasis on preparation for and involvement in original inquiry and investigations (individually or in groups).

- **Effective Acceleration.** Programming that expands, extends, or enhances students' learning experiences through instruction in a specific area of study at advanced levels, with greater complexity of content and process, and/or at a faster pace, in accord with the students' demonstrated ability to learn quickly and easily in that area.

- **Independence and Self-Direction.** Programming that enables students to develop proficiency as autonomous, self-reliant learners in relation to (a) setting goals, (b) identifying and managing resources and activities, (c) monitoring and modifying plans and actions while carrying out projects, (d) creating and sharing products, and (e) evaluating their own work.

- **Personal Growth and Social Development.** Programming that guides and supports students in recognizing and responding to their own strengths and needs, participating with confidence and conviction in challenging activities, maintaining their mental and emotional well-being, and recognizing and responding appropriately to the strengths and needs of others.

- **Career Perspectives and Futuristic Orientation.** Programming that challenges students to consider many and varied career possibilities, assists and supports students in personal and professional life planning, enables students to manage change effectively, and guides students in preparing for life in a world of rapid change.

Figure 6.1   Needs Assessment Inventory form

Directions

Each of the statements on the following pages describes a programming activity or service related to one of the six areas described above. Please read each statement and then circle the choices that best describe your assessment of your present school program for that activity or service. Please consider two issues: (a) the IMPORTANCE of that activity or service for students and (b) the AMOUNT OF ATTENTION OR EFFORT the activity now receives in your school.

Example

Items	Importance	Present Attention/Effort
1. Collecting milk money	(−2) −1 +1 +2	1 2 3 (4)
2. Teaching problem solving	-2 −1 +1 (+2)	(1) 2 3 4

The sample responses indicate that this person does not regard "collecting milk money" as an important activity (−2), although it now receives considerable attention (4). This person regards "teaching problem solving" as a very important activity (+2), although it is now receiving little or no attention (1).

Please respond to each item on the basis of your best impression, even if the decision is difficult to make. Give your own impression, even if you feel that the opinions of others might differ. Respond only in relation to the part(s) of the school's program in which you are directly involved. There is also an opportunity for you to offer general comments at the end of the inventory. THE RESULTS OF THIS INVENTORY WILL BE USED ONLY TO GUIDE PLANNING FOR INSERVICE AND DEVELOPMENT OF NEW OR IMPROVED PROGRAMMING. THE RESULTS WILL NOT BE USED FOR COMPARISON OR EVALUATION OF INDIVIDUALS OR SCHOOLS.

(Continued)

I. Differentiated Basics

Programming that takes into account students' unique characteristics, talents, interests, abilities, skills, and learning style preferences as the basis for providing individualized and varied learning opportunities.

Items	Importance				Present Attention/Effort			
1. Including varied learning activities in the classroom at any one time	−2	−1	+1	+2	1	2	3	4
2. Grouping students for instruction in multiple ways	−2	−1	+1	+2	1	2	3	4
3. Using questions and activities that call for higher-level thinking	−2	−1	+1	+2	1	2	3	4
4. Using tiered lessons to differentiate activities for students	−2	−1	+1	+2	1	2	3	4
5. Providing cooperative planning time among various staff members	−2	−1	+1	+2	1	2	3	4
6. Identifying students' learning style preferences and using them to differentiate instruction	−2	−1	+1	+2	1	2	3	4
7. Emphasizing quality and standards extending beyond knowledge/recall	−2	−1	+1	+2	1	2	3	4
8. Fostering active student participation in hands-on, minds-on activities	−2	−1	+1	+2	1	2	3	4
9. Using technology to individualize skill instruction and practice	−2	−1	+1	+2	1	2	3	4
10. Specifically assessing students' interests and using the results to plan activities	−2	−1	+1	+2	1	2	3	4

OPEN-ENDED COMMENTS

Add any general comments or suggestions regarding this section of the inventory.

_____

_____

_____

_____

Figure 6.1 (Continued)

II. Appropriate Enrichment

Programming that expands, extends, or enhances students' learning experiences above and beyond minimum expectations, integrating process and content skills with an emphasis on preparation for and involvement in original inquiry and investigations (individually or in groups).

Items	Importance				Present Attention/Effort			
1. Providing a variety of activities to help students discover areas of interest	−2	−1	+1	+2	1	2	3	4
2. Providing explicit instruction in tools and strategies for creative and critical thinking	−2	−1	+1	+2	1	2	3	4
3. Giving opportunities for students to choose to participate in varied programs (e.g., Future Problem Solving, Destination ImagiNation)	−2	−1	+1	+2	1	2	3	4
4. Using resource people, groups, and materials to stimulate curiosity and expose students to new areas	−2	−1	+1	+2	1	2	3	4
5. Providing instruction in skills and methods for research, inquiry, and presentation	−2	−1	+1	+2	1	2	3	4
6. Providing thematic or problem-based tasks or materials for problem solving activities	−2	−1	+1	+2	1	2	3	4
7. Providing opportunities for community service and "service learning"	−2	−1	+1	+2	1	2	3	4
8. Engaging students in working on identifying and solving real problems (personal, school, and community)	−2	−1	+1	+2	1	2	3	4
9. Locating audiences and outlets for students' projects, products, and results	−2	−1	+1	+2	1	2	3	4
10. Appropriately using Internet resources to expand curriculum and students' projects	−2	−1	+1	+2	1	2	3	4

OPEN-ENDED COMMENTS

Add any general comments or suggestions regarding this section of the inventory.

_____

_____

_____

_____

(Continued)

III. Effective Acceleration

Programming that expands, extends, or enhances students' learning experiences through instruction in a specific area of study at advanced levels, with greater complexity of content and process, and/or at a faster pace, in accord with the students' demonstrated ability to learn quickly and easily in that area.

Items	Importance				Present Attention/Effort			
1. Compacting or streamlining assignments and eliminating duplication or unneeded repetition of tasks	−2	−1	+1	+2	1	2	3	4
2. Explicitly assessing students' mastery or instructional level as a basis for continuous progress	−2	−1	+1	+2	1	2	3	4
3. Flexibly grouping and regrouping students to respond to their needs	−2	−1	+1	+2	1	2	3	4
4. Making special provision(s) for any highly advanced student (e.g., "testing out," advanced classes, double promotion)	−2	−1	+1	+2	1	2	3	4
5. Offering special courses, sections, or programs for highly advanced students	−2	−1	+1	+2	1	2	3	4
6. Providing acceleration opportunities across grade levels or school boundaries	−2	−1	+1	+2	1	2	3	4
7. Providing early graduation or dual enrollment options for very advanced students	−2	−1	+1	+2	1	2	3	4
8. Providing opportunities to replace low-level required courses with individualized choices or independent study	−2	−1	+1	+2	1	2	3	4
9. Providing opportunities for mentorship placements for students with exceptional needs	−2	−1	+1	+2	1	2	3	4
10. Providing access to correspondence or Web-based advanced courses for credit	−2	−1	+1	+2	1	2	3	4

OPEN-ENDED COMMENTS

Add any general comments or suggestions regarding this section of the inventory.

_____

_____

_____

_____

Figure 6.1 (Continued)

IV. Independence and Self-Direction

Programming that enables students to develop proficiency as autonomous, self-reliant learners in relation to (a) setting goals, (b) identifying and managing resources and activities, (c) monitoring and modifying plans and actions while carrying out projects, (d) creating and sharing products, and (e) evaluating their own work.

Items	Importance				Present Attention/Effort			
1. Using contracts, learning agreements, independent projects	−2	−1	+1	+2	1	2	3	4
2. Gradually involving students in independent learning decisions	−2	−1	+1	+2	1	2	3	4
3. Providing time for students to work on projects and to share the results	−2	−1	+1	+2	1	2	3	4
4. Encouraging independent research in cooperation with librarian/media specialists	−2	−1	+1	+2	1	2	3	4
5. Providing time and opportunity for students to work on projects with outside resource people or organizations	−2	−1	+1	+2	1	2	3	4
6. Providing opportunities for students to learn goal setting methods and tools	−2	−1	+1	+2	1	2	3	4
7. Involving students in locating and using a variety of resources to pursue a topic of special interest	−2	−1	+1	+2	1	2	3	4
8. Encouraging students to actively participate in evaluating and documenting their own progress and results	−2	−1	+1	+2	1	2	3	4
9. Providing mentorship placements for students pursuing their own inquiry or research	−2	−1	+1	+2	1	2	3	4
10. Providing opportunities for students to participate in projects, groups, or performances outside the school setting	−2	−1	+1	+2	1	2	3	4

OPEN-ENDED COMMENTS

Add any general comments or suggestions regarding this section of the inventory.

_____

_____

_____

_____

(Continued)

V. Personal Growth and Social Development

Programming that guides and supports students in recognizing and responding to their own strengths and needs, participating with confidence and conviction in challenging activities, maintaining their mental and emotional well-being, and recognizing and responding appropriately to the strengths and needs of others.

Items	Importance				Present Attention/Effort			
1. Assisting students in clarifying their values and character traits and in developing a positive self-image	−2	−1	+1	+2	1	2	3	4
2. Encouraging students to have trust and confidence in their personal goals, plans, and decisions	−2	−1	+1	+2	1	2	3	4
3. Guiding students in learning and applying teamwork, collaboration, and leadership skills	−2	−1	+1	+2	1	2	3	4
4. Ensuring that counselors are available to help students recognize and deal with personal and interpersonal challenges, fears, and concerns	−2	−1	+1	+2	1	2	3	4
5. Helping students learn to demonstrate caring, respect, and empathy for others	−2	−1	+1	+2	1	2	3	4
6. Providing systematic instruction and involvement in personal goal-setting and life planning	−2	−1	+1	+2	1	2	3	4
7. Providing guidance and support to help students develop intrinsic motivation	−2	−1	+1	+2	1	2	3	4
8. Helping students learn to manage stress and reduce the harmful effects of too much stress	−2	−1	+1	+2	1	2	3	4
9. Helping students to recognize the cost and benefits of their own talents and to manage demands for well-roundedness	−2	−1	+1	+2	1	2	3	4
10. Guiding students in recognizing, appreciating, and responding effectively to diversity	−2	−1	+1	+2	1	2	3	4

OPEN-ENDED COMMENTS

Add any general comments or suggestions regarding this section of the inventory.

_____

_____

_____

_____

Figure 6.1 (Continued)

VI. Career Perspectives and Futuristic Orientation

Programming that challenges students to consider many and varied career possibilities, assists and supports students in personal and professional life planning, enables students to manage change effectively, and guides students in preparing for life in a world of rapid change.

Items	Importance				Present Attention/Effort			
1. Providing career fairs or other opportunities for students to explore many possible career directions	−2	−1	+1	+2	1	2	3	4
2. Providing opportunities for students to assess their personal strengths and interests and the implications of those for future studies or careers	−2	−1	+1	+2	1	2	3	4
3. Providing group activities that challenge students to think about and discuss the future	−2	−1	+1	+2	1	2	3	4
4. Providing activities that help students to understand and deal with rapid change	−2	−1	+1	+2	1	2	3	4
5. Considering changing trends and directions in any curriculum area	−2	−1	+1	+2	1	2	3	4
6. Providing students with access to "shadowing," internship, or mentoring experiences for career exploration	−2	−1	+1	+2	1	2	3	4
7. Challenging students to investigate the lives and careers of talented people in many talent areas	−2	−1	+1	+2	1	2	3	4
8. Providing access to personal career counseling services as well as educational guidance	−2	−1	+1	+2	1	2	3	4
9. Using teaching tools and strategies for change management, problem solving, and decision making	−2	−1	+1	+2	1	2	3	4
10. Using the Internet to examine and investigate trends, issues, and emerging directions in the world of work	−2	−1	+1	+2	1	2	3	4

OPEN-ENDED COMMENTS

Add any general comments or suggestions regarding this section of the inventory.

_____

_____

_____

_____

(Continued)

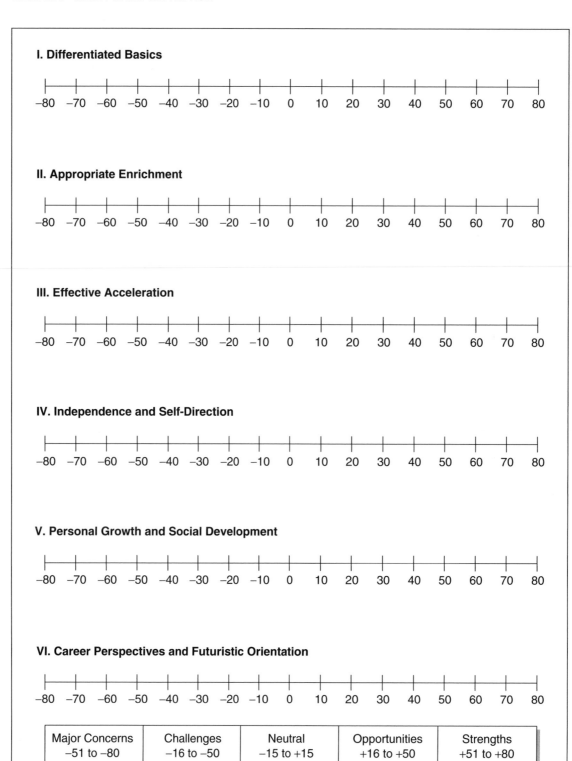

Figure 6.1 (Continued)

Source: Copyright © The Center for Creative Learning, Inc.

In each of these six areas, respondents rate both their perception of the importance of 10 specific items and the present level of attention or effort they believe the items currently receive in their setting.

After carefully explaining the purposes and goals of the Needs Assessment Inventory, you may find it helpful to ask all school personnel to complete it. Be sure to explain that its purposes and uses are not evaluative in nature and that the results will be useful in planning for talent development programming. After tabulating the results, you can easily prepare an individual report for each person as well as a summary of the means and ranges for each of the six areas for all respondents. Your summaries might include an overall profile of the results for a school, an entire district (with separate summaries for each school), or more specific subgroups, such as grade levels or content areas.

All six programming areas, and the 10 items in each section, are intended to represent curriculum or instructional activities or practices that are positive and that add value in any school setting implementing a contemporary approach to talent development. Of course, it is highly unlikely that, in any single group, *everyone* would actually be carrying out *all* the activities (all 60 items) equally effectively and to the same extent. It may also be possible that, for very good reasons, some settings might place greater or lesser emphasis on one or more of the six areas, or on specific items within any area. There are, therefore, no absolute, "correct" responses to the inventory. Use the summary of results to stimulate and guide discussion regarding your school's current positives—the work you are already doing that represents constructive, challenging programming for talent development—and regarding the areas that might be the primary focal points for improvement or innovation.

INTERPRETATION OF NEEDS ASSESSMENT RESULTS

After you have administered the Needs Assessment, consider how you will provide feedback and what the implications of the results might be for staff development or for designing and implementing talent development programming.

Providing Feedback and Discussing Results

After you gather everyone's responses, consider how it will be most helpful and meaningful to analyze the results. One starting point, of course, is to provide a chart or graph of the overall results for the entire set of data—an overall "snapshot" of the group's perceptions. You might include the mean score for each of the six dimensions as well as a measure of the variability of the responses, such as the standard deviation or simply the range of scores. Be certain to respect the privacy of all individual respondents, and do not label any score point with an individual's name in handouts, on a graphic, or orally. In addition to overall group results, consider sharing results for various subgroups that might be meaningful to compare. For example, you might compute separate summaries of the results for each grade level or subject in a school, or (at the district level) present overall district results with separate subreports for each school.

Provide each person with a report that presents his or her own results along with the overall group and/or appropriate subgroup results so that individuals can examine their responses in comparison with those of their peers. If individuals choose to state or describe their results in group discussions, permit them to do so. The principle of confidentiality suggests that they can share their results, but someone else should not do so without their permission. If you have prepared subgroup summaries (e.g., grade level results), provide time for the members of each group to review and discuss their results. Prepare tables or graphs for presentation in which you present group results, and provide time for the group to discuss the overall results, to raise and discuss questions, and to explore possible implications for future programming activities and commitments.

Encourage the group to consider their positive results, rather than just focusing on the "lowest" scores. Remind them to celebrate the positives, but also to keep in mind that those strengths must continue to be supported and nurtured, too. Investigate actions that will help those areas remain strong and flourishing in the school. Consider whether different subgroups have different strengths, and why that might be natural, healthy, and important to sustain. Then consider the lower scores, discussing which ones may require new or increased attention and effort, what kinds of action might be important to consider, and which group members might have the greatest interest and expertise in working on those topics. Be certain that the group's discussion focuses on the six programming areas as they are defined in the inventory. Prepare summaries of the definitions of each of the six dimensions on overheads, slides, or posters to help clarify them as needed.

We do not report normative data for the Needs Assessment Inventory, because the inventory's primary importance and use involves using the data to guide your own discussion and planning. Comparing your numerical results with those of another school or another school district—in which there may or may not be any reasonable basis for comparison—will not guide you in understanding your present practices or in designing programming for the future. If you review results among several local buildings, do it in a spirit of discussion and mutual support, not to seek ways for one school to gain competitive advantage over another. Keep in mind your shared goal of serving all your district's students as effectively as possible.

The chart on the final page of the inventory identifies five general score ranges for interpreting the Needs Assessment results. For each of the six dimensions, the scores can range from −80 (each of the 10 items rated −4 on importance times +2 for present level of activity) to +80 (10 items rated +4 on importance times +2 for present activity). Some general guidelines for interpreting the scores for each dimension are:

+51 to +80   **Strength**

A major commitment to excellence that is being implemented effectively.

+16 to +50   **Opportunity**

A positive commitment that is being implemented consistently. Attitudes are generally positive (since the total is on the positive side), but perceived implementation may be low or moderate.

−15 to +15   **Neutral**

Participants feel "mixed responses" in relation to importance and/or implementation and some uncertainty or hesitation about importance and/or action.

−16 to −50   **Challenges**

There are clear misgivings about support and commitment, even though there is some perceived emphasis on implementation. People may feel "pressured" to do some things they are not certain they really support or consider valuable.

−51 to −80   **Major Concerns**

Despite strong pressures to take action, there are strongly held concerns and possibly vocal opposition. Scores in this range are likely to indicate the presence of disagreement or conflict within the group. (Note especially that, since all the items on the inventory are practices we view as constructive in relation to talent development programming, we would feel very uncomfortable about these scores!)

Implications for Staff Development and Training

In addition to using the Needs Assessment Inventory results to stimulate discussion regarding your present practices and areas to develop for programming in the future, you can use the results to provide insights into opportunities for professional development and training.

Strengths

For dimensions that are your strengths (scores ≥51), it is not necessary to provide basic, informational staff development programming, except to help new members of your staff get up to speed. Basic or awareness level programs in these areas will be boring and redundant to your staff, and might even have negative impact on staff morale and commitment to programming. However, you should not assume that your strengths can simply be ignored. Discuss the activities and resources that will maintain those strengths, as well as new directions that will extend them and help you reach new levels of accomplishment and success. Some possible activities to consider in these areas include:

- *Celebrations.* Encourage people to share and communicate their successes with each other and in other appropriate forums (e.g., newsletters, reports to parents and community, recognition programs, conference presentations).

- *Professional sharing.* Create mentor programs for interested teachers or through partnerships with area teacher preparation programs; create opportunities for staff to share their expertise by serving as model sites for other schools.
- *Advanced training.* Encourage staff members to participate, individually or in teams or groups, in advanced training courses, seminars, or programs to expand and extend their expertise.

Opportunities

Dimensions for which your scores are in this range (+16 to +50) are natural areas for professional development focusing on "how to" and skill building. You can capitalize on positive attitudes and interests to provide professional experiences that will help individuals and teams be successful and enthusiastic in implementing programming activities and services related to the dimensions on which they score at this level.

Neutral

If scores are from –15 to +15, or at the Neutral level, it may not yet be wise to introduce professional development that focuses on skills or applications. Instead, you might do well to focus on activities that will create buy in and help people to understand the relevance and importance of the dimension. This can be a good situation, for example, to establish topical reading and discussion groups or study circles, through which you provide resources (e.g., new books or a set of current articles on the topic) and structured opportunities for participants to discuss them and to build a foundation of readiness and preparation to move forward.

Challenges

Activities similar to those recommended when scores for a dimension are at the Neutral level may also be appropriate when scores are at the Challenges level (–16 to –50), although at this level it is good to emphasize voluntary participation, allow extended time for discussion and reflection, provide an experienced facilitator who can manage the groups without being (or appearing) manipulative, and locate and use supportive professionals (especially other practitioners) who can share successful experiences.

Major Concerns

For dimensions with scores at the Major Concerns level (–51 to –80), we recommend resolving other issues before initiating any new professional development work on that topic. There are usually other serious concerns that must be addressed!

ADDITIONAL SOURCES OF DATA

To clarify or take stock of your current situation in relation to talent development and gifted education programming, you might explore a variety of additional kinds of information. In any careful planning, a balance must be struck between, on the one hand, gathering *so much* data that the committee is over-whelmed, and, on the other hand, gathering *enough* data to be able to make good decisions. Consider several additional sources of data that will help you to clarify your current situation; these include:

- *District and school data.* Data collected here should help you identify the interested parties in the district or school, identify the programs or modifications already in existence, and understand staff attitudes and needs.
- *Programming model data.* Collect information about contemporary programming approaches and the people in your area who have training and experience with various approaches. Meet with committees from schools in which particular approaches have been used successfully. Consider ways in which a contemporary programming approach can be compatible with your district's (or school's) values, goals, philosophy, and vision.
- *Resources and available funding.* Compile a list of available grant monies, materials, and human resources, and gather information about the district's commitment to allocating resources to the program.
- *Inservice and other staff development opportunities.* Collect data on available training resources, information about who will participate, schedules, program formats, and follow-up plans.

These four categories encompass a wide variety of possible data sources and needed information. If we cross these categories with the news reporter's familiar "who, what, when, where, and how," we can create a matrix. This matrix can help you determine which questions to ask and also guide you in setting priorities by determining which issues need to be addressed first. A sample of such a matrix is presented in Figure 6.2. The questions in the sample matrix are intended to be illustrative, not prescriptive, and are certainly not comprehensive. We recommend that you examine this matrix carefully, noting your ideas for questions that should be asked based on the unique needs of your district. If answers to some of the questions leap out at you, record those answers as data already available for your planning.

We have also developed another set of questions that can be useful for educators and parents to consider regarding the school's talent development programming. The document "Dear School People: What Are You Doing to Recognize and Develop My Child's Strengths and Talents?" poses 25 questions that "are more important than, 'Is my child in the gifted program?'" You can download or print these questions by visiting the Center for Creative Learning's Web site at http://www.creativelearning.com and clicking on "School People."

Type of Data	Who	What	When	Where	How
District and School Data	1. Who is interested in talent development programming? 2. Who has training in the field? 3. Who will be the "assisters" and who will be the "resisters"? 4. What parents might be willing to contribute? 5. Who else will be important to contact or involve?	1. What already exists in our school or district? 2. What are teachers already doing/feeling? 3. What resources do we already have? 4. What do we need? (immediately? soon? in the future?) 5. What have we tried? 6. What are the major interests among school staff and administrators?	1. When should planning begin? 2. When will programming efforts begin? 3. When should meetings be held? 4. When will we report the results of our planning efforts? 5. When will we conduct inservice and community awareness programs?	1. Where should we start? (schools? grade levels? tasks?) 2. Where are examples of excellent programming? 3. Where can we learn more? 4. Where can we find observers or others to help document our efforts?	1. How should we divide or share the planning tasks? 2. How will priorities be established? 3. How might we build motivation and support among staff and community members? 4. How might the plan be phased in gradually?
Programming Models Data	1. Who has expertise in various programming models? 2. Who might be willing to research and make presentations about various models? 3. Who else in our area uses various models in their district? 4. Who has interest in advanced study in talent development?	1. What are the important elements of contemporary approaches? 2. What are the pluses and minuses for us? 3. What books or materials do we have or need? 4. What will our approach actually look like in practice?	1. When was the approach developed that we plan to use? 2. When have research or evaluation data been reported? 3. When is the best time to introduce or review programming in our setting? 4. When and how will programming be updated or revised?	1. Where are other districts in which this approach is or has been used? 2. Where is support and advanced training available for our staff? 3. Where was the approach tested and evaluated? 4. Where was the model not successful?	1. How might we learn as much as possible about the models? 2. How might we compare various models? 3. How might models be adapted to our needs? 4. How might several models be synthesized?

Figure 6.2 Sample data matrix

Type of Data	Who	What	When	Where	How

Resources and Funding Data	1. Who can provide or help us find resources?
	  • community groups?
	  • businesses?
	  • governmental (local, state, federal) aid?
	2. Who is experienced, skilled, willing to help in fund-raising?
	3. Who makes budget decisions?
	4. Who might help us write grant proposals?
		1. What resources do we need? (staffing? materials? conferences? inservice? transportation?)
		2. What existing resources can be used?
		3. What contributions might be obtained?
		4. What needs are most pressing or immediate?
		5. What changes must we expect over time?
			1. When are various resources needed?
			2. When must we apply for support?
			3. When must a budget be proposed?
			4. When are funding decisions made?
			5. When can funds be available and used?
				1. Where can we look for help with funding?
				2. Where can we get help in preparing grant proposals?
				3. Where can proposals be sent?
				4. Where can we get free or inexpensive help or resources?
				5. Where might we use trading services or "barter" for support?
					1. How might we gain community support?
					2. How can funding priorities be set?
					3. How can limited resources be overcome creatively?
					4. How might we use volunteers?
					5. How might more people become involved in support?

Inservice and Staff Development Data	1. Who will benefit from inservice?
	2. Who is seeking inservice?
	3. Who can provide inservice for us?
	4. Who has heard various presenters?
	5. Who in our area might share their experiences and expertise with us?
		1. What options might be considered? (needs assessment? mini-grants? team projects?)
		2. What are the goals?
		3. What increases the effectiveness or impact of inservice?
		4. What present inservice programs can be related?
		5. What new approach should be considered?
			1. When should inservice work begin?
			2. When is the best time for inservice?
			3. When can staff be involved in planning?
			4. When can staff members observe other teachers or programs?
			5. When are training programs or conferences held?
				1. Where might inservice programs best be held?
				  • schools?
				  • hotels?
				  • retreats?
				  • college campus?
				  • conference center?
				  • other schools?
				  • community facilities?
				  • camps or lodges?
					1. How might staff support be increased?
					2. How might new forms of Inservice be tried?
					3. How might "rewards" be provided for new projects and ideas?
					4. How might cooperative programming efforts best be managed?

Figure 6.2 (Continued)

Checking the Climate 7

The planning committee should make an explicit commitment to setting goals and expectations for excellence. Contemporary, inclusive programming will be most effective when you build on knowledge of the factors that contribute to effectiveness and productivity in school programs. To accomplish this, and to create a foundation of "expectations for excellence," establish and sustain a productive context or environment for learning. This chapter involves checking your school's (or district's) expectations for excellence and then surveying your specific climate for implementing a contemporary approach to talent development.

A context in which contemporary programming will flourish is one in which "the life of the mind" and the examination of complex issues and ideas will be encouraged, and in which there are high expectations for everyone. In this climate, contemporary programming can be integrated in meaningful ways into the total school program. Without a clear, strong commitment to excellence in education and an ongoing effort to translate that commitment into action, statements about integrating talent development with regular school programming may become mere slogans.

Students' strengths and talents must be challenged at a high level, not merely tolerated. To help students to grow at an appropriate rate, commensurate with their abilities and interests, it is necessary to provide challenging materials and resources, high-quality instruction, and opportunities for students to work closely with adults who model reflective, analytical, and creative intellectual effort and productivity. How might you establish a context that supports and enriches students' talents and sustained interests—one in which excellence is not only encouraged, but flourishes?

You can profit from examining closely what is known about excellence in other kinds of organizations, such as those in business and industry. Knowledge from recent research in such fields as human relations, management science, and organizational development helps clarify the meaning of and conditions for organizational excellence and has significant implications for you in designing and conducting educational programs. For the present purposes, we will begin by considering the context for excellence as it pertains to adults (e.g., the staff and administration of the school or school district).

Many of these issues can also be readily translated into components of importance and concern in establishing and maintaining a context for challenge and productivity within the classroom and in relation to the transactions that occur between teachers and students.

ASSESSING THE SCHOOL CONTEXT FOR EXCELLENCE

The chart below presents several questions that can help you to assess your school or school district's context for excellence. This brief self-study audit may help you to examine these issues in relation to the unique aspects of your setting and to take stock of "where you are now" in relation to expectations for excellence in talent development programming in your school or school district.

The Context for Excellence—Some Self-Study Questions

- What are the positives that already exist in our school?
- How do we communicate and share these positives?
- How does our community recognize these positives?
- What is unique about our school as a place for teaching and learning?
- In what ways do we celebrate this?
- What five words or phrases best describe our school?
- What five words or phrases best describe our philosophy about education?
- What is the best thing that has happened in this school in the last two years?
- What is the worst thing that has happened?

For the next six questions, please rank the effectiveness of the school on a scale of 1 to 10 (1 = no effort in the area; 10 = a great deal of effort).

- To what degree is our school culture collaborative and supportive?
- To what degree is our school open to new ideas or suggestions?
- To what degree do we encourage and support people who take risks?
- To what degree do we recognize and reward staff members' efforts?
- To what degree do we use specific, definable criteria to rate performance?
- To what degree do we engage in long-range planning as opposed to reacting to crises?

Next, let us examine several important climate dimensions more specifically. Drawing from our work on climate (Isaksen, Dorval, & Treffinger, 2000; Isaksen, Treffinger, & Dorval, 1996), we pose the question, "Are you (and is your school) *ready*, *willing*, and *able* to work on implementing a contemporary, inclusive approach to programming?" Being *ready* means determining that the specific organizational climate and history are conducive to implementing a contemporary approach. *Willing* suggests that a contemporary approach to talent development will have a high strategic priority for your school or district, and that this effort will be recognized as important, worthwhile, and necessary to address.

Being *able* means that the resources are in place or available to support the work that will be necessary in order to implement a contemporary approach and to ensure that there will be follow-up and commitment to implementation.

Ready: Climate and History

The term *psychological climate* is used when people discuss individuals' feelings, reactions, and perceptions of the patterns of behavior in a group or organization. The term *organizational climate* is used to describe the overall response patterns of many individuals within the group or organization, or the shared perceptions that characterize life in the organization. Although climate is perceived by individuals within the workplace, Isaksen, Lauer, and Ekvall (1999) and Ekvall (1987) proposed that it exists independently of those perceptions and can be viewed as an attribute of the organization. Climate is distinct from culture in that it is more directly observable within the organization. Culture refers to the deeper and more enduring values, norms, and beliefs within the organization (Ekvall, 1997). Isaksen, Lauer, Ekvall, and Britz (2001) define climate as "the recurring patterns of behavior, attitudes, and feelings that characterize life in the organization" (p. 172). Climate involves the psychological or organizational dimensions that support or inhibit the development, adoption, and use of new and different approaches and concepts. It represents the patterns or procedures involved within the daily life of your school as they are experienced, understood, and interpreted by the people within it.

Building on Ekvall's work, Isaksen and others conducted research in a number of organizations and then reformulated the climate factors into nine major dimensions. Isaksen, Treffinger, and Dorval (1996) extended that work into educational settings. The nine factors in climate for creativity and innovation are:

Challenge and involvement: The degree to which students share in the daily operations, long-term goals, and vision of the school or classroom as a learning environment

Freedom: The extent to which students have the opportunity for independence in their behavior

Trust and openness: The extent to which students feel there is emotional safety in their relationships with each other and with the teacher

Idea time: The amount of time students can use (and do use) for identifying, exploring, and elaborating new ideas

Playfulness and humor: The extent to which the school and the classroom provide a setting for spontaneity and comfort or ease of behavior

Conflicts (low): The presence (or absence) of personal and emotional tensions in the school or classroom; the presence (or absence) of fighting and aggressive, hostile behavior among students, or overly stern, shouting, angry behavior by the teacher. (This is different from the tensions among ideas represented by the "debates" dimension.)

Idea support: The extent to which new ideas are treated with interest and respect

Debates: The extent to which encounters and disagreements among viewpoints, ideas, differing experiences, and knowledge will be encouraged in the class

Risk taking: The extent to which there is tolerance of uncertainty and ambiguity in the school or classroom

Readiness also involves "history." It necessitates understanding the historical experiences—the people, interactions, and events—that have shaped an organization over time and on which you can build for the present and future. Considering the history in relation to talent development and readiness for contemporary programming involves gathering data about a number of background themes and issues and sampling several different sources of information (since different people might have unique kinds of information to contribute, and also since several people might have differing memories and views of the same history and events). Some questions to explore relating to history are:

- What has been attempted in the past in relation to talent development? Have those efforts been successful? Why or why not?
- Have other people attempted previously to bring new approaches to talent development forward (or opposed efforts to address it)?
- Have there been champions or opponents? Were they credible and respected? Are they still around? Involved? Why or why not?
- What historical impressions, memories, and experiences might people have relating to talent development, and will those support current efforts or inhibit them?

Willing: Strategic Priority of Talent Development

It is also important to take stock of the extent to which there is commitment and support within the school or district that will enable a contemporary approach to talent development to take root and flourish. Some of the key questions to ask regarding willingness are:

- Does a contemporary approach to talent development relate clearly to a topic or area of high strategic priority as reflected in an established vision or mission statement? Are these efforts linked to specific goals or objectives that have been adopted?
- Can you relate contemporary programming directly to the needs, aspirations, or preferred future of . . . [this person, team, or organization]?
- Is there ownership, in the form of clear support from a sponsor, and well-established clientship (responsibility for taking action), for you to move forward with a contemporary programming approach?
- Do those who will be working on programming accept that a contemporary, inclusive approach is meaningful and worth doing? Are people inspired and eager to work on it?

Able: Setting and Resource Commitments

Your task will also include assessing the extent to which the resources and materials will be available within the school or district to support implementation of a contemporary approach to talent development. Some of the key questions to ask regarding availability are:

- Is there time available for people to come together to work on planning and implementing the approach? Is it genuine, or time that people must "take out of their own hide"?
- Will there be space or facilities available? Are they conducive to working effectively on talent development?
- Will the equipment, supplies, or material needed for working on programming be readily available? If they are not already present, will it be possible to obtain them in a timely way?
- Is there a budget for working on talent development programming? Is it realistic? Will it support the work that must be undertaken?
- Are there realistic goals and expectations about what will be accomplished, and by when?

THE CLIMATE SURVEY FOR CONTEMPORARY PROGRAMMING

The Climate Survey for Contemporary Programming (Figure 7.1, and also on the accompanying CD) is a practical tool that you can use to assess the extent to which your school or district is "ready, willing, and able" to begin working on a contemporary approach to talent development. It will help you to determine the areas in which you are prepared to move forward, as well as to identify the tasks that need to be addressed in order to establish a climate conducive to new programming directions.

LINKING THE INVENTORY RESULTS FOR "READY" WITH NINE CLIMATE DIMENSIONS

The nine major climate dimensions identified by Isaksen, Lauer, and Ekvall (1999) and Isaksen, Treffinger, and Dorval (1996) are represented in the "Ready" scale in the Climate Inventory. There are two items for each of the nine factors, as follows:

Challenge and involvement: items 1 and 2

Freedom: items 3 and 4

Trust and openness: items 13 and 22

Idea time: items 7 and 25

(*Text continues on page 96*)

Climate Survey

Name: _____   District: _____

Position: _____   Contact Information: _____

_____

_____

_____

This survey will help you to assess the climate in your school and/or district for implementing and maintaining a contemporary, inclusive approach to programming for talent development. Specifically, it will guide you in determining whether your school or district is ready, willing, and able to commit to a contemporary approach. The survey examines several aspects of the school environment in terms of organization, the delivery of instruction, and programming.

   Answer the statements on the next three pages as they relate to your own knowledge and experience in terms of individual students, classrooms, your individual school, and the district as a whole. Circle a number from 1 to 6 that indicates how strongly you agree or disagree with each statement. Circle 1 if you strongly disagree with a statement. Circle 6 if you strongly agree. At the bottom of the fourth page there are two narrative questions that ask you to comment on the climate in your school and district. Please think about the same situations that you used to answer the first 42 items.

	Strongly Disagree					Strongly Agree
1. We plan programs to challenge students to explore new topics and expand their interests.	1	2	3	4	5	6
2. Programs seldom give specific attention to individual students' characteristics and strengths.	1	2	3	4	5	6
3. We encourage students to explore many topics independently.	1	2	3	4	5	6
4. Teachers emphasize evaluation. Learning activities focus mainly on required or prescribed objectives.	1	2	3	4	5	6
5. Our mission statement encourages us to recognize and develop each student's strengths.	1	2	3	4	5	6
6. We do not have the resources needed to implement a new program.	1	2	3	4	5	6
7. Time is available to enable students to pursue meaningful and complex learning projects.	1	2	3	4	5	6
8. We view gifted education as most effective when focused on academic content.	1	2	3	4	5	6
9. When we are planning important programs like this, schedules are arranged to provide the necessary time.	1	2	3	4	5	6
10. Learning in our school is serious business; there is little room for activities designed to be "fun."	1	2	3	4	5	6
11. Our district recognizes the need to identify and develop talent in many domains.	1	2	3	4	5	6

Figure 7.1   Climate Survey for Contemporary Programming

	Strongly Disagree					Strongly Agree
12. It is very difficult for staff to adjust their methods to meet the demands of a new program.	1	2	3	4	5	6
13. There are opportunities for students to test new ideas and work on self-initiated projects.	1	2	3	4	5	6
14. If the district is to meet its objectives, we must focus on and remediate students' weaknesses.	1	2	3	4	5	6
15. In our district, when new programs are adopted the needed resources are always found.	1	2	3	4	5	6
16. Debate impedes progress and increases negative feelings.	1	2	3	4	5	6
17. We are enthusiastic about the implementation of a contemporary approach.	1	2	3	4	5	6
18. Time, resources, and personnel are spread so thin that no new programs stand a chance of success.	1	2	3	4	5	6
19. We respect and support students' ideas, and value their requests to pursue varied courses of study.	1	2	3	4	5	6
20. Individualized help and attention is required for only a relatively few identified students.	1	2	3	4	5	6
21. Our staff is able to make whatever adjustments are needed to implement a contemporary approach.	1	2	3	4	5	6
22. We encourage students to share their interests with others.	1	2	3	4	5	6
23. Our district's goals support the basic concept that each child has certain strengths that can be nurtured.	1	2	3	4	5	6
24. We are considering a new approach primarily in order to cut costs.	1	2	3	4	5	6
25. Every moment of the school day is accounted for with prescribed activities that "cover the material."	1	2	3	4	5	6
26. Our community believes that high-ability students will succeed; they have no need for special assistance.	1	2	3	4	5	6
27. All responsibility for talent development rests with our Gifted Coordinator and special-subject teachers.	1	2	3	4	5	6
28. We design activities so that students experience the joy of learning along with achievement.	1	2	3	4	5	6
29. Our district leaders are committed to a broad approach to talent development.	1	2	3	4	5	6
30. Our community will do whatever it takes to obtain the resources and people needed for student success.	1	2	3	4	5	6

(Continued)

	Strongly Disagree					Strongly Agree
31. We address conflicts that may arise with a sense of fairness that respects all views.	1	2	3	4	5	6
32. There is little enthusiasm on the part of district leaders to go beyond the status quo.	1	2	3	4	5	6
33. There are more demands in our district than there are resources to meet them. New projects are impossible.	1	2	3	4	5	6
34. It is difficult for students and staff to separate the issues of a disagreement from personalities.	1	2	3	4	5	6
35. Talent development is a top priority for our school and community.	1	2	3	4	5	6
36. There is a general understanding of contemporary approaches to talent development.	1	2	3	4	5	6
37. Novel ideas, requests, or points of view are frequently met with criticism and objections.	1	2	3	4	5	6
38. Our staff understands that implementing a contemporary approach will require sustained energy and effort.	1	2	3	4	5	6
39. Worthwhile projects require a lot of effort, but we have a dedicated staff that is up to the challenge.	1	2	3	4	5	6
40. We encourage people to express and discuss differing ideas and viewpoints.	1	2	3	4	5	6
41. It is part of our culture that we are all learning, and that there are often many right answers.	1	2	3	4	5	6
42. We encourage staff to develop open-ended projects even though there may be no guarantee of success.	1	2	3	4	5	6

A. What aspects of your district's environment will be most helpful in supporting the implementation of a contemporary, inclusive approach to talent development?

_____

_____

_____

B. What aspects of your district's environment will hinder the implementation of a contemporary approach to talent development?

_____

_____

_____

Figure 7.1 (Continued)

Scoring the Climate Survey

Name: _____ District/School: _____

Copy each rating from the survey in the space by the corresponding number below. Items marked "R" should use reversed scoring, so that a survey rating of 1 becomes 6, a rating of 2 becomes 5, a rating of 3 becomes 4, and so on. Total each column. A total above 63 indicates that the district is "ready" for the implementation of a contemporary approach. A total above 42 for the next two columns indicates that the district is "willing and able" to undertake the implementation of a contemporary approach.

Ready	**Willing**	**Able**
1. _____		
2. _____ R		
3. _____		
4. _____ R	5. _____	6. _____ R
7. _____	8. _____ R	9. _____
10. _____ R	11. _____	12. _____ R
13. _____	14. _____ R	15. _____
16. _____ R	17. _____	18. _____ R
19. _____	20. _____ R	21. _____
22. _____	23. _____	24. _____ R
25. _____ R	26. _____ R	27. _____ R
28. _____	29. _____	30. _____
31. _____	32. _____ R	33. _____ R
34. _____ R	35. _____	36. _____
37. _____ R	38. _____	39. _____
40. _____		
41. _____		
42. _____		

_____	_____	_____
Ready	**Willing**	**Able**

Playfulness and humor: items 10 and 28

Conflicts (low): items 31 and 34

Idea support: items 19 and 37

Debates: items 16 and 40

Risk taking: items 41 and 42

Considering these dimensions may also be useful in promoting analysis and discussion of the results and their implications. For example, you might discuss such questions as:

- How much agreement or variability is there among you in your perceptions of these nine dimensions, and of the three broader climate factors ("ready," "willing," and "able")? What might influence the similarities or differences among you in your perceptions?
- What implications do these results suggest in relation to the climate for program planning and implementation? Are you ready, willing, and able to move forward?
- What areas might need additional study or deliberate efforts to strengthen the climate? What steps might you take to work on those needs?

This chapter's goal has been to enable you to identify several key climate dimensions that are important for you to consider in clarifying your "current reality" (the present circumstances in your school or district that will encourage—or inhibit—your efforts to plan and implement a contemporary, inclusive approach to programming). When you address these dimensions, you will be able to build an effective foundation for programming and prevent a number of obstacles or challenges from hindering your programming efforts later. You can build a constructive climate in which programming will thrive, but it is important to address the perceptions of climate openly and honestly and not to assume that "everything is fine" or to attempt to avoid areas of concern or disagreement. Work collaboratively to understand the present conditions and to identify common needs and goals.

Programming Positives and Wish Lists 8

The final step in the "Clarify Where You Are Now" stage of the Six-Stage Systematic Planning model involves looking carefully at the activities or services relating to gifted education or talent development that are now occurring in your school or school district.

This step builds on the recognition that few, if any, schools are starting with a blank slate in relation to recognizing and nurturing students' strengths, talents, and sustained interests. We have never worked with a school district in which nothing positive was taking place, and we can't really imagine that happening. (If you are a cynic, you might say that such a school just would not call on anyone for assistance.)

During more than two decades of working with schools, school districts, and state education agencies on programming for giftedness and talent development, one strong lesson that we have learned is that it is very important to recognize and build upon the positives—to put your time, energy, and effort into finding what people are doing well and want to do even better instead of constantly harping on what they are not doing well and demanding that they get with the program. Perhaps Grandma said it best, after all: "You catch more flies with honey than with salt." (Others say that you catch more "with sugar than with vinegar," or various combinations; grandmas can be very flexible!) Or as business guru Ken Blanchard once suggested, it's a good idea to "sneak around and catch people doing things right."

In this chapter, then, our first step will be to guide you in looking for and documenting your "programming positives" (the valuable and worthwhile activities and services you are now providing). Then we will ask you to engage in some speculating and dreaming as you form your wish list of future programming possibilities.

YOUR PROGRAMMING POSITIVES

What kinds of activities or services does your school (or district) now offer that help your staff and your students to recognize any student's strengths, talents, or personal and sustained interests?

If you already have a gifted program in your school, you will probably be able to list quite a few activities and services that already take place there. However, as you consider a contemporary programming approach, don't stop there! Examine many activities that occur, day in and day out, anywhere in your school or district.

Some questions to consider are:

- What are some activities that stimulate students' curiosity and heighten their motivation and engagement or "wanting to know more" about topics?
- Who offers those activities?
- For what students? When? Where? Why?
- How do students find out about these activities or obtain an opportunity to participate in them?
- What activities are available to respond to students' special areas of personal interest, or to expose them to new areas they may not have encountered before?
- What do you now do to ensure that you are challenging and meeting the needs of students who excel in any academic or content areas (one or more areas; not necessarily in *every* area!)?
- What methods do you employ to find out about students' sustained interests (in school or outside of school)?
- What opportunities are now available for students who excel in areas outside the academic curriculum?

It is often helpful to pose these questions to a school's staff in a group setting (e.g., a workshop on talent development, or perhaps even as an idea generating activity in a staff meeting). Our experience has taught us that you and your colleagues will be quite likely to generate a fairly lengthy list of responses.

Some Tips for Identifying Programming Positives

- If you are working to implement programming on a districtwide basis, it might be valuable to investigate unique services that are offered within specific schools, activities that are offered in several schools (independently or collaboratively), and other services that may be offered on a districtwide basis. Seek ways to share and compare data from all schools that will emphasize collaboration and new opportunities rather than pit one school against another in a harshly competitive manner. Recognize that it may be helpful for schools to be aware of each other's unique strengths and offerings, and that sharing the results may also lead to collaborative efforts for the staff in two or more schools to learn with and from each other.

- If you are planning for implementation within a school, you may find it helpful to discuss the similarities and differences of results among grade levels, teaching teams, or content areas, as appropriate for your school's organization and structure.
- Be certain to consider activities within the school during the school day, after-school or out-of-school activities at the school, and community activities the school supports. Consider classroom-based activities as well as services that might already be designated specifically as "gifted" activities!
- Begin by considering six areas of your school educational program (from the dimensions of the Needs Assessment Inventory in the previous chapter); for each one, ask: "What are we already doing effectively to challenge our students in this area?" Then consider four Levels of Service: all students, many students, some students, and a few students, as illustrated in Figure 8.1. For more information about the four levels and examples at various grade levels and content areas, refer to Section V of this handbook or to *Enhancing and Expanding Gifted Programs: The Levels of Service Approach* (Treffinger, Young, Nassab, & Wittig, 2004b). Feel free to add boxes for other talent or content areas.

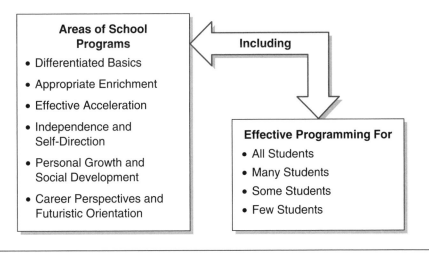

Areas of School Programs

- Differentiated Basics
- Appropriate Enrichment
- Effective Acceleration
- Independence and Self-Direction
- Personal Growth and Social Development
- Career Perspectives and Futuristic Orientation

Including

Effective Programming For

- All Students
- Many Students
- Some Students
- Few Students

Figure 8.1 Areas of school programs

Use the chart in Figure 8.2 (also on the accompanying CD) to record and categorize your responses. Taken together, these represent your *programming positives.* Take time to celebrate them, and to discuss how they contribute to your approach to programming for talent development. Discuss how they are important in helping your school in its efforts to recognize (or discover) and then to nurture and develop students' talents. The positives that you discover do not constitute a comprehensive talent development program, of course, but they are building blocks for your contemporary programming efforts.

What are your programming positives? What's already in place?

Area	Level I—All	Level II—Many	Level III—Some	Level IV—Few
Differentiated Basics				
Appropriate Enrichment				
Effective Acceleration				
Independence and Self-Direction				
Personal Growth and Social Development				
Career Perspectives and Futuristic Orientation				

Figure 8.2   Your programming positives

Source: Copyright © The Center for Creative Learning, Inc.

YOUR WISH LIST

After considering what positives are already in place, turn to the areas that you wish could be *created* or *expanded.* Approach this task from the standpoint of wishing and visioning rather than merely as a complaint session. To accomplish this, pose such questions as:

- What are some of the services you wish you (and your colleagues) could create or expand?
- What are we doing in only a small way that you wish could be expanded?
- What are some new possibilities we might experiment with or try?
- Are some things not working well that we might change, improve, or drop?
- What new directions have we read about or seen elsewhere that we might explore here?

Once again, it may be helpful to use the six programming areas and the four Levels of Service described above as a template or frame for organizing and categorizing your wish list. Figure 8.3 presents a chart (also on the accompanying CD) that will be useful for this purpose; you may add additional pages as needed.

At this point, look for exciting, challenging opportunities in the lists. We all want the best for our students, and it is refreshing and healthy to bring the recognition of this factor out and celebrate it. This is an important side benefit of the wish list language in contrast with the dreary, depressing "things we are failing to do" alternative!

Don't be concerned at this stage about priorities, costs, resources, or other limitations, nor about prioritizing the list. You will address those concerns in the next stage in the Six-Stage Systematic Planning Model. Your emphasis in this stage should be on wishing and dreaming, on identifying some new or improved or expanded opportunities for recognizing and developing students' strengths, talents, and sustained interests. The initial generating of ideas for your wish list can usually be accomplished easily in a faculty meeting.

SUGGESTIONS FOR SEARCHING SUCCESSFULLY FOR PROGRAMMING POSITIVES AND WISHES

Here are a few suggestions for carrying out the two main tasks in this chapter—searching for your programming positives and generating your initial wish lists—successfully and efficiently.

- *Involve everyone on the staff.* Include non-teaching staff and paraprofessionals to get input from many different sources.
- *Provide "time for incubation" before the meeting.* It will be helpful to inform the participants about the questions in advance and to invite them to think about some possibilities before they arrive at the meeting. This can be an effective way to start the generating session at a brisk and productive pace.

What does your wish list include?

Area	Level I—All	Level II—Many	Level III—Some	Level IV—Few
Differentiated Basics				
Appropriate Enrichment				
Effective Acceleration				
Independence and Self-Direction				
Personal Growth and Social Development				
Career Perspectives and Futuristic Orientation				

Figure 8.3   Your wish list

Source: Copyright © The Center for Creative Learning, Inc.

- *Use large chart paper to write down everyone's ideas.* Keep the ideas visible as you are generating them so that people can easily scan and review the list. This encourages "piggybacking"—building some ideas on others.
- *Accept every idea.* Invite people to express any ideas they have without holding back or censoring any of their thoughts. Do not criticize or praise any of the ideas, and do not stop for long explanations, discussions, or justifications. Just write down what people contribute! The ideas can be analyzed carefully as the planning process continues. Encourage people not to preevaluate or censor the ideas.
- *Keep the lists.* They will be useful to refer back to during your follow-up efforts.
- *Maintain an informal, constructive tone.* Strive to keep the discussion brisk and positive in nature.
- *Encourage the group to stretch their thinking.* Strive to search for novel and interesting possibilities and to find options that would add value to what you are already doing in the school.
- *Acknowledge the positives.* Many groups are quite surprised when they look at the results, especially for the "programming positives" list. A typical reaction is, "I never realized that we were involved in so many different things!" You might consider using your list to develop a catalog or brochure, for your own reference and for parent information or publicity purposes, describing the range of activities and services that are offered every year throughout your school.

Section IV

Stage Three—Decide Where to Go Next

S ection IV in the Six-Stage Systematic Planning Model deals with making decisions about your proposed future actions for implementing contemporary programming. The key tasks in this stage are as follows:

- Drawing on the work you have completed in the previous stage(s) of planning, set specific goals for sustaining your current programming positives and for attaining your wish list priorities.
- Develop a Master Plan to guide your overall implementation of programming.
- Develop specific Building Action Plan(s) to guide implementation of programming at the school level.

You will enter Stage Three of the Six-Stage Systematic Planning Model with an extensive foundation of information about your current situation and about the climate and needs of your school or district in relation to contemporary programming for talent development. You will exit Stage Three with a specific Master Plan and Building Action Plan(s) to guide your initial programming implementation activities. The three chapters in Section IV provide information and resources to help you in carrying out these tasks effectively and efficiently.

Setting 9 Goals for Your Desired Future

If you only do what you've always done, you'll only get what you've always gotten.

As you enter this stage of the planning process, you will already have clarified your present situation (or "current reality") regarding talent development programming. You will have examined your current programming positives and identified some initial items for the wish list for talent development in your school or district. Clarifying where you are now is just a beginning step toward innovation and improvement, however; it is the foundation for assessing where you hope to be in the future. The planning stage in this chapter guides you in shifting your focus from the current reality to the "desired future state." What will your schools be like three years, or five years, from now, if your improvement and program development efforts have been successful? Figure 9.1 poses the challenge: How will you move from your current reality to your desired future?

In the commitment to educational excellence that is fundamental to a contemporary approach to talent development programming, it is also important that you define, express, and communicate a vision of that commitment to excellence among all stakeholders—staff and administration, students, parents, and the community at large. Parker (1990) described several research-based dimensions of a powerful vision for an organization. She proposed that *powerful visions*:

- Describe a preferred and meaningful future state
- Evoke images in the minds of others
- Give people a better understanding of how their purpose could be manifested
- Are perceived as achievable
- Come from the heart—are genuine
- Are lofty, challenging, and compelling
- Are easy to read, concise
- Are free from statistics, numbers, and methods for achieving the vision
- Are expressed in the present tense
- Are free from negative or competitive phrases

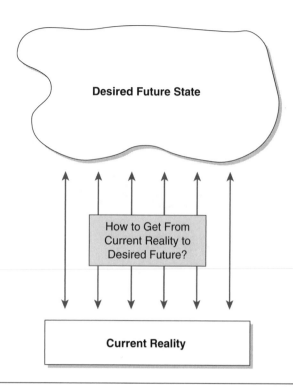

Figure 9.1 Moving to your desired future state

A shared sense of vision, mission, and purpose seeks "win-win" outcomes (rather than determining winners and losers), involves explicit goals in which there is a sense of direction or forward progress, and emphasizes a long view rather than being driven by immediate crises or the desire for quick ("Band-Aid") solutions. Compare these elements with your school or district's vision, mission, or purpose statements and identify specific points of agreement (or areas where clarification may be necessary).

Examining your desired future state involves forecasting or projecting your ideal—the contemporary, inclusive programming and school improvement results you hope to accomplish in three to five years. To create an effective vision for desired future programming, you might engage in five steps: (1) asking future-oriented questions, (2) finding a metaphor, (3) refining your wish lists, (4) writing a desired future statement, and (5) setting your vision.

1. *Asking future-oriented questions.* First, examine the programming positives you identified in the previous planning stage. In relation to those important positives already in place, what will change in the next five years? What will you need to do more? Do better? Do less? What programming positives do you hope will be the same five years from now as they are now? What do you most wish to keep and preserve? How do those things now take place? Does the staff do them? The students? Others? In what ways will the roles and activities of teachers and administrators change over the next five years? What are some ways in which your schools will be different in five years? (What facts and figures are at your disposal? What are your own wishes, hopes, or feelings?)

How will you ensure that your programming positives continue to remain strong and healthy? They will need continuing care and attention! Use the chart in Figure 9.2 (also on the accompanying CD) to consider ways to sustain them.

Area	Who? (Key Players)	What These Need to Thrive:
Schoolwide		
Grade Levels or Subject Areas		
Team or Individuals		

Figure 9.2 Maintaining your programming positives

Source: Copyright © The Center for Creative Learning, Inc.

2. *Finding a metaphor.* Your next step in defining your desired future state is to find and develop a metaphor for your school or school district. Although this is not the desired future statement, it will help you to identify and describe more accurately the components you wish to include in that statement. A metaphor is a figure of speech in which you take a common term (an object, an event, a person, or a time or place) and use it to describe something else that seems to be similar to it in a number of ways. Review your responses to the questions in step one. Try to think of something you consider a good comparison or metaphor for describing the way you would like to see your school five years from now. Use the chart in Figure 9.3 (and on the CD) to describe your metaphor.

When you find a metaphor that seems to do the best job of describing your vision of your school in five years, use a large sheet of chart paper and some markers to *draw* it. Make it good sized, using the whole sheet of paper, so others with whom you are working will be able to see it easily. Don't worry about artistic ability—the emphasis here is on ideas, not drawing skills. Use words or phrases to help clarify your drawings. Keep the metaphors created by all participants for reference later. (In a group meeting, hanging everyone's drawings around the room can be a useful, and sometimes even inspirational, activity.)

Figure 9.4 gives an example of a metaphor for a school.

3. *Refining your wish lists.* Your metaphors will guide you in investigating the *new directions* you need and want to follow for effective implementation of your programming approach. When you were working in the previous stage, you developed some wish list items for future implementation. Revisit those in relation to your metaphor for your school's future. Do you see ways those wishes fit into the metaphor? Does the metaphor suggest any changes or additions? Record these as another element to consider in relation to your desired future state. Use the charts in Figures 9.5 and 9.6 (and on the accompanying CD) to update or expand your wish lists and to begin thinking about who might work on them and how they might be attained.

As you consider "who," think about people in your school who have the most interest, energy, and excitement about those wishes. Are they willing to be "champions" for those ideas, people who will assume the initial responsibility for working to attain them?

Keep in mind that there might be two kinds of items in the wish lists. Some of the wishes might be very direct and easy to attain, and they might be wishes rather than current positives only because they haven't been considered previously. Others might be much more complex, challenging, or long-term wishes, dreams, or hopes. These may require extended time and effort to attain. For either kind, make some notes about some initial steps that will begin to help you move forward. (The "S/L" column in Figure 9.6 refers to whether the wishes are short- or long-term possibilities.)

4. *Writing a desired future statement.* Use your metaphors and drawings, along with your updated wish lists, to formulate a statement describing what you want your school to be like in five years. From your metaphor statements and drawings, list the most important elements to include in your desired future statement. Then capture the most important and intriguing elements

(*Text continues on page 115*)

My metaphor for our school (or district) five years from now is:

Because:

That object or thing is . . .
(List several words or phrases that describe it!)

And our school is similar in these ways:
(For each item, show how your school or district is similar to the metaphor.)

Feel free to experiment with more than one metaphor!

Figure 9.3   My metaphor for our school

Source: Copyright © The Center for Creative Learning, Inc.

My metaphor for our school (or district) five years from now is:

Rain Forest

Because:

Rain forests are important, but many people don't think too much about them. They are feeling the impact of change, progress, and inappropriate behavior.

That object or thing is . . . (List several words or phrases that describe it!)	And our school is similar in these ways: (For each item, show how your school or district is similar to the metaphor.)
Full of life; several "layers" deep	*Staff, students, community context provide similar depth of life*
Great quantity but also great diversity of both plants and animals	*Lots of people and activities already taking place*
Has some strange and beautiful plants and animals (some we may not even know yet!)	*Students and adults have many talents and strengths (many may yet be undiscovered)*
Sources of many vital medicines	*Students and adults may add great richness, excitement, and value both within and outside the school*
All rain forests resemble one another in many ways, but contain rich differences, too (among them and within any one)	*All schools also resemble one another in some ways, but also differ widely (within any one and across schools)*
Humans are destroying the rain forests at an alarming rate (timber, mining, agriculture, settlements) for many reasons (including many negative motives). Consequences of their destruction may be very serious.	*We are also dealing with many forces and pressures that can make it difficult for strengths, talents, and interests to be recognized and nurtured. This may have serious consequences.*

Feel free to experiment with more than one metaphor!

Figure 9.4   Sample metaphor

Area	Level I—All	Level II—Many	Level III—Some	Level IV—Few
Differentiated Basics				
Appropriate Enrichment				
Effective Acceleration				
Independence and Self-Direction				
Personal Growth and Social Development				
Career Perspectives and Futuristic Orientation				

Figure 9.5   Worksheet for refining your wish list

Source: Copyright © The Center for Creative Learning, Inc.

Area	S/L*	Who? ("Champions")	What's Needed (What? When? Where?)
Schoolwide			
Grade Levels or Subject Areas			
Team or Individuals			

Figure 9.6   Preliminary planning worksheet for attaining your wishes

*Short term or Long term

Source: Copyright © The Center for Creative Learning, Inc.

from your wish lists to include in your statement. From these, synthesize a statement that will capture the essence of where you are going, and ideally, where you hope your school will be five years from now. The form in Figure 9.7 (and on the CD) may help you to summarize this step.

Metaphor Elements:	Wish List Elements:

Desired Future Statement:

Figure 9.7   Desired future statement worksheet

Source: Copyright © The Center for Creative Learning, Inc.

Here is an example of some desired future statements that came from the rain forest metaphor in Figure 9.4.

Five years from now our school will be a place that:

- *Looks for, values, and nurtures the different strengths of each individual student*
- *Celebrates the school as a place where individuals can connect as a unified community*
- *Enables individuals to reach out, in positive ways, to benefit the larger community*
- *Is recognized for the good work that is done within and without its walls*
- *Is valued by all and protected from outside forces and pressures*

5. *Setting your vision.* Now you are ready to create (or update) a vision statement to serve as the foundation for future planning and implementation. The vision statement serves as the starting point for creating a Master Plan, which will be the focus of the next chapter. Your vision statement should describe succinctly the dynamic tension between your current reality and your desired future state. It will give you a concise, challenging, and inspirational overall picture of where you hope to be in the future in relation to contemporary talent development programming.

Here is an example of a vision statement that emerged from the rain forest metaphor and its desired future statements. It is somewhat longer than some vision statements, but it communicated what its creators wanted to say!

We celebrate our school as a place in which the strengths and talents of all are recognized and nurtured. Through the talents and interests of our staff, students, and parents, we add value to our community, and our efforts are valued. Talent development helps us to be a positive force in many lives and contributes to the outcomes and results we value most highly.

Use the form in Figure 9.8 (and on the CD) as a vision worksheet. Keep your vision statement, along with your working notes (desired future state, current reality, programming positives, and wish lists), as valuable input data for constructing your Master Plan (Chapter 10) and your Building Action Plan (Chapter 11).

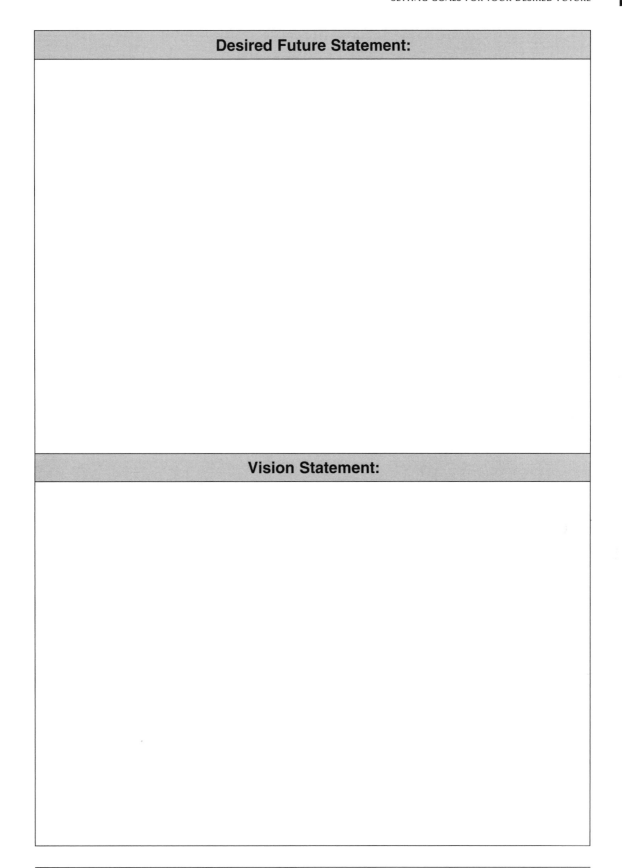

Figure 9.8   Vision statement worksheet

Source: Copyright © The Center for Creative Learning, Inc.

Constructing the Master Plan 10

The vision statement you created in Chapter 9 should guide you as you now begin to create your Master Plan and your Building Action Plan(s). Refer to your vision statement frequently to maintain an effective and appropriate focus. It is a good idea to create a poster of your vision statement and to display it where all can see it as you work on the Master Plan. Your wish lists and programming positives will also help you as you formulate specific goals and objectives in subsequent planning stages.

The distinction between the Master Plan and the Building Action Plan is most important when you are planning to implement programming on a districtwide basis. The Master Plan is generally the districtwide "umbrella" that sets out the major decisions and commitments that will apply to all schools. Building Action Plans are specific for implementing programming at the local school level. Individual schools are responsible for implementation within the broad guidelines presented in the Master Plan. There may be unique components in any school's specific plan. This chapter refers primarily to the Master Plan as a district level document. However, if your initial implementation plan focuses specifically on an individual school rather than a whole district, we recommend that you review this chapter first and then combine the necessary elements of it into your Building Action Plan, creating a single written plan rather than two separate documents.

THE MASTER PLAN

The planning committee's major responsibility is to develop a specific, comprehensive written Master Plan. This plan is important for several reasons:

- It expresses the commitments that have been made at the district level to create and support contemporary programming in all schools.
- It guides and directs the development, implementation, and evaluation of individual school plans.
- It provides a foundation for proposals for resources and support for programming.

- It establishes the "history," or context, upon which subsequent efforts (e.g., program evaluation or modification) can build.
- It facilitates communication and coordination among individual schools within the district.
- It provides a foundation for clear, consistent, accurate communication with others outside the schools.

Specific Components of the Master Plan

Ensure that all members of the planning committee recognize that, as you proceed through each step in creating a Master Plan, all decisions are tentative or working conclusions until the entire plan can be reviewed and tested for consistency. In the fray of planning, certain decisions may well seem appropriate, but later it will become evident that, in view of subsequent decisions, changes will need to be made.

The Master Plan includes 11 specific components; these are:

1. Philosophy and vision statement

2. Definitions

3. Goals and objectives

4. Identification policies and procedures

5. Programming commitments

6. Implementation guidelines

7. District time line

8. Resource considerations

9. Coordination and staffing

10. Professional development

11. Evaluation plans

Philosophy and Vision Statement

The Master Plan should begin with your specific philosophy and vision statement. This establishes the importance of and rationale for programming and identifies the important ways in which programming will be linked with the overall mission and goals of the district. The statement should be concise—probably less than one page. It should also be consistent with contemporary views of quality education, school effectiveness, and the nature of human talents and abilities. Review and work from the vision statement developed in the preceding chapter. Your statement should present concisely your fundamental beliefs and commitments regarding programming.

An effective philosophy statement should address three basic issues:

1. What do you mean by giftedness and talent? (Review Chapter 3 of this handbook)

2. What kinds of programming will you provide? (See Chapter 12 of this handbook and additional publications relating to your programming approach)

3. What does identification mean, and what are its purposes? (See Chapter 13 of this handbook and additional publications relating to your programming approach)

The text in the box below provides a sample of a philosophy statement created by a district whose contemporary programming emphasized our Levels of Service (LoS) approach.

General Sample of a Philosophy Statement for LoS Programming

Giftedness and talent refer to students' potential to become healthy, independent, creatively productive people. Programming is an ongoing process, through which we recognize and nurture each student's potentials. It is intended to create an environment in which we make deliberate efforts to recognize students' emerging strengths, talents, and interests and then nurture them through appropriate and challenging experiences and activities.

This process leads to modifications of instructional activities and services based on students' unique characteristics and needs. We affirm that outstanding potentials among students, which may lead to expertise and outstanding accomplishments, create the need for experiences and services both within and extending beyond the regular program. We are committed to systematic and deliberate programming to respond to those needs.

Rather than labeling some individuals as gifted (hence implying that all others are nongifted), identification should focus on recognizing and responding to students' needs that arise from their strengths, talents, and sustained interests. Identification should be positive, dynamic, flexible, inclusive (not exclusive), and ongoing. Identification is a process that helps us to recognize students' characteristics and guides us in effective instructional planning.

Talent development programming is concerned with expanding or enhancing learning opportunities for all students, through four Levels of Service. Developing and fulfilling students' strengths and talents is accomplished through a wide variety of opportunities and experiences. We recognize that the regular school program serves as a foundation upon which many activities and options can build, and in many cases must also be augmented through additional opportunities and experiences.

Many districts also find it important and helpful for their school board to formulate and adopt a formal policy statement in which the district's commitments and priorities for talent development programming are stated explicitly. The box on page 122 provides a sample of such a board policy statement (again, from a district in which programming followed our Levels of Service approach to programming).

Sample Board Policy Statement

The School Board affirms the responsibility for providing educational programs which are designed to maximize the development of all of its students. The Board further believes that deliberate and explicit efforts should be made to recognize and nurture students' emerging strengths, talents, and learning potentials in ways that are consistent with their needs for personal fulfillment and the best interests of society.

The School Board is, therefore, committed to these specific efforts:

- *Establishing and supporting an inclusive and contemporary definition of giftedness and talent*
- *Enabling and supporting staff involvement in comprehensive planning at the district and school levels, which reflects our commitment to collaborative planning and decision making by faculty and administration*
- *Developing appropriate and flexible procedures for recognizing students' unique strengths, talents, and interests. The district will make systematic and deliberate efforts to recognize and respond to students' potentials for creative, productive accomplishments. These potentials among our students indicate the need for modification or extension of the regular school curriculum*
- *Developing and supporting programming at four Levels of Service to encourage or foster the development of giftedness and talents*
- *Developing and supporting appropriate professional development opportunities for teachers and administrators, to stimulate innovation and excellence in educational programming*
- *Communicating with parents and other community members regarding programming for talent development*
- *Providing for ongoing evaluation of the effectiveness of talent development programming, and implementing improvements as warranted*

Definitions

The Master Plan should state clearly your definition of giftedness and talent. To clarify issues relating to definitions, review Chapter 3 of this handbook.

Goals and Objectives

The Master Plan identifies goals and objectives for talent development programming. Goals are broad statements of major outcomes or purposes to be attained. They are general statements of the major concerns of programming. Objectives are more specific; they are commitments to particular actions which, when taken as a group, will lead to the attainment of the goals that were stated. Each broad goal statement should be accompanied by one or more specific objectives. One effective approach to formulating goals and objectives emphasizes the intended outcomes and benefits in four categories: (a) students, (b) staff, (c) institutional and process, and (d) community. The goals and objectives should arise from your district vision statement and philosophy statements and will also draw on the goals and student outcomes for programming (review the programming goals and student outcomes in Chapter 3). Some examples include:

Student outcomes. These should draw upon and be interconnected with content, and contemporary views of workplace basics.

Goal: To foster productive thinking among our students.

Objective: Students will demonstrate proficiency in creative and critical thinking (as evidenced by pre-post test gains in appropriate creative and critical thinking assessments and portfolios of student projects).

Staff outcomes. This category of outcomes involves opportunities for continuing personal and professional growth for staff members.

Goal: To promote staff involvement in curriculum planning and revision for differentiation.

Objective: Teachers will create and carry out (individually or in groups) curriculum modifications or innovation projects that will result in new materials for classroom use and will incorporate principles of differentiation into their classroom instruction.

Institutional and process outcomes. Institutional outcomes should relate to school improvement goals and objectives. Process outcomes should target ways of making decisions, ways of monitoring school improvement and programming goals, and strategies for effective teamwork.

Goal: To improve school management team decision making processes.

Objective: Members of the school management team will learn and use structured group decision making techniques.

Community outcomes. Community outcomes should focus on active participation, lifelong learning, and collaboration between school and community agencies and organizations. These can be mutually beneficial.

Goal: To increase opportunities for local groups to communicate with and participate in the school's talent development programming and to promote talent development in students.

Objective: Local organizations will provide opportunities for students through visitations, shadowing, internship, or mentorship experiences that help nurture students' talents and interests.

Two Examples of General Goal or Mission Statements From School Districts for a Contemporary Programming Approach.

Example #1

The goals of the [District's] gifted programming services are to search for and recognize talent and strengths in all children. Gifted programming seeks to recognize those children who demonstrate strengths, talents, and sustained interests that are expressed at a high level and to provide appropriate program options for students to develop and apply their talents and skills.

Giftedness is represented through achievement and creative productivity over a sustained period of time in a domain that matters to the child. This conception of giftedness includes characteristics or traits that can be nurtured or enhanced through appropriate instruction and experiences. Talent denotes the increasingly specialized aptitudes or abilities that develop in youth as a function of general intelligence and experiences at home, school, and the community. Talent grows as students develop specific skills, interests, and motivations. When talent and expertise unite with creative abilities, the achievement and productivity that mark giftedness become evident.

In [the School District], a gifted programming specialist and [an additional professional support team member] provide gifted programming in each elementary building. These teams coordinate services for all children, Grades K–4. A gifted programming specialist also coordinates each middle school program.

A gifted programming plan outlining the full range of opportunities for students is available in every building. [The District's] gifted and talented program has been distinguished as a national model and the District's faculty has received national recognition as leaders in the field.

Example #2

The mission of [Name]Public School District is to provide educational opportunities that challenge all students to reach their potentials. The Gifted and Talented Levels of Service mission is to recognize, challenge, and support gifted students.

- *Recognize—We acknowledge and embrace giftedness and realize the diverse ways giftedness is exhibited.*
- *Challenge—We seek to expand and enhance learning opportunities for students who demonstrate high ability in academic areas. We help gifted students develop the skills for lifelong learning.*
- *Support—We make deliberate efforts to identify gifted students. We provide them with challenging learning opportunities and advocate challenging curriculum. We offer resources to families so they might better understand their gifted children.*

Identification Policies and Procedures

The goal of this component of the Master Plan is to develop and communicate the rationale, policies, and procedures for identification. In most school settings today, state or local requirements call for, and may even mandate, certain parameters regarding identification. The challenges created by emerging contemporary programming approaches involve balancing those requirements with the important need to look at students in ways that are flexible, diagnostic, and ongoing. Keep in mind the larger goal of creating and sustaining opportunities for nurturing students' potentials.

From a district standpoint, make efforts to inform individual schools about the opportunities that a contemporary, inclusive approach provides to (a) search for all students' strengths and talents; (b) document students' strengths, talents, and sustained interests; and (c) respond to students' need for appropriate services in varied ways. This implies moving away from focusing exclusively on inclusion or exclusion of students from certain categorical designations. From a school standpoint, be certain to let parents and teachers know about your commitment to seeking many different strengths, talents, and interests among students and to provide appropriate and challenging instruction that is linked specifically to each student's strengths, talents, sustained interests, and needs. Chapter 13 provides more information about the implications of contemporary programming approaches for identification.

Programming Commitments

Following contemporary, inclusive approaches to programming usually leads to a Master Plan that contains a menu of programming options and opportunities rather than a single, one-size-fits-all program (see Chapter 12, for example, for a discussion of programming options drawing on our Levels of Service approach). Consider the unique dimensions of your setting, your existing programming positives, and your wish list for programming as you construct your specific menu of options and services.

Implementation Guidelines

While each Building Action Plan will reflect the unique structure and concerns of that school and its administration, staff, students, and community, there is also a need to ensure a degree of consistency or comparability on a districtwide basis. Balancing these concerns can be attained by creating a clear set of guidelines for schools to follow in creating their Building Action Plans. Ensuring that each school is represented on the district planning committee also helps to address these concerns. The planning committee's efforts can support and enhance subsequent planning at the school level in a number of ways, including:

- Communicating with all schools to promote awareness
- Sharing the planning committee's efforts to develop philosophy and policy statements
- Sharing information obtained from the planning committee's study of definitions, identification, and programming options
- Initiating systematic needs assessment among the staff to determine areas in which additional information or inservice may be needed
- Creating opportunities for careful discussion of both the district's proposed Master Plan and the criteria for reviewing the Building Action Plan
- Developing and sharing a time line giving dates for the start-up of various aspects of the program

- Disseminating information regarding conferences, workshops, site visits, and other study opportunities or resources which may be available to all interested staff members
- Sharing policies and plans for program resources and support and information about possible funding opportunities (e.g., grants, special projects)
- Identifying resource or contact people in each building

The Time Line

The entire planning process requires time. There are no quick fixes, nor any simple, prepackaged or ready-made programs for instant adoption. An effective planning process represents an ongoing commitment characterized by continuous efforts to review, innovate, revise, and improve.

Some planning committees invest from 6 to 12 months in the initial development of a Master Plan. Extensive review and discussion among staff, administrators, and the school board may also require additional time. While each school's informal planning may occur simultaneously with the development of the Master Plan at the district level, the development of a comprehensive Building Action Plan may require at least another year after the guidelines have been provided through the Master Plan. Time will also be required for the development and implementation of flexible, diagnostic identification procedures and the gradual expansion of services to pupils. In addition, there will need to be careful consideration of the time needed for inservice or professional development.

A sample of a general three-year time line is summarized in Figure 10.1. You may wish to duplicate this page, or make a list of the major topics with target dates for completing each task, to distribute to all planning committee members at your initial meeting. Within any school, while the planning process is under way, many staff members may be highly motivated and eager to initiate direct services for students. With this in mind, some suggestions regarding the sequence or time line for such efforts seem warranted:

1. Take actions that will support and extend existing programming positives.

2. In considering the wish list, begin with the modifications that are easiest, least disruptive of scheduling and resources, and for which there are champions within the group (i.e., individuals or groups who are eager to take ownership of them).

3. Begin by seeking modifications or enhancements of the school program that will benefit the greatest number of students (a good strategy both philosophically and from the standpoint of marketing your program to the parents and the community).

4. Start with modifications for which you have the most expertise. For example, if no one in the building has ever run a mentor program, it is probably not wise to begin one as your first effort.

Resource Considerations

Determine what resources will be available for programming, at the district level and for each school. While most aspects of contemporary programming can begin with very modest resources, the level of support offered by a district

District Time Line		
Year One	**Year Two**	**Year Three**

A. Organize the district committee
• Establish general goals and purposes
• Provide overview of planning model
• Define tasks for the committee
 	
B. Preliminary data gathering
• Within district
• From outside sources
• State consultant input
• Attend conferences, workshops
• Consultant input
• Visit model programs
 	
C. Read, observe, study, reflect, compare, analyze
 	
D. Draft Master Plan for district
 	
E. Obtain input, reactions to Master Plan
• Staff, through awareness, review, discussion
• External review
	A. District committee
	• Review Building Action Plans and give feedback
	• Plan and conduct inservice
	• Institute resource recommendations (budget, staffing)
	• Initiate design and data collection for evaluation
	• Exchange Building Action Plans, discuss together
	• Monitor Building Action Plans
	  o Consistent with Master Plan
	  o Verify that action occurs
	• Seek new directions, new resources
	• Troubleshooting and problem solving as needed; new questions
	
	B. Building committees
	• Draft Action Plans
	• Input from staff
	• Submit plans to district committee
		A. District committee
		• Expand linkages with other areas of involvement
		  o School improvement
		  o Professional development
		  o Curriculum development
		  o Special curriculum areas
		  o Counseling, pupil services
		  o Community resources
		• Expand or revise Master Plan
		• Monitor Building Action Plans
		• Ongoing review, recommendations regarding resources and budget
		• Troubleshooting, problem solving
		• Evaluation support
		• Encouragement of new services
		
		B. Building committees
		• Review, revise Building Action Plans

Figure 10.1 Sample three-year planning time line   *(Continued)*

District Time Line		
Year One	**Year Two**	**Year Three**

F. Present Master Plan to Board
 	
G. Community awareness and information activities
 	
H. Formulate the charge to each building
  • Organize building committees
  • Begin preliminary tasks
  • Start work on Building Action Plans
 	
I. Formulate criteria and process for review of Building Action Plans
	• Initiate actions
	  ○ Staff awareness
	  ○ Programming positives, wish lists
	  ○ Initial implementation decisions
	  ○ Identify inservice needs, targets
	• Continuing input and discussion with district committee
	• Participate actively in evaluation efforts
	• Consider opportunities for innovation
	• Initiate gifted education programming on a pilot basis
		• Expand programming positives
		• Expand work on wish list priorities
		• Begin problem solving on wish list
		• Review, modify Action Plans
		• Continuing professional development
		• Link gifted programming with other services
		• Evaluate pilot programming activities and modify as warranted
		• Ongoing participation in evaluation, other district activities
		• Publicity and communication activities
		  ○ Brochures, newsletters
		  ○ Communications with parents and community
		• Monitor articulation among schools

Figure 10.1 (Continued)

in any new or expanding programming area is often an indicator of the degree of interest and commitment to the program that exists on the part of the board and the administration.

The planning committee may have the charge of developing a budget plan for training (courses, workshops, seminars, or conferences, for example), resources and professional study materials, supplies and services (paper, document preparation, and duplication), and program visitations. If you plan to use consultants to provide input and support to the planning committee, allocate resources as needed for fees and expenses. It is generally best not to expect the planning committee to meet after school or on the personal time of its members; this means that released time or substitute costs may need to be included in determining your resource requirements for the committee's work.

As the Master Plan emerges and the criteria for Building Action Plans are established, it will also be necessary to determine the resources that will be available to the school-based planning committees. Their expenses may involve many of the same general categories as those of the district level planning committee, even though they may benefit from the experiences and resources of that committee. They may receive some initial support from the planning committee's resources. Additional questions will arise at the school planning level. These include determining what resources, if any, will be made directly available to the schools for planning, for inservice, or for direct services to students, and how those resources will be allocated. Will each school receive resources on the basis of head count or pupil enrollment? Or by teacher units, with support for a part- or full-time staff person in the school? Or on the basis of projects or proposals they have developed?

Although budgets may need to be formulated and approved one year at a time, long-term projections of resource requirements will help the district to analyze and prepare for its needs more effectively than it can if each year's budget request is a surprise. General commitment to supporting the development of talent development programming may also be more likely if you have anticipated thoughtfully the long-range costs and needs of programming. In addition, plan specific resource commitments for professional development for staff and for expanding and extending each school's regular program. It will be important for the district to acknowledge and support the efforts of many staff in implementing contemporary, inclusive programming on a day-to-day basis.

Coordination and Staffing

The Master Plan also addresses the need for trained personnel to coordinate programming, on both the districtwide level and in each building. Effective, successful programming is more likely to take place in districts in which there is a professional commitment to searching for, selecting, and supporting staff members who have (or who are willing to pursue) appropriate professional training in talent development. A district coordinator can bring experience and knowledge of relevant theory and research to the work of the planning committee and can also support the efforts made by each school. In addition, the planning committee needs to work closely with the schools as they develop their own Building Action Plans to assist them in determining their staffing needs and in designing strategies for meeting those needs in coordination with other buildings.

Professional Development

Professional development is a critical component of your programming effort. Without adequate preparation and expertise, programming will lack support and effectiveness. Modern practice views staff development as an ongoing process involving several stages:

- Conducting a Needs Assessment to determine areas of concern and interest and to plan for appropriate professional development opportunities
- Establishing ways to meet the stated needs within existing staff development models and programs or by developing new initiatives
- Planning and implementing a variety of staff development options or activities
- Assessing the effectiveness of the staff development program
- Revising and recycling

In viewing staff development this way, districts encourage staff to expand their confidence and motivation as well as their skills.

Evaluation

Consider evaluation to be a natural and important process that guides you in sustaining or modifying programming and making it more effective. Evaluation is also addressed in greater detail in Chapter 14 of this handbook. Effective evaluation should be:

1. Closely linked to the goals and objectives laid out for programming

2. Inclusive of information gathered from all the people affected by the program. This includes, but may not be limited to, parents, staff, students, and administration.

3. Qualitative as well as quantitative; it documents the real activities and accomplishments of those who are involved

4. Diverse and linked to the information desired or needed by various target audiences. The questions posed by teachers, building level administrators, board members, and parents may all be different, and may require different kinds of evidence or support.

THE MASTER PLAN: USES AND FORMAT

A comprehensive, written Master Plan represents a significant milestone in the planning committee's work. Your written Master Plan will be important to all board members, administrators, and staff members; each of these target audiences will have specific needs and concerns which should be considered. Figure 10.2 describes many of these needs and concerns.

Target Audience	Needs and Concerns	Implications for Master Plan
School board	Policy and budget input for them to consider	• Information regarding the importance of and need for programming • Resources needed for programming • Implications for staffing • Time line
District administration	Foundation for effective administrative management of policies, procedures, and resources	• Specify district functions • Specify schools' responsibilities • Procedures for monitoring and evaluating • Administrative and staff duties • Criteria for reviewing Building Action Plans • Resource needs and time line • Professional development plans
Building administration	Foundation for effective formulation of Action Plan, its implementation, support, and evaluation	• Schools' planning responsibilities • Components of Action Plan • Review of Action Plan • Available support and how to obtain • Evaluation of school's efforts • Staffing and professional development implications • Time line • Information to answer parent, community questions
Staff members	Awareness of district policies, procedures, and resource commitments; involvement in planning, implementation, and evaluation	• Information regarding philosophy, definition, Master Plan • Staff roles and responsibilities • Staff development opportunities • School planning committee tasks • Implementation guidelines and resources available • Evaluation activities • Information to respond to parent, community, student questions

Figure 10.2 Concerns of stakeholders

The format and length of the Master Plan may vary from one district to another. It should be read, studied, understood, and used by those concerned with the design, implementation, and evaluation of talent development programming throughout the district. If it is a long document (that is, more than 8 to 10 pages), it would be advisable to prepare an "executive summary" providing abstracts of the major topics and highlighting specific recommendations that will be of major concern for specific target audiences.

Since the Master Plan should be reviewed, updated, and revised on an ongoing basis, it may be helpful to prepare it with numbered sections and subsections in a flexible format (e.g., loose-leaf) so that you can easily modify and update it as changes arise.

There is a Master Plan summary checklist in Figure 10.3 (and on the CD) to assist you in keeping track of your progress. Appendix A provides a structured template to guide you in creating your Master Plan; this form is also included as a Word document ("Master Plan Constructor") on the CD that accompanies this handbook.

Has your district completed and shared:

❑ Philosophy and vision statement

❑ Definition

❑ Goals and objectives

❑ Identification policies and procedures

❑ Implementation guidelines for schools

❑ Philosophy and vision statement

❑ District time line

❑ Resource considerations

❑ Coordination and staffing

❑ Professional development

❑ Evaluation plans

Figure 10.3   Components of the Master Plan: A checklist

Constructing the Building Action Plan 11

This chapter deals with the development of your specific Building Action Plan. The Building Action Plan is based on your Master Plan (from Chapter 10) and guides implementation of contemporary programming at the school level.

THE BUILDING ACTION PLAN

The Master Plan provides a framework or "umbrella" to guide schools in their planning. Working within the general parameters established in the Master Plan, each school creates its own Building Action Plan, which addresses several major questions:

- What are we already doing to challenge our students and to recognize and nurture their strengths, talents, and sustained interests?
- What should we be doing?
- What needs to be changed, expanded, or added to help us do the best job possible in this area?

The staff of a school, or a building level planning committee, constructs the Building Action Plan. In the Building Action Plan, you will consider the school's staff (and their own talents, interests, and resources), the curriculum, the instructional program's strengths and activities, and the school's resources (looking at, for example, the use or redistribution of existing resources as well as requests for new resources). Use the following steps to encourage active involvement and the development of investment and ownership of programming by the school's staff.

Review and update your list of programming positives. Review the work you did previously and pose such questions as, "What kinds of activities already occur in our school to challenge students, to extend their learning, or to spark their interests and curiosity? What do we do to stretch our students and expand their talents?" Consider *any* activities: schoolwide, by grade level or subject area, or special projects conducted by one or more teachers. Include consideration of clubs, special areas, community service projects, or any other major commitments in which the staff and students are involved.

Next, take another look at your preliminary wish list. Once again, ask, "How might we increase or expand what we do to 'stretch' our students or bring out their best learning potentials, talents, and sustained interests?" Sort your wish list into two categories: the wishes and goals that can readily be accomplished, and the goals that will require more extensive planning and problem solving to attain.

Initiate a discussion of your school's possible "next steps." What are some of the specific actions that you can take to move programming forward? Who agrees to assume responsibility for action?

COMPONENTS OF THE BUILDING ACTION PLAN

A Building Action Plan generally includes 13 important components, each of which your planning committee (and perhaps your entire staff) should review and discuss thoroughly. Developing a Building Action Plan may require at least 6 to 12 months of careful planning and hard work. As we consider this baker's dozen of components briefly, we offer several sample questions to illustrate the kinds of discussion that will be helpful for each of them. In addition, each of the shaded boxes below provides an example of responses from actual Building Action Plans from schools.

Rationale and Benefits

What is your rationale for implementing a contemporary approach to talent development programming? What benefits do you anticipate from its implementation?

Example From an Elementary School

- *By involving a team approach to addressing talent development, we can address more needs of students and develop a stronger team.*
- *We can continue Level 3 and 4 services while meeting the needs of more children, giving all students access to creative problem solving and critical thinking skills. We have the potential to increase the achievement of all children.*
- *There are multiple intelligences and many students' gifts and talents are outside of our current program.*
- *Talent development complements and is in alignment with district initiatives.*
- *A Levels of Service approach opens the door for more students to be serviced and more content areas to be explored.*
- *Talent is recognized across the curriculum and services are provided for all students.*

- *Students become productive thinkers.*
- *All children possess special talents and strengths. Through talent development we can build upon those strengths through activities that are designed to help students reach their academic potential.*
- *Talent development is a model that provides for flexible implementation with the ability to add services as the need is identified and resources become available.*
- *Evidence indicates that our top-performing students are currently not demonstrating high levels of learning. By implementing our talent development program, there will be more of an emphasis on challenging our top performers.*
- *Self-esteem and acceptance levels of students are better addressed through this type of program.*
- *The research and program evaluation support the shift in providing gifted services from a few students to all students through a Levels of Service approach.*

Establish Your Philosophy and Definitions

What decisions, if any, have been made at the district level, or in your Master Plan, regarding your philosophy and definition of key terms relating to contemporary programming? What impact do those decisions have on your school? How will you explain them in a clear and concise way to your staff, students, and parents?

Example From a Middle School

We believe that all students have unique interests and strengths. Our mission is to recognize, nurture, and enhance the development of those talents by providing educational experiences that will allow students to pursue their interests and reach their greatest potential.

Giftedness and talent refer to students' potential to become healthy, independent, creatively productive people. Programming is an ongoing process, through which we recognize and nurture each student's potential. An environment is created where students' strengths and talents are recognized and enhanced through specialized learning experiences that are challenging and developmentally appropriate.

We believe that identification of students should be based on the characteristics derived from strengths, talents, and sustained interests. Identification is a continuous process that occurs as a result of Talent Spotting, interest-based surveys, and referrals. Identification is inclusive as it enables us to better recognize the varying strengths of our students on an individual basis.

Our program's effectiveness is based on the premise that opportunities for all students to learn will be offered through the four Levels of Service. We believe that our regular school programming is the foundation for learning. The Levels of Service approach offered through our talent development program builds upon differentiated classroom experiences. In addition, our program establishes a link to the community as a partner in learning.

Stating Goals and Objectives

What general goals and specific objectives have you established for implementing programming? Are they stated in ways that describe important outcomes and results for students? How will you promote those goals and objectives to key participants (e.g., teachers, students, parents)?

Example From an Elementary School

➢ Help students better understand learning styles
➢ Incorporate more critical thinking and divergent thinking into the regular classroom
➢ Address student strengths in providing learning opportunities
➢ Expand the areas of interest and nurture talents in more areas across the curriculum
➢ Match identification to interests and strengths of students
➢ Assist students in discovering their own strengths and interests
➢ Improve test scores of upper quartile students

Identify Your School's Uniqueness

What key elements of your culture, mission, values, and climate are important to consider when designing your Building Action Plan? How are they reflected in your proposed actions or responses? What are the established operations in your school—the expectations, traditions, rituals, and rewards that everyone comes to know and expect? What is the climate like? How do people feel about being there, about the way the school operates, and about each other? How are your culture and climate reflected in your wish lists? How might your Building Action Plan reflect your best understanding of your unique identity, your school's strengths, and what you hope to accomplish together?

Example From an Elementary School

Our school is known to possess and display a very open, caring, and friendly environment. We are not a large school and the staff has many opportunities to interact. . . . Our staff has a "kids first" attitude. We want to do what's right. Talent development is best for kids.

Example From a Middle School

Strengths

• Faculty and staff are very willing to provide students with additional time, remediation, acceleration, or classroom differentiation.
• Teachers provide a warm and welcoming environment in which brain compatible teaching strategies are used.

> - *Classrooms are grouped heterogeneously, providing students with opportunities to receive individual assistance that meets their needs.*
> - *Students respect authority and school policies and generally reflect a positive experience.*
>
> **Needs More Work**
>
> - *Bring more teachers on board with differentiated instructional practices.*
> - *Increase teacher awareness so they become better talent spotters.*
>
> **Uniqueness**
>
> - *Specified class time is available to meet with students for mini lessons.*
> - *Teachers are willing to provide additional opportunities for students.*
> - *Fine Art Department has a wide range of unique opportunities such as Jazz Band, Midpoint, Spring Musical, and a variety of art contests.*

Assessing Students' Characteristics and Needs

In what ways might you search deliberately for students' strengths, talents, and sustained interests? How might you increase your ability to recognize and respond to your students' unique characteristics and needs? What steps can you take to avoid merely labeling or categorizing your students?

> *Interest inventories, standardized test results, and anecdotal observations are currently used in the identification process. It is our intent to expand training to enable teachers to become better talent spotters through observation through classroom projects and tasks. Multiple intelligences, Habits of Mind, learning styles, and higher-level thinking skills will be integrated into training sessions and collaborative discussions. Building-based collaborative meetings provide opportunities for teachers to share findings and concerns on student progress. Better coaching/facilitation, dialogue around student artifacts, and analysis of student data are current topics at collaborative meetings.*

Examining the Regular School Program's Strengths

How does your school ensure challenge, recognize diversity, and offer opportunities for student productivity? What programming positives describe the areas in which you are already doing well to challenge your students and to build on their talents and interests? Do you balance concern for remediation and deficiencies with efforts to locate students' strengths?

> *We use an eclectic approach to balanced instruction that honors the developmental level of the student. We base strategy and skill development on student need, and we use a scaffolded approach to allow opportunities for appropriate practice and progress.*
>
> *(Continued)*

> (Continued)
>
> *We are strong in literacy skills in the content areas, integration of multiple intelligences, and Habits of Mind. We have many community connections, including businesses and area colleges and universities. We have excellent opportunities in sports, fine arts, music, and drama. We strongly encourage and develop teacher understanding of how best to identify talents/strengths as a "tool" for individual growth. Our strongest areas in Needs Assessment were in differentiated basics and personal growth/social development. Next were independence and self-direction, appropriate enrichment, and effective acceleration. Careers and futures was the lowest area.*

Extending, Enhancing, or Expanding the Regular Program

What are the items on your wish list toward which you are already making new or expanded efforts? What initial steps have you taken to address the difficult areas of the wish list? What are some changes, expanded services, increased activities, or innovations you will attempt to bring about through your talent development programming? How will you link these efforts to other components of your ongoing commitment to quality instruction and school improvement?

> *Stronger community connections/reciprocal support*
> *Cross-content services; project-based learning*
> *Service learning projects*
> *Increased use of videoconferencing to share differentiated practices*

Identifying Active Participants and Leaders

What will be the roles of classroom teachers and of administrators in implementing your Building Action Plan? Who else will be involved? Will staff members be available to work with other staff members and students to facilitate the development and implementation of new services and activities? How will you support faculty members' efforts to improve planning, student diagnosis, and delivery of instruction? What age or grade levels will be involved? In what subject or program areas will students be involved in programming? Who in your school will provide leadership to help talent development programming move forward successfully?

Staff Development

What new skills, resources, or methods and techniques will you need to carry out your Action Plan? How will you ensure that these will be available, and that your staff will learn how to use them effectively? What training opportunities will you need to ensure the staff's competence and commitment, and how will you provide those opportunities? How will you determine their impact?

Talent Spotting needs to be further developed so students are not overlooked or underserved; we will provide ongoing training at the district and building levels to address this need. Thinking skills coaches and building representatives provide direct support at the building level. They are working on videotaping and videoconferencing to build the focus on these strategies.

Resource and Budget Implications

What school resources will you obtain and use to carry out the Building Action Plan? What new resources will you require? From what outside sources might you obtain additional resources (financial, people, materials), and how might you obtain their support? What are the long-range resource implications? When you initiate programming, what ongoing resources will you need to ensure its successful continuation?

The Implementation Time Line

When will you begin to implement the Action Plan? When will you review and evaluate it? When will you consider modifications? How long will it require for you to initiate each component of the Action Plan and bring it to full implementation?

Links With Other Initiatives

Talent development programming is not an isolated concern; it can and should be related to many other important initiatives within the school. Is there an explicit school improvement plan in your school? If so, how will it relate to your Building Action Plan for talent development? If there is no current school improvement plan, how will your talent development programming contribute to the overall quality and effectiveness of your school? *Suggestion:* Go on an "advance" together (we don't talk about "retreats") for staff to set a vision and develop a three- to five-year plan.

Our talent development steering committee meets regularly with our school improvement team, and we have integrated many of our talent development programming goals and objectives with our annual school improvement goals. We also coordinate talent development programming with our district's ongoing commitment to differentiating instruction in the classroom.

Evaluation Plan

What specific plans and commitments have you made to evaluate the school's Building Action Plan and its implementation? What criteria will you use to document the effectiveness or impact of the components or activities in the Building Action Plan? How will you use evaluation data to refine or modify your talent development programming efforts?

MOVING FORWARD

When you have completed your work on a Master Plan (from Chapter 10) and your Building Action Plan, you will be ready to implement a contemporary, inclusive approach to talent development programming. The next sections of the Six-Stage Systematic Planning Model provide additional implementation suggestions and support. We recommend that you study the "Carry Out Programming" and "Seek Talents and Strengths" sections of the Six-Stage Systematic Planning Model before you finalize your Master Plan and your Building Action Plan. These sections include information and resources that may stimulate your thinking and decision making regarding the activities and services you plan to carry out.

Use Figure 11.1 (also on the CD), the Building Action Plan checklist, to assist you in keeping track of your progress. Appendix B of the handbook provides a structured template to guide you in creating your Building Action Plan; this form is also included as a Word document on the accompanying CD ("BldgPlanConstructor").

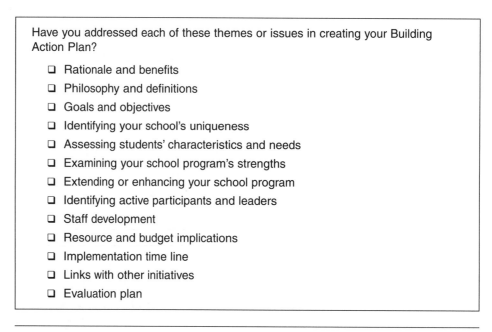

Have you addressed each of these themes or issues in creating your Building Action Plan?

- ❑ Rationale and benefits
- ❑ Philosophy and definitions
- ❑ Goals and objectives
- ❑ Identifying your school's uniqueness
- ❑ Assessing students' characteristics and needs
- ❑ Examining your school program's strengths
- ❑ Extending or enhancing your school program
- ❑ Identifying active participants and leaders
- ❑ Staff development
- ❑ Resource and budget implications
- ❑ Implementation time line
- ❑ Links with other initiatives
- ❑ Evaluation plan

Figure 11.1   Components of the Building Action Plan: A checklist

Section V

Stage Four—
Carry Out
Programming

In the first three stages of the Six-Stage Systematic Planning Model, you prepared your context for programming, clarified your current situation, made decisions about your next steps, and then created a Master Plan and a Building Action Plan. Stage Four involves carrying out programming effectively.

The key tasks in this stage are:

- Considering four Levels of Service for implementing a contemporary, inclusive programming approach
- Exploring six broad areas of excellence in programming
- Determining how you will move forward effectively at the classroom, school, or district level

Chapter 12 provides information and resources to help you implement these tasks effectively and efficiently. This chapter is intended to serve as an overview and illustration of contemporary programming, drawing specifically on our experience in implementing a Levels of Service (LoS) approach in many schools and school districts. This section supplements other published resources about the LoS approach (e.g., Treffinger, Young, Nassab, & Wittig, 2004b). You may also choose to supplement this chapter with additional published resources from other contemporary approaches to programming (as described in Chapter 1).

You will enter this stage when your planning efforts have progressed to the point at which you have a clear picture of your programming positives and a variety of services that you can provide in your school setting. Since effective programming is an ongoing process, it is not appropriate to state an exit point for this stage.

Implementing Contemporary Programming 12

This chapter deals with implementing a contemporary, inclusive approach to programming. It provides a brief overview of four "Levels of Service" in contemporary programming. The examples are drawn from our *Levels of Service* approach (LoS; Treffinger, Young, Nassab, & Wittig, 2004b) to illustrate important considerations in implementing a contemporary, inclusive approach to programming. They are not intended to be a comprehensive discussion of programming.

Programming concerns are at the heart of the LoS approach, and they are central in many contemporary, inclusive approaches to talent development. *Programming* has to do with the activities, services, or instructional practices that exist in any school to respond to students' strengths, talents, and sustained interests. Programming deals with what you actually *do* with students, day in and day out. It involves what happens in every classroom, and beyond—in the library, the gym, the auditorium, or anywhere in the community. Figure 12.1 summarizes the key elements in our view of talent development programming.

Programming for Talent Development Involves . . .

Activities based on students' strengths, talents,
and sustained interests in many talent areas or domains

Challenges in which students apply knowledge creatively

Many options or services, with considerable flexibility in how and
when services are offered

Activities that emerge from, extend, and enhance
(strong) regular curriculum

Shared ownership and participation by many staff, students, and
community resources

Figure 12.1 Key elements of talent development programming

In the LoS approach, and in several other contemporary approaches as well, we have moved away from the view that there is a single, fixed program or curriculum for all "gifted and talented" or high-ability students ("the program"). We have moved instead to an emphasis on programming that is dynamic, multidimensional, flexible, and responsive to many talent domains, strengths, and interests among students. It is usually best to emphasize what an approach is "for" rather than what it is "against," and to let an approach stand (or fall) on its own merits. However, the major shift in our approach to programming challenges older views in many ways, and so it may be important for you to be able to identify and analyze the contrasts in some detail. These are summarized in Figure 12.2.

Programming emphasizes the importance of providing activities and services that are *appropriate*, *challenging*, and *developmental*; Figure 12.3 summarizes these three essential factors. Programming must be directly relevant to each student's characteristics and needs; it is not a matter of one-size-fits-all services!

THE FOUR LEVELS OF SERVICE

The LoS approach to programming centers around four Levels of Service that are important components of an effective instructional program.

Level I: Programming for All Students

Level I involves providing instructional activities aimed at all students. Level I activities are often completed in a single event, lesson, or unit, after which students move on to other exploratory experiences. The objective is to build a foundation of experience through which students discover and begin to pursue personal interests, strengths, and talents. These activities might take place in the classroom, as services for students in several classrooms at a grade level, or in activities for an entire student body (e.g., class trips or schoolwide assemblies). High-quality classroom instruction is a key factor, based on best practice, and differentiated to meet the needs of individual students. As students participate in Level I activities, they may exhibit strong interest and talent potential. Upon observing a learner's strengths, teachers and parents encourage him or her to follow up with more in-depth and demanding involvement in a particular area of interest. Level I activities also provide a foundation for students to become aware of their personal learning style preferences, to learn and apply creative and critical thinking tools and independent learning skills, and to begin managing and directing their own learning.

Level II: Programming for Many Students

Level II programming invites students to build on their initial curiosity about or interest in particular subjects or talent areas and to explore them in more depth. All students *might* participate in any Level II activity; however, not every student *will*. While others might direct or encourage students to become involved, voluntary participation is a key element of this level, building students' ownership in and responsibility for talent development. Their interest in the subject or activity has reached a point at which they are ready to invest their time and effort in its pursuit. Activities may vary in scope and duration

Traditional Views	Contemporary Views	Why?
• Adopt a model	• Draw on many models, according to your circumstances and goals	• The context and needs of every school differ; it's not a one-size-fits-all matter
• Create a gifted program	• Offer a variety of different activities and services in response to varied student needs, talents, and interests	• The diversity of strengths and talents among students requires varied responses
• Provide a special, separate program (e.g., pull-out, resource room, or special class) or identify "cluster groups" to be served more effectively in the regular program	• Strengthen the regular program for all students and augment it as needed to provide for students' talents and interests	• No individual teacher can be everything to everyone. However, many aspects of traditional gifted/talented programs are important and appropriate for all students.
• Provide a gifted/talented teacher who attends to the instructional or programmatic needs of identified students	• Create a team effort, including one or more staff with appropriate training and experience	• It is important to create a balance of collaborative instructional responsibility between leadership and trained personnel
• Create and follow a "differentiated curriculum" for the identified population	• Provide differentiated instruction	• Giftedness is in the response—what people do with what they learn and know—not in the material we present to students
• Provide services only to identified students	• Provide services that are appropriate and challenging for all students, based on their characteristics as learners	• It is important to design instruction for students' actual characteristics, not stereotyped assumptions about categories of people

Figure 12.2   Traditional and contemporary views of programming

Appropriate	Challenging	Developmental
• Especially well suited • Consistent with needs and characteristics • Fits well • Makes sense • Wisely and carefully designed • Compatible	• Invitingly provocative • Arousing competitive interest, thought, or action • Energizing and stimulating; exciting and motivational • Expanding, "stretching" • Forward looking • Capacity building • Inspiring, stirring passion and intense involvement	• Designed to assist or encourage growth • Gradually becoming manifest or apparent • Helping to bring about improvement • Making active and available • Enabling progress or advancement to new or higher levels

Figure 12.3   Activities and services should be appropriate, challenging, and developmental

but generally have fixed points at which students can decide whether to continue or move on to other interests. They often involve creating some product or taking part in a public performance or presentation. During their work, students practice and apply their knowledge and their self-directed learning skills, with adult oversight, in a relatively low-risk environment. They have opportunities to test their level of interest and commitment to a particular field while supportive adults work with them to observe and record their accomplishments and urge them to move on to more demanding and in-depth work. As teachers discover talents, even if no existing school service is available, they search for or create ways to respond. As students excel, they come to feel affirmed and encouraged to achieve excellence.

Level III: Programming for Some Students

Level III programming offers services for students who are enthusiastic about a particular field of study or talent area. Students aspire (and are expected) to perform at a high level of engagement and accomplishment. In Level III the focus shifts away from foundation-building or exploratory activities to differentiated responses to a student's maturing strengths and talents. Students sustain their participation in Level III activities over an extended period of time and devote a considerable amount of time on their own to study, practice, or preparation. In a school setting, Level III opportunities might include selection for an advanced study group or class; auditioned musical, speech, or theatrical groups; extended science, social studies, or art projects; inventing or community service programs or competitions; creative writing for publication; individual study; or clubs and organizations with selected membership. Opportunities outside the school might include private lessons or advanced tutoring, participation in auditioned community-based performing groups, or selection to play on a community sports team such as an all-star Little League or traveling soccer team. Mentors, teachers, parents, and coaches continually challenge the students to stretch and move on to more demanding work and a greater sense of accomplishment.

Level IV: Programming for a Few Students

Level IV programming responds to the exceptional needs that may be demonstrated by a few students in any domain who have outstanding records of expertise, experience, dedication, passion, and ability to attain or approach a "professional" level of performance and accomplishment in that subject or talent area. Instructional goals for Level IV programming address four dimensions of talent development: content, process, affect, and product. Content is expected to be high level, complex, and challenging. Students will often share the results of their work, including authentic products, with others in their field and with the public. They may receive recognition and support for these products with advanced academic credit, publication, having their work patented, professional performance, and selection for highly competitive programs or groups. The school's role involves helping to locate appropriate resources, providing the means for a student to take advantage of those resources, supporting the student's pursuit of appropriate opportunities, and enabling the student to document and earn credit for advanced work and accomplishments. Programming may include grade level acceleration, multiple grade advancement, independent work with teachers, or dual or part-time enrollment and participation in higher-level courses. Level IV services often extend beyond the school setting, through connections with mentors who are successful in their field, internships, active involvement in professional organizations or societies, or advanced learning through Web-based distance education courses or projects.

Figure 12.4 summarizes the four levels graphically, and Figure 12.5 provides several illustrative examples of services at each level. Figure 12.6 illustrates parallels among the LoS approach, the talent development model widely applied in music education, and examples from other talent areas. We chose the music model as an example specifically because music programs are widely familiar and offer clear examples of how the Levels of Service are already being applied in specific domains in school settings today.

All four levels of programming are equally important in meeting the needs of students; therefore, it is necessary to provide a full range of programming options, spanning all four Levels of Service. Traditional gifted programs have too often been viewed as providing only a few specific services at Levels III and IV for a small, narrowly defined and identified group of students. This often leads to providing too few services for too few students. At the other extreme, some schools have contended that the needs of all students can (and should) be met only through provisions made by classroom teachers in the regular program. These programs focus only on Levels I and II. This creates a risk that schools offer "a little something for everyone" but fail to make any deliberate efforts to recognize or respond to the needs of students with specific, high-level strengths and talents. The optimum response is to ensure that programming takes into account all four Levels of Service, and to challenge schools to provide appropriate and challenging instruction for all students. Instructional programs should enrich and expand learning opportunities for all students commensurate with their strengths, talents, and sustained interests. This is essential for any school with a commitment to excellence and continuous improvement.

It is often said that "all children can learn." In some ways, this assertion is so obvious that it is a platitude. It certainly does not mean that all children learn

I. Services for ALL Students—

Providing foundational skills and tools
"Discovering and Building"

II. Services for MANY Students—

Engaging and verifying interests
"Curious and Exploring"

III. Services for SOME Students—

Meeting the need for alternative opportunities
"Enthusiastic and Performing"

IV. Services for A FEW Students—

Responding to blossoming expertise and the need
for highly individualized services
"Passionate and Soaring"

Figure 12.4   Programming for talent development: Levels of Service

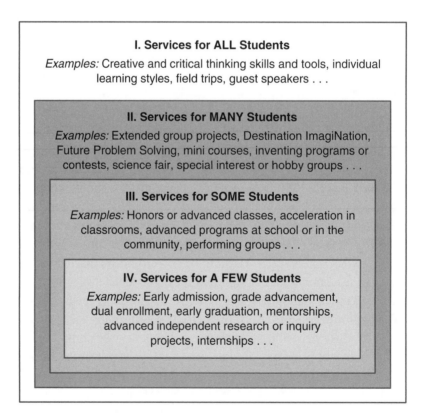

I. Services for ALL Students

Examples: Creative and critical thinking skills and tools, individual
learning styles, field trips, guest speakers . . .

II. Services for MANY Students

Examples: Extended group projects, Destination ImagiNation,
Future Problem Solving, mini courses, inventing programs or
contests, science fair, special interest or hobby groups . . .

III. Services for SOME Students

Examples: Honors or advanced classes, acceleration in
classrooms, advanced programs at school or in the
community, performing groups . . .

IV. Services for A FEW Students

Examples: Early admission, grade advancement,
dual enrollment, early graduation, mentorships,
advanced independent research or inquiry
projects, internships . . .

Figure 12.5   Levels of Service examples

Levels of Service	The Music Model	Other Talent Areas
Level I: All • Instruction builds foundations and basic skills in the area of study • Exploratory experiences are part of the regular instruction program, usually in group settings • Talents, strengths, and interests are allowed to emerge	**Exposure** • All students are exposed to music in a variety of ways • Students gain a basic familiarity with musical terms and notation • Students explore as audience members and music makers	**Exposure Examples** • All students receive instruction in specific content areas • Students take part in developmentally appropriate science experiments and creative writing lessons • Students attend science and theater assemblies
Level II: Many • Activities and instruction are open to all but not all will participate • Activities are inclusive, usually involving group participation • Activities allow for a closer exploration of the subject and of the student's level of interest and motivation	**Voluntary Participation** • All students are invited to join a vocal or instrumental group • Music electives are provided in upper grades • All students are provided opportunities to attend special performances	**Voluntary Participation** • All students are invited to join the science, literary, or drama clubs • Specialized science, creative writing, and theater electives are offered • Science fairs, special trips, and theatrical presentations are open to all
Level III: Some • Activities and instructional programming are offered based on evaluation of the student's specific learning needs and performance • Services are provided individually as well as in small and large groups • Activities and mentoring are provided outside of the regular school program	**Limited Participation** • Performing group membership is based on audition • Memberships are available in community-based groups and other selective performance venues • Student learning needs are continually assessed in private lessons	**Limited Participation** • Successful science projects are selected for presentation at larger venues • Creative writing pieces are selected for publication • Students are accelerated or placed in advanced study groups • Students belong to various clubs and organizations
Level IV: Few • Opportunities are developed in response to the unique skills and needs of each student • Relationships are established with mentors who are highly successful in their field	**Targeted Programming** • Students are encouraged to join an all-state band, chorus, or orchestra • Students are encouraged to participate in the governor's or county's school for the arts • Opportunities to study with a highly regarded professional are provided	**Targeted Programming** • Students attend a regional math competition • Students enter various state and national competitions • Mentorship with a leading scientist or writer is provided • Students take high-level courses online

Figure 12.6   Programming parallels: LoS, the music model, and other areas

Source: Adapted from Selby and Young, 2003.

in the same ways, and at the same rate, nor that all children will have the same strengths, interests, and talents. "Democratic" instruction means that every student has the challenge and opportunity to discover and use her or his best potentials and talents and to develop those talents as fully as possible. This implies that it is essential for schools to recognize that many programming options (from Level I through Level IV, in the language of our approach) must be sustained in an effective instructional program.

DIMENSIONS OF EFFECTIVENESS AND CRITERIA FOR HEALTHY SCHOOL PROGRAMMING

Your Building Action Plan should be directed toward establishing, maintaining, or expanding efforts that lead to a "healthy" school program. No matter what specific model or approach to talent development you choose, including the LoS approach, the healthier your regular school program, the greater the likelihood of your success in talent development. Conversely, without the strong foundation of a healthy school program, it is very probable that any talent development model will be very limited in its impact and success in the long run. Thus, it is very important to consider the following questions:

- Is our school program healthy?
- How can we determine its health in several areas?
- What are some of the indicators and criteria that might be used to take stock of, or subsequently to enhance, the health of the school program?

Some educators express concern that these questions deal with the overall school program and not specifically with gifted/talented programming. The greater your concern and commitment to programming that nurtures and expands the strengths and talents of many students, however, the less bothersome is such a concern. In addition—under any contemporary view, such as the LoS approach—there should be systematic efforts to link or "bridge" talent development programming with the total school program. Thus, all efforts to enhance or strengthen your regular program will lead to a more constructive foundation for talent development. The general characteristics of a healthy school program might be described in a variety of ways, of course. In this handbook, we have used six general dimensions (presented in the Needs Assessment Inventory in Chapter 6) as a basic structure. Use these dimensions, reflected in the results of your Needs Assessment, to consider your specific plan for carrying out programming. Which areas should be represented in your programming positives, and which might be important elements of your wish list? Are these areas represented in your Building Action Plan? Do some of them suggest unique strengths of your school, or areas in which you need to engage in some long-range planning and problem solving?

In addition, examine how each of these six indicators might be reflected in programming at all four Levels of Service. Figure 12.7 provides examples of possible combinations. The specific array of activities and services for your school will depend on many factors that are unique to your setting and resources.

Level of Service	Differentiated Basics	Effective Acceleration	Appropriate Enrichment	Independence and Self-Direction	Personal and Social Growth	Careers and Future Orientation
Level I—Services for ALL Students	All levels of Bloom's taxonomy; exploration of various talent areas; exposure to many and varied topics; learning through preferred styles	Each student in any class progresses at his or her own individual pace (e.g., by the use of mastery learning or differentiated instruction)	General exploration; field trips; guest speakers; special films; videos; assemblies; interest centers; after-school/Saturday programs	Varied teaching styles to stimulate varied student activities, individual or small group classroom projects	Class activities or projects that help students understand their own styles; thematic studies of interpersonal or group skills	Activities, units, or experiences to make students aware of change, futures, and careers; development of forecasting skills
Level II—Services for MANY Students	Opportunities to pursue additional work in areas of particular interest	Opportunities for "testing out" in specific units of content	Self-selected programs based on student interests; clubs, hobbies; Future Problem Solving, Destination ImagiNation, Junior Great Books, inventing	Individual, small group, or team projects based on student interests as extra credit; opportunities to participate in projects conducted by student clubs or activity groups	Simulations for students to explore special needs and circumstances, group relations; involvement of many students in varied roles in class or school projects or programs	Guest speakers or field trips to expose students to careers and future issues; involvement in programs such as Future Problem Solving or World Futures programs
Level III—Services for SOME Students	Advanced courses providing the basics of more complex content areas for qualified students	Opportunities for testing out, credit-by-exam, or challenging of final exams to earn course credit; Talent Search programs	Independent or small group investigations of real problems and challenges; instructional groups for specific talent or interest areas	Individual, group, or team projects extending students' current level of interest, knowledge, or experience and giving them new opportunities to extend their learning	Leadership programs or activities for students; involvement in small groups to address personal and interpersonal skills and tools	Young Entrepreneur, Junior Achievement, or other career/future-related program opportunities based on students' interests, experience, and application or nomination

Figure 12.7   Levels of Service by area

(Continued)

Level of Service	Differentiated Basics	Effective Acceleration	Appropriate Enrichment	Independence and Self-Direction	Personal and Social Growth	Careers and Future Orientation
Level IV— Services for A FEW Students	Independently planned and managed learning programs or contracts for individual students with particular strengths	Early admission, early graduation, grade advancement, dual enrollment in courses at varied levels and sites	Application to and participation in special programs or projects away from school; mentorships; advanced independent projects	Extended individual or group projects or investigations; opportunities to do research/projects with mentors or organizations; high-level contests, competitions, or service projects	Leadership roles in clubs or at the class or school level; participation in community activities and forums	Internships, job shadowing, and mentoring opportunities based on students' future personal and career goals

Figure 12.7 (Continued)

Source: From the Center for Creative Learning, Inc.

152

EFFECTIVE IMPLEMENTATION OF PROGRAMMING

The following four general suggestions will help increase the likelihood of your success in implementing contemporary programming at the school or building level. You can also find specific keys for success in implementing programming at each of the four Levels of Service in Treffinger, Young, Nassab, & Wittig (2004b).

1. Phase in programming "action" gradually; begin with services for many or all students, then expand to more complex services. Begin to take action at the school level *gradually*, and begin with consideration of several important directions that involve many (or all!) students and staff. Examples of activities or services for many students, readily incorporated into any school's program, include:

• *Thinking skills for all students.* Many programs and resources are now available to guide educators in their efforts to promote higher-level, productive thinking among all students. Costa's (2001) *Developing Minds* is a useful collection of brief descriptions of many such programs. The *Thinking with Standards: Preparing for Tomorrow* volumes (Treffinger, Nassab, Schoonover, Selby, Shepardson, Wittig, & Young, 2004a, 2004b, 2004c) provide examples of activities to integrate content standards with creative and critical thinking tools. The *CPS Kit* (Treffinger, Nassab, Schoonover, Selby, Shepardson, Wittig, & Young, 2006) provides a comprehensive program to guide students in learning and applying Creative Problem Solving, working independently or with a team, small group, or class. Many publishers also provide a wide range of practical resources for promoting creative and critical thinking, problem solving, and decision making.

• *Programs that offer motivating opportunities for students' creativity, imagination, and inquiry skills to be expressed and developed.* Some examples include Future Problem Solving (www.fpsp.org), Destination ImagiNation (www.destination imagination.org), and the Camp Invention program (www.invent.org).

• *Systematic efforts to learn about student differences, such as methods for recognizing and responding to students' learning styles.* There are many practical resources for both adults and students to learn more about learning styles and preferences. Visit the International Learning Styles Network Web site (www.learningstyles.net) or the VIEW problem solving style Web site (www.ViewStyle.net), for example, for more information on a number of resources and instruments.

• *Increasing community resource use and involvement.* This may include efforts to develop or expand community resource and mentor programs, involvement of community organizations or businesses in partnership programs, such as the Adopt-a-School program, and development of "artist in residence" or other similar programs. Parents and parent groups may be effective support systems for the establishment of such efforts on a schoolwide basis.

2. Establish ways to search for and review new instructional resources and to create and implement new programming opportunities. Begin to work on several steps of your wish list. Seek many and varied ways to increase the number and kinds of services that are offered—to all students, and, on the basis of students' particular interests and needs, to individuals and groups. Some examples include:

• Conducting specific activities and making deliberate efforts to notice and respond to students' interests.

• Creating opportunities for students to participate in interest development or exploratory activities, such as listening to guest speakers, field trips, and special interest programs or resources. They may be provided on a voluntary attendance basis, by invitation (when students with particular known interest areas, for example, are invited to a special follow-up session with a guest speaker after an introductory program for a larger audience), or by grade level, subject area, or even by individual class participation.

• Helping teachers to be alert to opportunities to identify students' special interests, talents, or strengths, which may emerge naturally as an outgrowth of their participation in a unit of study or a project in any classroom. That is, within the regular instructional program—when appropriate and challenging learning experiences are offered—individuals or groups of students may identify their own strengths through the questions they raise or the complex or sophisticated work or projects they do (in response to assignments or on their own), or by declaring their enthusiasm for learning more or digging more deeply into a topic. These natural identification opportunities provide a strong foundation for effective programming responses.

3. Create opportunities for advanced and higher-level instruction. While programming opportunities that arise naturally, as described in the preceding item, are strong and positive, it is also important for the school to include in its programming deliberate efforts to stimulate those opportunities. Such efforts may be related to ongoing inservice for the staff, but they can also include other kinds of direct services to students. For example, these may include:

• Advanced courses, seminars, or independent study for students with exceptional background, proficiency, and interest. Students who participate in such courses should be identified on the basis of their specific background, experiences, interests, and ability in that area, rather than merely selected on the basis of global ability scores or ratings.

• Special sections of academic classes in which the regular curriculum can be condensed to provide opportunities for investigation of more complex issues, themes, and problems. Such sections should not consist merely of piling on more or more difficult content to be "covered," but should involve complex thinking, problem solving, and research or inquiry skills.

• After-school or summer opportunities for enrichment and advanced study, which may also be undertaken in cooperation with other agencies such as state-sponsored special programs or special programs conducted by colleges and universities.

4. Respond to individual cases as needs arise. Contemporary, inclusive programming challenges the school to respond with flexibility and imagination to meet unique or unusual needs of students as they arise. Such circumstances may not readily fit the current school schedule, "the way we've always done things in the past," or the need we feel to treat everyone "fairly" or "equitably."

Consider asking, "How might we avoid homogenizing students, or treating everyone alike?" There are real differences among peoples' abilities, skills, and interests; the issue has often been posed this way: "Nothing is more unequal than the equal treatment of unequals."

Your efforts to implement programming should provide clearly for deliberate efforts to recognize and respond appropriately and supportively to the unusual learning needs and characteristics of *any* student. Test scores in themselves do not define a specific learning need from which appropriate instruction can be planned; as such, then, test scores should not be considered a defining criterion or entitlement for advanced services. It is more powerful and productive to examine specific information regarding a student's background, achievement, skills, goals, and interests. Such an investigation may include test data as part of a more complete profile, of course. The questions to be posed should be: "What are the student's actual needs? How might we best provide a response to those needs?"

Implementation of programming can begin within a classroom, a school, or a school district. The three charts below provide suggestions for initiating programming at each of those three levels.

Implementing Contemporary Programming . . .

. . . In a Classroom

- LOOK every day for students' strengths and talents in many different ways. Be a talent spotter.
- TALK with students about their strengths, special interests, and talents.
- Encourage students to EXPLORE different areas and LOOK for their own strengths.
- ASSESS students' learning styles and help them to understand the results and to know how they learn and work best.
- Construct TALENT PROFILES and TALENT ACTION OR GROWTH PLANS and involve the students in the process.
- DESIGN the classroom as a flexible, multitalent learning laboratory; create a CLIMATE conducive to creative learning and inquiry.

(Continued)

(Continued)

- Teach students how to use many kinds of TOOLS to extend their own learning and productivity (e.g., technology, thinking tools, time/organization tools, product and presentation tools).
- Teach METACOGNITIVE and SELF-DIRECTION skills and help students use them.
- Use a variety of learning activities, including CIRCLE OF KNOWLEDGE, TEAM LEARNING, and varied "hands-on, minds-on" activities.
- Discuss and apply criteria for QUALITY work and CREATIVE products.
- Incorporate PRODUCTIVE THINKING (creative thinking, critical thinking, problem solving, and decision making) into instruction for all students on a daily basis.
- Be ALERT for students with special talents and interests that relate to any topic or curriculum area, and for students who may need more challenge or advancement in learning activities.
- INVOLVE parents and community resource people or groups in search for talents and strengths and in learning projects.
- GUIDE all students in planning, carrying out, sharing, and evaluating learning projects and independent inquiry (individually and in small groups).
- LINK classroom learning with out-of-school events, places, and resources.

Implementing Contemporary Programming . . .

. . . In a School

- Create, monitor, follow, and revise a SCHOOL ACTION PLAN with specific vision and goal statements for talent development.
- Support LEARNING STYLE and PROFILING processes schoolwide.
- Create opportunities for teachers to SHARE ideas and resources.
- Provide MATERIALS and TIME for curriculum and instructional development.
- Provide support and guidance for teachers to DISCUSS students' strengths and talents and to work together to respond to student needs.
- Provide access to TECHNOLOGY in all classrooms, not just in one lab.
- Examine SCHOOL CLIMATE and work to sustain or enhance a healthy climate.
- Create CURRICULUM ENHANCEMENT teams to stimulate innovation.
- CLUSTER students in talent and interest areas for parts of the school day to provide services that cut across classroom or grade level boundaries.
- Offer time and opportunities on a weekly basis (at least!) for talent EXPLORATION and SHARING on a cross-age basis. Involve staff and community resource people, too.
- Create and draw upon a COMMUNITY RESOURCE POOL (places and people). Develop opportunities for MENTORING and ROLE MODELING in talent and career areas.
- Form PARTNERSHIPS with community agencies, organizations, and businesses.
- Make your school a LIGHTHOUSE for LEARNING—a place where people of all ages can pursue learning in various talent areas.

- Support a variety of OPTIONAL and INVITATIONAL learning activities and programs (e.g., contests, quiz bowls, Destination ImagiNation, Future Problem Solving, Young Inventors).
- Provide scheduled time and support for staff to review and discuss all students' TALENT PROFILES and TALENT ACTION/GROWTH PLANS.
- BENCHMARK and CELEBRATE exemplary progress and products. DISPLAY and PROMOTE creative accomplishments of staff and students.
- Create a BANK of enrichment units or learning projects for staff to exchange.
- Provide time for one or more staff to serve as programming specialists or CATALYSTS.

Implementing Contemporary Programming . . .

. . . In a District

- Create a DISTRICT MASTER PLAN to guide policy and program development. Strive for support and commitment to sustain programming efforts.
- Provide regular opportunities for teachers (individually, in groups or teams, and within or among schools) to SHARE both successful practices and concerns.
- Adopt a PHILOSOPHY STATEMENT consistent with the fundamental tenets and belief statements, and provide resources to support its implementation.
- Promote COMMUNITY AWARENESS of your approach and its benefits.
- Provide opportunities and support for appropriate, sustained PROFESSIONAL DEVELOPMENT; move beyond one-shot or "entertainment" presentations.
- Initiate, conduct, and use the results of a systematic EVALUATION of programming.
- Encourage and support programming that CUTS ACROSS age, grade, and building lines.
- Support initiatives that contribute to CONTINUOUS IMPROVEMENT and to INNOVATION at the classroom, school, and district levels.
- Be open to EXPERIMENTATION, and share the results.
- Work together to use structured problem solving and decision making methods and tools to ADDRESS NEW OPPORTUNITIES, CHALLENGES, OR CONCERNS.
- Promote CONTINUOUS LEARNING by staff, including involvement in professional literature and organizations.
- Seek CREATIVE FUNDING through grants and special project funding.

A PROFESSIONAL PARTNERSHIP

Effective implementation of programming depends on cooperation and collaboration among regular classroom teachers and professionals with training, experience, and specific responsibilities for carrying out programming effectively. We do not believe that classroom teachers can do everything that is needed, on their own and in their classrooms, to provide appropriate, challenging, and developmental experiences for students in all talent areas. On the other hand, we do not believe that it is effective and appropriate to expect "the gifted teacher" to assume the entire responsibility for meeting every student's needs in a comprehensive way. Effective programming involves a partnership in the service of the students. Some of the major roles and responsibilities in that partnership are illustrated in Figure 12.8.

Classroom Teacher	Programming Specialist
1. Being a talent spotter; searching actively for all students' strengths, talents, and sustained interests.	1. Facilitating planning at school and district levels.
2. Teaching with multiple groupings, varied activities, and assignments.	2. Initiating, coordinating, and supporting many classroom services.
3. Providing time and support for student initiated projects.	3. Leading, networking, and supporting advanced services.
4. Engaging students in productive thinking.	4. Facilitating contacts and connections with outside resources.
5. Designing and using authentic learning experiences or activities.	5. Serving in liaison role (staff, students, parents, administration, and the community).
6. Offering and supporting many exploratory activities.	6. Assisting in documenting students' activities and accomplishments.
7. Recognizing, responding to unique, high-level needs.	7. Assisting and supporting curriculum planning and individualized modifications.
8. Using many, varied materials and resources.	8. Collaborating in projects for instruction and staff development.
9. Collaborating with the programming catalyst.	9. Coordinating evaluation and public relations.

Figure 12.8   A professional partnership for talent development

Rather than creating a single, fixed program for one selected group of "identified gifted" students, LoS and other contemporary, inclusive approaches challenge schools to plan and carry out many services to find and develop the strengths, talents, and interests of many students. Figure 12.9 summarizes how these approaches "shift the paradigm" in your approach to carrying out talent development programming.

The response is . . .

Single program for all or
limited options for
"categories" of students

Prespecified curriculum—
fixed content

Separate from
(and at a "higher level" than)
the regular curriculum

Ownership centralized
in the gifted/talented teacher

Derived from "generic"
inferences about gifted/
talented student needs

Focus on applying, using
knowledge creatively

Options, flexibility in
how/when services offered

Emerging from, extending,
and enhancing the (strong)
regular curriculum

Many staff share ownership

Based on students' strengths,
talents, and sustained
interests

Figure 12.9   Changing our approach to talent development programming

Section VI

Stage Five— Seek Talents and Strengths

Section VI deals with seeking talents and strengths in students. This is the fifth stage of the Six-Stage Systematic Planning model. Gifted education has traditionally placed considerable emphasis on "identification." Contemporary, inclusive approaches to talent development place considerable emphasis on appropriate and challenging programming; this may lead to new directions in understanding and implementing identification. This stage offers a number of hypotheses about new possibilities and options.

The key tasks in this stage are to:

- Describe emerging modifications and directions in the concept of identification in talent development
- Explore and examine ways to make your identification efforts more natural, flexible, dynamic, inclusive, and relevant to programming
- Describe new opportunities and directions for Student Action Planning for talent development

There is one chapter in Section VI. You enter this stage when you are ready to explore new ways to search actively for the talents, strengths, and sustained interests of your students and to use them to create and implement powerful approaches to identification. Identification is an ongoing process, so it is not appropriate to define an exit point for this stage.

Identification in Contemporary Talent Development

13

In 1981, Renzulli, Reis, and Smith expressed a concern about common practices in identification in gifted education:

> Although most people will not admit it, up to this point in our history, we continue to view giftedness as an absolute concept—something that exists . . . by itself without relation to anything else. . . . This absolute conception causes us to act as if giftedness is something that "you have" or "you don't have" and consequently, we still think in terms of a child being "in" or "not in" a program. (p. ix)

Today, despite decades of experience and discussion about goals and procedures for identification, there is still a great need for a substantial shift in thinking and practice regarding "identification" and its challenges. Some discussions seem still to focus on ways to find new answers to old questions, in effect tinkering with traditional screening and selection procedures; others focus primarily on comparing, selecting, and using specific instruments.

CHANGING VIEWS OF IDENTIFICATION

The major shift underlying contemporary, inclusive approaches involves refocusing our view of the major force that energizes, moves, or drives all talent development programming efforts. This is a shift away from using identification as the primary "engine" that drives our approach to a view that programming is the central concern (Treffinger, 1998). Viewing programming as the primary consideration driving talent development reminds us that our goal is to provide appropriate and challenging services for students, not merely to assign a label to them or place them in a certain category. Figure 13.1 illustrates the key elements of the shift from identification-driven approaches to a programming-driven approach.

Identification-Driven Approaches

- Emphasize screening, selection, placement
- **"Medical" model** Does this student have "it"?
- **Comparative model** Who is "most in need"?
- **Percentage model** Based on statistical distribution
- Emphasize inclusion or exclusion ("in" or "out")
- Focus on categorical definition of giftedness
- May lead to emphasis on program as entitlement, reward, or status

Programming-Driven Approaches

- Provide opportunities for students to explore (from which strengths may emerge)
- Create new possibilities for recognizing and nurturing talents
- Link identification to specific talent, performance domains
- View identification as flexible, ongoing, dynamic, and diagnostic
- Emphasize providing appropriate and challenging instruction

Figure 13.1   A shift in approach

This is not an "anti-identification" view, but a shift that involves clarifying and realigning the relationship between identification and programming to create and implement new and more powerful approaches to identification. The identification process may be important not only because it is mandated in many places, but because it can provide information that will inform or guide meaningful educational or instructional programming decisions. While the needs of many (perhaps most) students can be met through the offerings of the regular education program, those efforts will not be sufficient to ensure that the strengths, talents, and sustained interests of students will be recognized and nurtured. Deliberate efforts to recognize strengths and talents and to extend, expand, or enhance the regular program must be carried out if the students' high-level potential is not to be lost.

The goal of identification in contemporary approaches to talent development is to create and sustain opportunities to recognize and nurture students' strengths, talents, and sustained interests. This view of identification involves a close, ongoing, supportive relationship with programming, as illustrated in Figure 13.2.

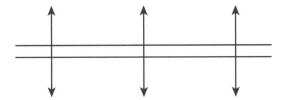

Programming

Carefully planned opportunities to provide . . .

Appropriate and challenging instruction
("expand—extend—enhance")
Options and choices
Opportunities for involvement
Commitment to quality and excellence

Identification

Deliberate efforts to search for, and to
recognize, each student's . . .

Strengths
Talents
Sustained interests
Learning and thinking skills and tools
Expertise
Unique learning and working styles

Figure 13.2   The relationship between identification and programming

Source: From the Center for Creative Learning, Inc.

Six principles express the implications of contemporary, inclusive approaches to programming for the identification process. These are:

1. *The principle of unique and varied strengths.* This principle emphasizes multiple talents, abilities, strengths, and interests across a wide variety of content areas or domains. Talent development involves seeking, recognizing, and responding to many talents in many students in unique, appropriate, and challenging ways. Contemporary programming for talent recognizes the importance of many talent areas or domains and the need for educators, families, and communities to work in harmony to nurture them.

2. *The principle of purposeful, authentic identification.* This principle highlights the importance of obtaining and using data that will contribute to the school's ability to plan and carry out appropriate instruction and learning experiences, based on students' documented needs. Emerging views of identification will focus on understanding what students can do, and what they need in order to grow in their talent and strength areas. It is always important to look at existing data that are readily available to you to identify students'

strengths, talents, interests, and needs. A student who has straight A's and a State Science Fair Award probably does not need to be tested to see whether she or he needs extended programming in science! A more diagnostic, purposeful (or authentic) view would address such questions as, "What activities or services will best continue to extend, expand, or enhance learning for this student? What will best serve this student in school? How might we provide those opportunities?" Emerging approaches to identification involve procedures that are flexible, inclusive, and diagnostic; they are more concerned with extending the student's strengths and talents than with determining whether or not the student "fits" in a certain category. (If one asks, "But is the student really gifted?" our answer would be, "Time will tell.")

3. *The principle of constructive inclusion.* This principle addresses the importance of recognizing "positive needs" (searching for what students do well). Contemporary approaches challenge you to transform identification in a systematic search for ways to bring out the best in students, rather than to find ways to include or exclude them from a fixed program. This principle opens the possibility that "identification" can be inspiring and motivational, stirring students' dreams and passions. It can become an empowering, collaborative process that contributes to self-assessment and self-direction—involving students themselves in the process of searching for, examining, and documenting their own strengths, talents, interests, and needs. Over time, and with guidance and supportive feedback, students can become powerful contributors to the process of identifying their talent development strengths and needs.

4. *The principle of continuous, dynamic search.* This principle expresses the importance of remaining open to continuously searching for and discovering student strengths, using any and all data that become available to you at any time. A continuous, dynamic approach to identification suggests that whenever strengths, talents, and positive needs become evident, you can begin to design and offer appropriate responses. Rather than treating identification as a once-a-year search for a small set of students to place in a fixed program, contemporary approaches transform identification into a fluid, flexible, ongoing process that can be responsive to changing data and new insights about students and their needs.

This also emphasizes the need to keep in mind during the identification process that the data you obtain give you information about strengths and talents that are *now present* in a student. If, at one time, you do not find particular strengths, it does not mean that there are no strengths or talents in the students. Strengths may reside in ways you did not locate, or might emerge at another time. It was once said that "lack of evidence does not mean evidence of lack." In contemporary views of identification, searching for students' strengths, talents, and sustained interests is an ongoing process.

5. *The principle of diverse perspectives.* The need to look at students' characteristics using many tools, data sources, or assessment strategies is also an important element of contemporary approaches to identification. This principle highlights the need for identification to become a process through which you can use a wide array of methods and resources to guide your efforts to provide effective programming for all students. Searching effectively for

students' needs may draw on both qualitative and quantitative data. Searching for students' strengths and needs (rather than simply using scores as a cutoff for program placement) also expands your perspective about the kinds of data that will be helpful to consider. For example, learning style data, student interest assessments, and anecdotal records about activities and accomplishments out of school may be informative and valuable tools in a diagnostic approach and may offer rich insights for planning appropriate services. In different talent areas, among different students, and with many kinds of programming options from which to choose, the sources of data you use should provide information that will guide you in identifying the student's strengths and needs for specific kinds of programming activities and experiences. Data about a student's strength in mathematics or technology, for example, inform you about programming needs in mathematics or in technology. Your goal involves understanding the student's specific strengths, talents, interests, and programming needs, rather than a global judgment (i.e., declaring that the student is or is not "a gifted student"). Be open to information of many kinds, and from many sources, in order to obtain as rich and complete a picture as possible of any student's characteristics and programming needs. One person (the source is not known to us) stated the concern clearly: "Using one source of data in assessing a student would be like using only a blood pressure reading to assess the treatment needs of a trauma victim with multiple injuries; it simply wouldn't provide the information needed for effective treatment."

6. *The principle of responsible assessment.* This principle underscores the importance (in any identification process, not just in emerging contemporary approaches) of using data with sensitivity to the strengths and limitations of the tools you are employing. If your data sources include quantitative data such as test scores, for example, pay careful attention to basic measurement issues such as validity and reliability evidence, and to the standard error of measure associated with an observed score on any test. Study test manuals and standard test review resources (such as the *Mental Measurements Yearbook*) before adopting instruments. When you are using qualitative data, be aware of appropriate guidelines for interpretation and use, as well as possible challenges in comparing students or combining qualitative and quantitative data sources.

EXPLORING NEW OPPORTUNITIES AND DIRECTIONS

As contemporary, inclusive programming approaches have emerged (the "fourth generation" described in Chapter 1), it has become possible to envision new opportunities and directions for identification in both theory and practice.

From Identification to Student Action Planning

In exploring new directions, consider first the possibility of viewing identification less as a process that focuses exclusively on identifying *students* and more as a focus on identifying *needs*. This emphasizes students' educational needs as the focal point of our efforts, rather than simple inclusion or exclusion (or being "in" or "out" of a program). We envision this as a potential shift from *identification* to *Student Action Planning*. Student Action Planning for talent development is a constructive, active, and forward-looking process. It involves understanding student's strengths, talents, interests, and needs, then identifying ways to respond to them by offering appropriate programming opportunities. Student Action Planning involves three broad stages: *deliberate search*, *constructive design*, and *monitoring and managing*. Each stage includes several important tasks. The three stages and important tasks are illustrated in Figure 13.3; we will discuss each stage briefly.

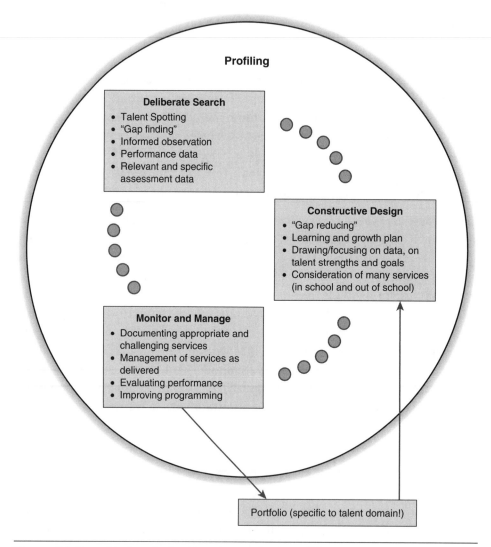

Figure 13.3   Student Action Panning circle: Overall design

Source: From the Center for Creative Learning, Inc.

Deliberate Search

Student Action Planning begins by searching deliberately and in many ways to recognize, discover, and even to stimulate students' strengths, talents, and sustained interests. It can involve recognizing strengths and talents that are obvious, right in front of you—the strengths that one person called "interocular" (so obvious that they hit you between the eyes!). Deliberate search can also involve taking the time and making the effort to discover strengths, talents, or interests that are present in a student but not evident without some explicit inquiry or probing. Sometimes deliberate search can involve uncovering hidden talents, or awakening talent and interest possibilities that are exciting new opportunities for the students themselves—creating a platform for the emergence and development of new strengths, talents, and interests that may prove to be more than a passing fancy or curiosity and may become very powerful factors in the person's development. Deliberate search involves asking (and answering) some very important questions about students. These include:

- What strengths or talents do we see in this student?
- What data give us a full picture of this student?
- What additional data are needed?
- What particular interests and accomplishments tell us about this student's learning needs?
- How might information about the student's ability, interests, and motivation inform us about her or his learning needs?

Multiple data sources. Deliberate search for students' strengths and talents involves gathering and using several kinds of data. These may include tests, ratings or referrals, performance data (such as feedback from teachers, classroom test results, report card grades, or anecdotal records), and authentic assessments of student products or accomplishments (such as student products, work samples, or portfolios).

Talent Spotting. In Student Action Planning, the deliberate search stage also involves "Talent Spotting," or explicit, constructive efforts to find students' strengths and talents (Young, 1995a, 1995b, 1995c, 1995d). This term can be helpful, since it reminds people of the process often used to locate or discover talents in many real-world settings (such as music, dance, drama, and athletics). By listing the attributes of an athletic scout, for example, we might find some helpful insights into the behaviors of an educator who is a talent spotter. An athletic talent scout:

- Knows the sport
- Knows about the needs of the field
- Knows the benchmarks of talent development
- Knows the difference between potential and performance
- Knows the standards of excellence within the field
- Has a historical perspective and knowledge of the field
- Is able to recognize talent in raw form
- Is patient and persistent but knows when to move on to new prospects
- Relies on many sources of data—observations of performance, study of films, interviews with the prospect and others (coaches, players, etc.), player statistics, press clippings

- Has sharp powers of observation
- Sees possibilities for playing other positions and roles on the team
- Takes risks based on assessment of data and potential for talent development
- Spends a great deal of time in the field
- Understands that there are many factors to consider in addition to physical skills (attitude, opportunity, training, coaching, etc.)

How might these attributes of an athletic scout inform us about the role of a classroom talent spotter? In what ways is an athletic talent scout like a classroom talent spotter? What does it mean to be a talent spotter in the educational setting? There are several similarities between the athletic scout and the classroom talent spotter: They both must have thorough knowledge of and experience with the task, the people with whom they are working, and the methods and techniques they will need to use. They both deal with assessments that are complex, "tricky," and in some ways, may involve as much "art and luck" as "science." Spotting talents, like finding the next athletic superstar, is hardly an exact science!

Just as in the athletic setting, in which the scout might look at many different variables depending on the player's age, experience, and position played, the classroom talent spotter must be able to deal with many different factors or dimensions of talent. Both must be able to consider potential as well as current performance. While natural ability might be an important issue, the scout usually looks closely at what the prospect does with that ability. In either context, work habits, motivation, and perseverance can often be even more important than "raw power."

Athletic scouts believe that a talented player might be found in a small town or a rural setting just as likely as in a more metropolitan area. In fact, one can never be sure of where a superstar athlete might be found. Similarly, classroom talent spotters believe that any students in their classrooms might have valuable potentials that can be recognized and developed.

Furthermore, athletic scouts, like classroom talent spotters, possess both general knowledge and specialist knowledge. Scouts know and understand the sport and the general needs of their field. They are familiar with specific benchmarks of talent development, such as various stages of physical and motor development. Scouts also know and understand the standards of excellence within their field. Classroom talent spotters know and understand the skills, processes, and attitudes associated with productive thinking. As generalists, they are aware that productive thinkers apply both creative and critical thinking when processing information and solving problems. As specialists, they have in-depth knowledge of the organization and structure of productive thinking (Treffinger, 1994). They know that the foundations for productive thinking include a strong knowledge base, personal motivational elements, and metacognitive controls. Finally, talent spotters know and understand the basic competencies required for creative productive accomplishments in the future.

Based on their beliefs and knowledge, athletic scouts and classroom talent spotters spend a great deal of time gathering clues. They keep notes about their observations of performances and inferences about potentials. Clue gathering is also done during informal discussions and in social situations through active listening and asking questions. Scouts interview the prospect, coaches, and other players. Talent spotters ask students, their peers, and parents about outside interests and activities. They are both persistent in looking for talents over a sustained period of time.

There are also some differences between athletic scouts and talent spotters. For example, athletic scouts are paid just to look for and evaluate talent, while teachers must deal with all students all of the time. As a result, classroom talent spotters have to be developers as well as finders of potentials. While scouts are usually on the lookout for specific talents within one sport, classroom talent spotters recognize that there is an enormous amount and variety of human potential available within society and are personally committed to increasing the amount and kinds of talent developed by schools. Scouts ask themselves if a prospect is truly talented. Talent spotters, on the other hand, believe that it is more productive to ask, "In what ways is this student talented?" Talent Spotting involves:

- Examining many different variables (students' characteristics and styles, context, operations, and desired outcomes)
- Considering work habits, motivation, and task commitment as well as "natural ability"
- Asking, "In what ways is this student at his or her best?"
- Searching for strengths over an extended period of time
- Designing lessons that allow for talents to be expressed and applied
- Acting like a detective gathering clues
- Recording observations
- Talking with and listening to students about their strengths, special interests, goals and aspirations, and talents

You can use the "Classroom Teacher's Talent Spotting Indicators Worksheet" (Figure 13.4) and the "Teacher's Talent Spotting Checklist" (Figure 13.5), which are also on the accompanying CD, as resources to initiate and document Talent Spotting activities.

Constructive Design

The second stage of Student Action Planning involves examining the data you gathered during the deliberate search stage and formulating ideas or options about what responses might be appropriate, challenging, and developmental for the student.

The constructive design stage poses the question, "Given the student's strengths, talents, sustained interests, and needs, what might we consider doing about them?" If there is a gap between the needs that are evident and the ways you are now serving the child (or the educational programming you are now offering), what changes might you consider to close that gap? This stage involves comparing a student's needs with many programming options, activities, and services and making the best "connections" that will respond effectively to those needs.

During the constructive design stage, you may begin developing a *student talent profile* or growth plan that will document the key information you gathered about the student's interests and needs and the decisions you made regarding

Talent Spotting Indicators Worksheet

List the names of students who fit each description below.

1. Finishes most assignments in one or more subject areas quickly and easily, with satisfactory (not necessarily "perfect") accuracy and comprehension; may seem bored with regular school assignments.

   _____

2. Reads widely about a topic, including many sources that are advanced or technical.

   _____

3. Asks many questions about a topic, frequently reflecting prior study or complex understanding.

   _____

4. Has a "one-track mind"; eats, sleeps, breathes, walks, and talks the topic—sometimes to the distraction of others.

   _____

5. Frequently brings projects or products to school to share with classmates and/or teachers.

   _____

6. Asks the librarian for many books or resources on special topics; searches widely on the Internet for resources on a special topic.

   _____

7. Uses his or her own special interests and talents as topics for other assignments (e.g., themes, art projects, book reports) whenever possible, or as alternate products when a choice is given (e.g., submitting a play or a song instead of a written report).

   _____

8. Participates in outside activities or is involved in special activities or groups (e.g., membership in groups, outside lessons, after-school or weekend programs at other agencies, camp or summer program experiences).

   _____

9. Keeps a log, journal, or diary of her or his activities and experiences in areas of special talent or interest.

   _____

10. Talks often about his or her hobbies or career aspirations related to his or her special talent or interest areas.

   _____

Figure 13.4   The classroom teacher's Talent Spotting indicators worksheet

---

Talent Spotting Checklist

Student _____   **Date** _____

Circle each item that helps describe this student's strengths and characteristics.

1. Challenges assumptions

2. Unafraid to make mistakes

3. Goes against the odds

4. Turns obstacles into challenges

5. Looks beyond the obvious

6. Looks at things in new or different ways

7. Asks many questions

8. Is curious

9. Searches widely for information

10. Has many interests

11. Connects ideas

12. Predicts, speculates, forecasts

13. Uses metaphors or analogies

14. Is persistent

15. Displays confidence

16. Becomes absorbed or passionate

17. Carefully and constructively evaluates ideas

18. Produces quality work, beyond average

19. Pays attention to details

20. Demonstrates advanced vocabulary

Figure 13.5   The teacher's Talent Spotting checklist

Source: Copyright © The Center for Creative Learning, Inc.

appropriate activities and services to respond to them. Figure 13.6 summarizes the components of a student talent profile. You will also find a sample of one form that might be used in constructing such a profile in Figure 13.7 (and on the CD).

Talent Profiles Are . . .

1. **Flexible.** May include a variety of data and forms of documentation (not a fixed format).

2. **Developmental.** Change as new or additional data become available.

3. **Focused on Strengths.** Identify what student can do well, and on special areas of talent, ability, or interest.

4. **Diagnostic.** Use data to help us plan for appropriate and challenging instructional activities or experiences.

5. **Functional.** Guide instruction; they are "file drawer" documents.

6. **Dynamic.** May be initiated or updated at any time, not just at certain "deadlines" for an identification or selection decision.

7. **Based on Varied Data Sources.** Can include many kinds of information (qualitative and quantitative).

8. **Action Oriented.** Document actions to take; include goals, objectives, person(s) responsible, evaluation, and time line.

Figure 13.6   Components of a student talent profile

Source: Copyright © The Center for Creative Learning, Inc.

Monitor and Manage

The third stage of Student Action Planning involves actively monitoring or keeping track of the activities and services in which a student participates in any content or talent area. It also involves managing the student talent profile or growth plan to ensure that it is being implemented and that it is meeting the student's needs as intended. During this stage you will also carry out several other tasks: recognizing when the plan needs to be modified or updated, convening key people to review and revise the plan, and documenting the student's work, accomplishments, and future plans.

The monitoring and managing stage may also involve guiding students in developing, reflecting on, maintaining, and sharing portfolios. Student portfolios may serve several purposes that students should know and take into account as they create and modify them; these include showing examples or samples of their best work, demonstrating breadth or variety of accomplishments, and documenting growth and improvement over time.

STUDENT ACTION PLANNING PROFILE

Student _____ Grade _____ Date _____

Planners: _____

Programming Decisions	Who	Where	Time Line		Document/Evaluate
			Start	Review	

Data used to develop programming decisions:

	Important Student Characteristics				Task and Environment Dimensions
Data Sources	Strength in Talent Area	Creativity	Learning Style	Sustained Interests	Knowledge and Experience Foundations
Test Data					Goals, Expectations, and Assessed Needs
Ratings					
Self- or Peer-Reports					Specific Context/Climate or Environmental Considerations
Observations and Products					

Figure 13.7 A Student Action Planning profile form

Monitoring and managing also involves ongoing efforts to document and evaluate the student's progress and accomplishments, updating the profile and instructional plan of action in light of new and ongoing information, and refining plans for differentiating instruction or varying learning experiences and activities as appropriate. As suggested by the Action Planning "circle" (Figure 13.3), the process of Student Action Planning is ongoing. It is not a single event in which you categorize the students and determine whether they will be "in" or "out" of a specific program.

Student Action Planning as a Collaborative Problem Solving Process

Another promising direction for contemporary identification involves approaching Student Action Planning as an opportunity for collaborative problem solving. Student Action Planning and the major activities in its three stages can be a collaborative enterprise in which several people come together cooperatively to consider ways to assess and respond to a student's characteristics and needs. Depending on the student and the circumstances, the group might include talent development specialists, classroom teachers, curriculum specialists, counselors, mentors, parents, and students themselves. Their "problem solving" efforts might focus on questions such as:

- What do we know about this student's strengths, talents, sustained interests, and needs?
- What are we doing now to meet the student's needs?
- Are there additional (or different) kinds of services we should consider for this student?
- How might we ensure that the student's educational program is the best it can be?

The group may draw upon many different kinds of data as part of their review and analysis of the student's characteristics and needs, including both quantitative and qualitative data. The group may approach their task as a specific application of a structured Creative Problem Solving (CPS) process (e.g., Isaksen, Dorval, & Treffinger, 2000; Treffinger, Isaksen, & Stead-Dorval, 2006). Figure 13.8 illustrates how CPS methods and tools are related to the deliberate search, constructive design, and monitoring and managing stages of Student Action Planning.

SUMMARY

As you work to implement contemporary, inclusive approaches to programming for talent development, new opportunities and directions for student identification may also emerge. Promising new directions in identification emphasize recognizing student's strengths, talents, sustained interests, and needs in ways that pave the way for appropriate, challenging, and developmental learning opportunities. Student Action Planning is not simply selecting,

Student Action Planning Task	CPS Component or Stage
Clarifying the student's strengths, talents, interests, and needs ("Deliberate Search") • What opportunities and needs do we see? • What information do we have to document strengths, talents, interests, needs? • What are we really striving to accomplish or provide?	Understanding the challenge • Constructing opportunities • Exploring data • Framing problems
Deciding how we might respond ("Constructive Design")	Generating ideas
Establishing a specific "growth plan" or educational design for the student • Evaluating and choosing options • Formulating a detailed plan for the student • Monitoring and managing the plan's implementation	Preparing for action • Developing solutions • Building acceptance

Figure 13.8   Student Action Planning and Creative Problem Solving

labeling, or placing a single, fixed group of students. We seek to recognize and nurture students' individual talents, strengths, and sustained interests. Students' talents may take time to "emerge" and to enable you to observe them. They cannot show up if opportunities are not provided for them to be expressed. Therefore, new approaches must be both flexible and ongoing; you need to look continuously for opportunities to enhance, extend, and expand learning opportunities for your students.

Section VII

Stage Six—
Ensure Quality,
Innovation,
and Continuous
Improvement

This section deals with ensuring quality, innovation, and continuous improvement. This is the sixth stage of the Six-Stage Systematic Planning model. This stage addresses the important topic of program evaluation. We view evaluation as more than simply judging programming as "good or bad" or characterizing it as "successful or unsuccessful." Effective evaluation guides educational decision making and planning for the future. The key tasks in this stage are:

- Identifying the purposes and goals of evaluation and documentation of programming
- Defining ways to assess and determine the quality of programming
- Identifying ways to support and sustain programming through continuous improvement of current efforts
- Establishing new opportunities and directions for innovation in program development

There is one chapter in this section, which provides information and resources to help you in carrying out these tasks effectively and efficiently. You will enter this stage as you prepare to document your efforts to plan and carry out contemporary programming. You will exit this stage with a specific plan for evaluation and a commitment to ongoing improvement and innovation.

Quality, Innovation, and Continuous Improvement 14

The planning process does not end when you have prepared a Master Plan and your Building Action Plan(s), nor even when you've begun implementing them. In this chapter, we consider several interrelated issues and concerns that address the sixth stage of the Six-Stage Systematic Planning model: ensuring quality, innovation, and continuous improvement.

How will you determine the quality, effectiveness, and impact of your programming efforts? How will you document whether you have done what you intended and planned to do, and what the results or outcomes of those efforts have been? What components or aspects of your programming have been most and least successful? What should be done to sustain exemplary practices, or to modify and improve practices that have not been successful?

Most educators will recognize these as questions pertaining to evaluation. Everyone evaluates many activities and experiences, formally or informally, every day. These include:

Job satisfaction
Career progress
Spouse/relationships
Readiness for new roles
    or responsibilities
Financial "health"
Our housing
Our transportation
TV programs (us/for kids)
Charity contributions
Reactions to people we meet
Our children's behavior
Grocery stores

Babysitters we hire
How well the kids mowed the lawn
Educational options or choices
Service we receive from a store/agency
Health and fitness
Sermons we hear
Movies, plays, concerts we attend
Credit card offers in the mail
Getting a new or used [whatever]
    versus repairing the old one
Restaurants (food, price, service, value)
Insurance (coverage, needs)

However, we don't evaluate all these the same way, or for the same reason. We might also ask why we evaluate any of them at all! In this chapter, we address these issues in relation to talent development programming.

Rather than just "evaluation," we used the longer phrase "quality, innovation, and continuous improvement" in this chapter for several reasons. First, the word *evaluation* often suggests, especially in informal or nontechnical conversations, "making a judgment," with a ring of absolute finality and certainty. In a programmatic context, however, evaluation should provide information that will help you in a variety of ways. Common reasons for evaluating many kinds of programming include:

- To provide a basis for effective policymaking and decision making
- To assess the strengths and weaknesses of any programming effort
- To assess achievements and accomplishments
- To analyze program quality, curriculum, and instructional methods thoroughly, carefully, and constructively
- To accredit schools or validate program claims
- To monitor and justify the investment of funds
- To encourage and support both continuous improvement (enhancing your programming in an ongoing commitment) and innovation (preparing for new initiatives or directions)

A comprehensive discussion of appropriate methods, procedures, and resources for evaluating talent development programming is beyond the scope of this handbook. We will summarize briefly some fundamental considerations.

When you are planning to evaluate *any* programs that take place in complex, real-life settings, sometimes described as "naturalistic" evaluation, you must consider a number of issues or concerns that can make the task complex. These include:

1. Desirable or undesirable consequences of a decision or course of action that has been chosen

2. Confusion regarding courses of action

3. Desirable or undesirable deviations from older practices

4. Perceived value discrepancies or conflicts (institutional, societal, or personal)

5. Issues relating to sources, changes, or uses of power

6. Economic issues or impact

7. Perceived inconsistency with input or suggestions

8. Perceived inequity or disparity of treatment among groups

9. Understanding (or lack of it) regarding rationale or goals

10. Good (or poor) fit with exemplary practices or standards

11. Desirable or undesirable side effects or "spin-offs"

12. Effectiveness (or lack of it) in communication

13. Equity or inequity of administration of policies or procedures

14. Availability of training or support to enable successful implementation

More specifically, evaluating gifted and talented programs is a difficult but important task. Complex outcomes, such as those commonly stated for gifted and talented programming, are not easy to measure. In addition, the full impact or benefits of programming for students may require an extended period of time to become evident. There are also many unique challenges in evaluating contemporary, inclusive programming approaches in contrast to traditional gifted programming approaches. Figure 14.1 describes seven of these unique concerns and identifies several constructive possibilities for dealing with them.

Evaluation is not a one-shot, one-time event; thorough, effective, useful evaluation should be an ongoing or continuous process of identifying ways to strengthen or improve your efforts. Evaluation should be a natural process that enables programs to be modified and made more effective. In contemporary, inclusive programming (as in many school improvement initiatives), a sense of incompleteness can be healthy—recognizing that accomplishing one's goals and attaining excellence in any programming area is an ongoing process.

For several important areas of concern in contemporary programming, Figure 14.2 illustrates sample evaluation questions that might be posed, representative data that might be used to respond to those questions, and people or groups who might provide that data. (The CD accompanying the handbook includes a folder containing several sample evaluation survey instruments we have developed and used to gather these kinds of data in schools and districts implementing our Levels of Service approach to programming as well as sample record keeping forms.)

ELEMENTS OF EFFECTIVE EVALUATION

There are many models of or approaches to program evaluation. In general, however, there is substantial agreement that effective evaluation involves:

- *Advance planning.* Plans for evaluation should be made as part of the initial planning process, not after program implementation has already begun. A common error, for example, is to defer consideration of evaluation until it is too late to gather appropriate pretest or "baseline" data upon which later assessments of change or growth may depend.
- *Agreement on the purposes to be served.* The purposes and need for evaluation of programming efforts should be clearly understood by everyone involved before the evaluation process begins.
- *Recognition of the varying needs of different stakeholders.* While there may be many questions of common interest or concern to all who will be involved in the evaluation process, certain objectives of the evaluation, and the kinds of data needed to assess them, may vary or be quite

(*Text continues on page 188*)

Traditional Programs	Contemporary, Inclusive Programming	Challenge for Evaluation	Constructive Responses
1. Program has a separate, stand-alone identity.	1. Programming strives to be integrated as seamlessly as possible into students' total school experience.	1. No single focus can be defined as the experimental condition or "treatment."	1a. Use naturalistic evaluation approaches that extend beyond traditional designs from experimental research. 1b. Document services offered and student involvement at each level of service. 1c. Document collaborative projects and services, including participation (adult and student) and responses.
2. Services are provided for a fixed, constant group of students; students are "in" or "out."	2. Services are provided for many students; students may vary across services.	2. Whom to study?	2a. Gather data from teachers and students during participation in specific activities. 2b. Gather responses from teachers, students, and parents regarding value and impact of specific services (then group the responses by the level of service represented).
3. All students who are "in the program" receive the same services.	3. Depending on their unique characteristics and needs, students participate in different services.	3. What to study?	3a. State specific objectives and formulate specific evaluation questions for each level of service and for specific activities. 3b. Gather data from "clusters" of students who participate in group activities. 3c. Include case studies for students who are involved in advanced, highly individualized services.
4. The time students are "in the program" is constant for all participating students.	4. Students participate in services that may vary substantially in duration.	4. It is difficult to treat "the program" as if it were constant intervention.	4a. Provide detailed documentation of the number, range, and variety of services provided. 4b. Gather data from those who participate in specific activities. 4c. Gather schoolwide data relating to broad goals and purposes of programming, but describe the overall context thoroughly. 4d. If possible, gather data regarding other factors and conduct multivariate analyses of effects and impact.

Figure 14.1 Unique challenges in evaluating contemporary, inclusive programming

5. The program is delivered by specific gifted/talented staff members.	5. What staff provide data?	5a. Develop evaluation questions that will be appropriate for various respondents across activities. 5b. Include specific questions for various activities that are unique to the specific activity.
6. The program has a specifically defined curriculum and comparable objectives for all participating students.	6. What content or outcomes to evaluate?	6a. Frame research questions that are appropriate to the specific activities or services. 6b. Gather data and report results for varied activities and services. 6c. The overall evaluation may incorporate and synthesize several "mini" evaluations for specific service areas. 6d. Use case study methods for highly individualized services (e.g., Level IV).
7. The program is a "visible" one to which many stakeholders can react.	7. How to obtain informed responses?	7a. One aspect of evaluation might investigate the awareness of various stakeholders regarding LoS activities and services. 7b. Provide questions regarding the stakeholders' reactions to a variety of activities (but include the opportunity for a "not applicable" response). 7c. Document awareness and informational activities regarding LoS and evaluate responses by various stakeholders. 7d. Use a structured interview format to probe awareness and response to various LoS services.

Figure 14.1 (Continued)

185

Area of Concern	Sample Questions	Representative Data	Who Provides Data
District Master Plan	Has the plan been developed? Was it created appropriately? Is the plan complete? Did appropriate constituents have input and involvement in creating the plan? Has the plan been disseminated and reviewed appropriately?	Written plan exists Survey or interview data from committee members, staff, administration, Board, community Verification and external review of the plan	Committee members Other constituents External reviewers or outside experts
Each School's Plan of Action	Has the plan been developed? Is it complete and appropriate? Does it reflect unique concerns? Is it consistent with the district Master Plan? Did appropriate constituents have input and involvement in creating the plan?	Written plan exists Review and approval by staff and district Survey or interviews with staff and administrator(s)	School staff and administration District administration District coordinator External expert audit or review
Diagnostic Identification Procedures	Do policies and procedures focus on recognizing students' characteristics, needs, talents, and interests? Do procedures provide for flexibility and inclusiveness? Are procedures applied appropriately? Are student needs being recognized?	Survey, interview data from classroom teachers, catalyst teachers Direct review of student records	External evaluator or auditor District coordinator Catalyst teachers Classroom teachers Review by outside experts
Programming for All Students	Are many activities offered to challenge students, develop student interest, and enrich student learning opportunities? Are students' unique learning styles recognized and dealt with? Do students demonstrate progress in achievement and in process skills?	Logs of activities (schoolwide, grade level, subject areas) Learning style profiles Survey, interview, and/or observation data (teachers, students, parents) Student achievement data (teacher/test) Process skills data (teacher/test/products)	Catalyst teachers District coordinator Classroom teachers School administrators Students Parents External auditor review of data

Figure 14.2   Evaluation questions, representative data, and sources

Programming for Many Students	Do students who demonstrate special interest and involvement in topics have appropriate enrichment opportunities? Are appropriate options offered? Does "compacting" of regular curriculum and requirements occur? Is there follow-up to extend Level I?	Student profiles (diagnostic) and portfolios (accomplishments) Logs or records of activities Varied classroom assignments/projects Documentation of special activities and group programs Survey, interview, observations	Catalyst teachers District coordinator Classroom teachers School administrators Students Parents, community resource people External auditor review of data
Programming for Some Students	Are students' special talents and sustained interests recognized? Are options provided or created to respond? Are responses linked clearly and appropriately to students' needs and interests? Are student/staff efforts encouraged?	Student profiles (diagnostic) and portfolios (accomplishments) Logs or records of activities Documentation of special activities and group programs Contract or independent study records Survey, interview, observations	Catalyst teachers District coordinator Classroom teachers School administrators Students Parents, community resource people External auditor review of data
Programming for a Few Students	Are opportunities provided for advanced study, acceleration, dual enrollment, early admission or graduation? Are students enabled to progress at their own, appropriate pace? Are mentorships sought and established? Are other, independent options used?	Student profiles (diagnostic) and portfolios (accomplishments) Logs or records of activities Documentation of special services and student products Contract or independent study records Survey, interview, observations	Catalyst teachers District coordinator Classroom teachers School administrators Students Parents, community resource people Mentors, instructors of advanced courses External auditor review of data

Figure 14.2 (Continued)

187

unique from one target audience to another. That is, the questions and concerns of parents, administrators, board members, and staff members may differ and may also involve different kinds of evidence or documentation. These differences should be taken into account when planning the evaluation.

- *Clear goals and well-defined objectives.* In order to facilitate effective and useful evaluation, the goals and objectives for programming should be stated as clearly as possible, in terms that make clear the kinds of data (or evidence) that will permit them to be assessed.

- *Specific recommendations.* The evaluation effort should result in specific recommendations regarding modifications or revisions of support, action, or content of programming that will enhance program effectiveness. Good evaluation efforts lead to improvement planning and decision making.

- *Both qualitative and quantitative data.* Evaluation of complex outcomes that are typical of programming for high-ability students cannot be accomplished solely by the use of standardized achievement tests or other strictly quantitative data and test scores. Effective evaluation documents the real activities and accomplishments of students. Test data may be *one* valuable component of program evaluation, but they are not likely to be the *only* data, and in many cases, they will not even be the primary data for evaluation. For example, a 15 percent increase in students' fluency scores may be impressive to some people, while actual evidence of students' applications, such as their solving problems at home or in school, may be much more important and impressive for many others.

- *Emphasis on benefits for students.* Effective evaluation addresses more than just attitudes or measures of satisfaction and documents that programming leads to important and lasting benefits or effects for students.

- *Authentic tasks and authentic assessment.* As we begin to focus more and more on creating tasks or learning experiences that relate instructional content to the ways it will be used or applied in real-world contexts (authentic tasks), we also face the need for new ways of assessing students' attainment of those outcomes. As a result, there has been growing interest in authentic assessment, including nontest demonstrations of performance by individuals or groups on real or realistic tasks, open-ended project evaluation, and documentation of student outcomes using a portfolio approach.

Callahan (1986) proposed that asking the right questions is a critical factor in designing and conducting effective evaluations. She proposed that questions should be *relevant* (bearing directly on the program), *useful* (providing information that will guide decisions and action), and *important* (questions for which the answers will lead to genuine improvement). Callahan proposed five guidelines for formulating evaluation questions; these were:

1. Construct and give priority to questions of concern to *internal* and *external* audiences.

2. Emphasize questions that relate to areas of the program or activity that are of central functional importance (i.e., elements that are vital to the program's success).

3. Identify questions that suggest problems or areas that need clarification, diverse viewpoints, or controversy.

4. Identify questions for which information is needed in a timely way.

5. Determine whether questions address context, input, process, or product (or several).

These foundations lead to a number of general recommendations for effective evaluation of talent development programming. These include:

- Plan early; don't wait too long to obtain "baseline" data.
- Involve many stakeholders.
- Be clear about the program's goals and objectives and address them in the evaluation.
- Ask important questions that are meaningful to stakeholders.
- Don't ask people questions that they have no basis to answer in meaningful ways (or that you wouldn't expect them to know about).
- Don't ask for opinions about matters that should be answered by data and evidence.
- Emphasize evaluation questions and procedures that guide decision making and improvement.
- Use many relevant data sources and documentation.
- Provide adequate funding and time to conduct the evaluation effectively.
- State recommendations and encourage follow-through.
- Share the results with all key stakeholders.

Figure 14.3 (also on the CD) provides a number of sample questions that may be useful in evaluating contemporary programming (based, as an example, on our LoS approach). These are not intended to serve as a complete or comprehensive "instrument," but rather to offer illustrations of questions that might be helpful in addressing some of the unique dimensions of a contemporary, inclusive approach such as LoS. You might select questions that are relevant for your setting, or use this set as a starting point for framing your own questions.

Figure 14.4 presents a summary list of resources to consider including in your efforts to document programming, once again using the LoS approach as an example.

Figure 14.5 provides examples of possible applications of interviews for documenting and evaluating programming (also using the LoS approach as an example).

LoS Program Evaluation

Please read each of the following statements and circle the number that best describes your assessment of our LoS programming. If you have not had any opportunity to assess a particular statement, leave that item blank.

Please use the following scale:

1 = Strongly Disagree; 2 = Disagree; 3 = Neutral; 4 = Agree; 5 = Strongly Agree

1. I understand the rationale and goals for the LoS approach.   1   2   3   4   5

2. I support the rationale and goals for the LoS approach.   1   2   3   4   5

3. Our school makes effective efforts to provide appropriate and challenging activities at all four Levels of Service.   1   2   3   4   5

4. Our staff communicates about students' strengths, talents, and interests.   1   2   3   4   5

5. Students in all classrooms have many opportunities to learn and apply creative and critical thinking daily.   1   2   3   4   5

6. Our school sponsors, hosts, or supports a variety of before-school, after-school, weekend, or summer enrichment activities.   1   2   3   4   5

7. LoS programming fits well with our commitments to differentiate instruction for all students.   1   2   3   4   5

8. Our school provides many appropriate opportunities for our most able students.   1   2   3   4   5

9. Our school is successful in discovering and developing strengths and talents among many students whose potential might otherwise go unnoticed.   1   2   3   4   5

10. We recognize and respond to students' strengths in many different talent areas.   1   2   3   4   5

11. We receive the support and resources necessary to implement LoS programming effectively.   1   2   3   4   5

12. We conduct activities to discover students' interests.   1   2   3   4   5

13. We assess students' learning style preferences.   1   2   3   4   5

14. We provide instruction and activities that help students become independent learners.   1   2   3   4   5

15. We offer many enrichment activities for students to choose on a voluntary or self-selecting basis.   1   2   3   4   5

16. We make it possible for students to move forward at an advanced rate in any subject area if they are able to do so.   1   2   3   4   5

17. We offer advanced classes or sections for students who have academic strengths in specific subject areas.   1   2   3   4   5

Figure 14.3   Sample LoS program evaluation questions

1 = Strongly Disagree; 2 = Disagree; 3 = Neutral; 4 = Agree; 5 = Strongly Agree

Circle Your Assessment

18. Our school provides opportunities for students with high ability and interest in specific talent areas to work together.   1 2 3 4 5

19. Students have opportunities to work on individual or group projects in their areas of strength.   1 2 3 4 5

20. Our school offers high-level content instruction for advanced students.   1 2 3 4 5

21. We help students to understand and appreciate their personal strengths and talents.   1 2 3 4 5

22. We help students to understand and appreciate the strengths and talents of other students.   1 2 3 4 5

23. Our school provides students with opportunities to learn and practice teamwork and collaboration skills.   1 2 3 4 5

24. Students in our school have few opportunities to demonstrate or develop leadership skills.   1 2 3 4 5

25. Our staff has not had access to training or inservice about the LoS approach.   1 2 3 4 5

26. Parents have had opportunities to learn about and discuss the LoS approach.   1 2 3 4 5

27. Our school is effective in involving parents in carrying out programming activities.   1 2 3 4 5

28. We use community agencies or personnel to participate in our LoS programming activities.   1 2 3 4 5

29. Our school board is knowledgeable about LoS.   1 2 3 4 5

30. Our school board supports the LoS approach.   1 2 3 4 5

31. Our administrators are knowledgeable about the LoS approach.   1 2 3 4 5

32. Our administrators support the LoS approach.   1 2 3 4 5

33. Parents and staff members communicate effectively about students' strengths, talents, and needs.   1 2 3 4 5

34. Our LoS programming has helped us accomplish growth in these areas this year:
    a. Differentiated Basics   1 2 3 4 5
    b. Appropriate Enrichment   1 2 3 4 5
    c. Effective Acceleration   1 2 3 4 5
    d. Independence and Self-Direction   1 2 3 4 5
    e. Personal Growth and Social Development   1 2 3 4 5
    f. Career Perspectives and Future Outlook   1 2 3 4 5

35. LoS programming has distracted us from our work on state-mandated content standards.   1 2 3 4 5

(Continued)

1 = Strongly Disagree; 2 = Disagree; 3 = Neutral; 4 = Agree; 5 = Strongly Agree					
		Circle Your Assessment			
36. LoS programming will not be likely to have a positive impact on our school's test scores.	1	2	3	4	5
37. LoS programming is compatible with our school improvement goals and initiatives.	1	2	3	4	5
38. We have adequate staff to implement LoS.	1	2	3	4	5
39. We have adequate time to implement LoS.	1	2	3	4	5
40. We have adequate training to implement LoS.	1	2	3	4	5

Figure 14.3 (Continued)

We can identify four general stages in planning for effective evaluation and several key tasks or questions for each stage. (The evaluation folder on the accompanying CD includes a summary LoS Programming Evaluation Planning Guide with more information about these stages.)

1. Preparing for the Evaluation

- Is there a written plan for the evaluation?
- Are you clear about who will conduct the evaluation?
- Are there clear purposes and goals?
- Have you identified stakeholders?
- Has a time line been established?

2. Designing Data Collection

- Do you have clear and appropriate evaluation questions?
- Are questions worded to yield valuable data for documenting and improving the program?
- Does the evaluation examine different perspectives about key themes and issues?
- Are you using varied data collection methods (e.g., personal interviews, telephone interviews, Web-based or print surveys, classroom observations, test data)?
- Are all programming activities and services addressed?

3. Conducting the Evaluation

- Are the evaluators available to varied audiences to facilitate each audience's understanding of the evaluation process and procedures?
- Are multiple stakeholders consistently and appropriately involved with data collection and with monitoring and reviewing the evaluation process?

- Do you have a plan for timely data analysis and feedback, including the roles of individuals in meeting prescribed time lines?
- Is there a commitment from evaluators, key program personnel, and steering committee members to use the findings for positive program improvement?
- Is there an explicit plan for proceeding from evaluation findings into constructive action, and are the roles of evaluators, program personnel, and stakeholders included in that process?

4. Reporting Findings and Follow-Up

- Have evaluators, program personnel, and steering committee members assessed the impact of evaluation findings?
- Are the findings interpreted and presented accurately, comprehensively, and in ways that are attentive to the interests and concerns of all stakeholder groups?
- Are written reports clear; do they avoid the use of jargon and confusing, technical presentations and interpretations of data?
- Do evaluation reports describe thoroughly and clearly the nature of programming implementation, the evaluation questions, the evaluation process and procedures, the participants in the evaluation process, the data collection and analysis, the findings, and the evaluators' interpretations?
- Do the results and recommendations address all programming areas, activities, and services?
- Do evaluation reports include specific recommendations to guide and support follow-through and action?

INDICATORS OF QUALITY IN PROGRAMMING

How can you determine whether your programming efforts meet or exceed reasonable standards of quality? In areas as complex as teaching and learning and serving as diverse an array of stakeholders as schools must, it can be very difficult indeed to respond with confidence to this question. The search for an appropriate response that can be defended on the basis of research and theory as well as logic and personal values will probably begin with an examination of the school's results and outcomes in relation to its stated vision, mission, goals, and objectives. No universal agreement has been attained regarding how to compare or evaluate a school's selection of goals. In addition, it is often exceedingly difficult to attach specific performance standards or criteria to many of the goals we consider important, especially more complex outcomes at higher cognitive (e.g., productive thinking, creativity, and problem solving) or affective (e.g., resourcefulness, love of learning, self-management) levels. A school's ongoing analysis, review, and evaluation of its efforts should always seek ways, both quantitatively and qualitatively, to document the goals it holds important, and not to permit evaluation to be reduced only to the level at which the most easily measured outcomes (e.g., memorization and recall of information) become, by default, its most important outcomes.

- Lists pertaining to Level I activities and services
  Activities and services offered within classrooms
  Activities and services offered within grade levels, across classrooms
  Activities and services offered schoolwide
  Activities and services offered across multiple schools
  Documentation of numbers of students
  Documentation of leaders' names, duration of activities, goals/objectives

- Lists pertaining to Level II and Level III activities and services
  Description, duration, and objectives of activities
  Location(s) at which activities take place
  Names of leaders and supervisors
  Names of participating students
  Evaluation data from specific activities

- Documentation of Level IV services
  Student names and written plans for Level IV
  Name of teacher or supervisor
  Documentation of products, outcomes, or accomplishments (including work in
    progress)
  Copies of evaluations and/or feedback forms

- Materials from district level and building level committees
  District Master Plan (including mission/vision statements)
  Building Action Plans
  Planning committee minutes and notes
  Records of visitations or site visits

- Samples of letters, memos, brochures, or publicity pieces
  Material addressed to any stakeholders
  Public and media documents

- Data regarding student assessment to verify student needs
  Assessment data
  Rating scales, self-reports, checklists, observation reports
  Teacher, pupil, and/or parent conference records
  Student profiles and/or portfolios

- Documentation of district or building level dissemination activities
  Records of visitors to the school or district
  Conference presentations
  Articles for journals
  Awards or recognitions
  Self-study or self-assessment reports

Figure 14.4   Resources to incorporate in LoS documentation

Interviews With . . .	Types of Information
1. Students	Frequency of, type of, setting of, and satisfaction with services offered
2. Parents	Understanding of LoS philosophy and goals; understanding of frequency, type, and setting; satisfaction with student access to services as well as effectiveness
3. School personnel providing services	Awareness of and support for Los; extent of their involvement in planning and delivering services; effectiveness of support, resources, and coordination; effectiveness of relationship with LoS staff; involvement in and satisfaction with professional development services offered
4. Planning and/or steering committee	Satisfaction with planning, design, and delivery of programming
5. LoS programming specialist(s) and program coordinator	Range and type of services offered; relationships with regular education staff; parent and community relationships
6. Administrators	Understanding and support of LoS approach; awareness of services offered; relationships with staff, parents, students, community; support for schools provided by the district office
7. School board members	Understanding and support of LoS approach; current status of programming and written plans
8. Community agency personnel	Awareness and support of LoS; range and type of direct contacts with staff and students

Figure 14.5   Examples of interviews in LoS evaluation

Similarly, we recommend caution when using and interpreting standardized achievement test results, especially in relation to school improvement and programming outcomes for high-ability students. Minimum competencies are not necessarily indicators of effectiveness, even for at-risk students; schools should not permit minimum competencies to become maximum expectancies for any student. By the same token, high achievement scores are not necessarily indications of successful instruction or appropriate challenge for students. Some students may attain high scores on the basis of what they already knew prior to instruction, rather than as a reflection of high-quality, challenging instruction. In addition, some students who attain very high achievement scores may simply be getting by on what they already know, rather than being challenged to progress to higher or more complex levels. We must be mindful of the warning issued by Professor Julian Stanley of Johns Hopkins University that there is more variability in the 99th percentile than in the rest of the distribution. That is, when a student's score is at the 99th percentile, we only know that the test was not able to tell us about how much beyond its ceiling (if at all) a student might have been able to continue responding successfully. Some students might have reached their limit in the very next group of questions, if there had been another group, whereas others might have continued on successfully through many more complex and challenging levels.

In the chapters of this handbook on needs assessment (Chapter 6) and carrying out programming (Chapter 12), we presented six broad programming areas as a way of describing the foundation for a successful, challenging instructional program. They will provide a useful starting point for self-study of any school's instructional efforts.

INNOVATION AND CHANGE

Effective evaluation can also provide directions and challenge for innovation and change, identifying significant areas of need or opportunity for new activities or services. In Chapter 4, we discussed many of today's pressures for innovation and change. In order to be effective in dealing with or managing change, educators, administrators, and policymakers in today's schools must be prepared to gather data from many sources and to use those data to monitor and revise their present policies and actions. It is no longer possible in today's world to assume that curriculum, instructional methods and resources, or the characteristics, needs, and interests of students will remain static for long periods of time. Effective schools are those in which people work to establish and maintain relatively short cycles of response to change (that is, to create and apply flexible, responsive modes of action to effect change without long delays for review, analysis and reanalysis, and approval).

CONTINUOUS IMPROVEMENT

Obviously, no programming efforts are ever perfect; there is always room for improvement. Can our efforts ever be completely free of any error? "Zero defects" is often discussed as a goal, for example, in the world of business and manufacturing.

How many defective products can emerge from a factory before the owners and workers conclude that performance is unsatisfactory? (Is one in a thousand too many—or too demanding a standard? Would your response be different if you knew that the one defective product in a thousand would be the one you purchase?) If we set our standards as high as possible, toward the ultimate goal of zero defects, we will then be challenged to be constantly alert to new ways to improve and do things better—our goal, and our standard operating procedure, will focus on continuous improvement, rather than on "just good enough."

To be sure, educating children and youth is a much more complex challenge than mass-producing widgets, and it is often much more difficult to know what a "defect" represents. The better we become at defining the outcomes we consider essential for every student, the more we will be able to determine whether or not we have been successful. In the same sense as for the manufacturer, the zero defect principle is a worthwhile challenge for educators in that it encourages us to accept the goal of continuous improvement. We must always be examining our policies, practices, and results in order to be alert for better ways to recognize and develop students' strengths, talents, and sustained interests and to ensure their competence, confidence, and commitment as learners.

Similarly, school improvement is a continuous process, in which you are always seeking ways to enhance all aspects of your school's operation and services. We have never heard of a "New, Improved School!" (with a special, patented secret ingredient)—but we do encourage schools to think of themselves as continuously improving institutions.

Continuous improvement is not only a matter of finding things that are insufficient, wrong, inadequate, or deficient; it is not just fixing up something that is damaged or not working right. It will be just as important—and undoubtedly much more satisfying and renewing—to keep in mind that every good school always seeks ways to become better. Thus, as some important goals are attained, new ones emerge. As innovation occurs within a school, a climate is established in which more new ideas can be encouraged in the future. Growth must be planned and well managed, to be sure, to avoid a helter-skelter approach in which nothing seems stable for very long. But at the same time, it is also necessary to avoid the dangers of complacency, failure to examine carefully the strengths and weaknesses of the program over time, and rigidity in the face of changing circumstances and needs.

THE ROLE OF THE PLANNING COMMITTEE

The role of the planning committee does not end once the initial Master Plan or Building Action Plans have been prepared. Its role will change in several important ways as you progress from the planning process into actual implementation efforts. Give careful consideration to the continuing role and responsibilities of the planning committee's members after the initial completion of your written plans. These continuing tasks have been grouped into four general categories: preparation for implementation (the start-up phase), implementation and management, evaluation and long-range planning, and communication and school-community relations.

Preparation for Implementation

After you have drafted the Master Plan, it should be reviewed thoroughly by many stakeholders and adopted explicitly. To prepare for implementation of the Master Plan, the first group of tasks involves promoting and supporting school or building level planning efforts; supporting resource development and allocation; sharing, discussing, and updating the Building Action Plans; considering resources needed and resource allocations; and stimulating staff development opportunities.

Promoting and Supporting Building Efforts

The planning committee should assist and support the efforts of each school to create its own Action Plan. The planning committee's support for building level efforts should also extend into programming opportunities. For example, if special opportunities arise to bring in unique resource persons or groups (e.g., an artist or writer in residence or a performing arts group) on a districtwide basis, it may be more efficient to coordinate arrangements and to schedule individual building visits centrally than through each building independently. It may also be possible at the district level to help increase all schools' awareness of such opportunities.

Sharing, Discussing, and Updating the Building Action Plans

The Building Action Plan for each school is not a static, fixed document, but rather a flexible, dynamic plan that should be examined as an ongoing process. It is essential for the school's staff to have regular opportunities for input regarding the plan's implementation and growth. It can also be valuable to share the plan with parents and community members so that they will be knowledgeable about the school's programming philosophy and practices and to invite their contributions to carrying out the plan where appropriate. The building level Action Plans should also be reviewed and discussed regularly to support program development as well as to monitor or evaluate program implementation and outcomes.

Resource Development and Allocation

The planning committee can coordinate and review resource requests, synthesize individual requests into an overall fiscal plan or proposal for programming, and promote cooperative or shared use of resources among buildings. They may also take leadership in preparing grant proposals for various aspects of programming. The planning committee can serve as a conduit of professional resources and information for all staff members through such services as subscribing to and circulating appropriate magazines and professional journals; circulating information about conferences, workshops, or graduate study opportunities; or promoting opportunities for visitations to other programs or participation in networking or consortium activities within the local area, state, or region.

Stimulating Staff Development Opportunities

Another important continuing role for the planning committee involves designing, organizing, arranging, and conducting inservice or staff development opportunities. The planning committee can provide leadership at the districtwide or school level to ensure that provisions are made within existing professional development programs to help staff members throughout the district to increase their confidence and proficiency in recognizing students' unique characteristics, needs, and interests. The planning committee can also initiate new directions for inservice, or promote and enhance innovative staff development approaches that are already in place, to help support the district's overall efforts to apply contemporary principles and evidence regarding professional development.

Inservice or staff development within any building, or on a districtwide basis, should be designed to provide all staff members with new ideas and information; to be effective, however, it must also help the staff to use, practice, and modify in their own setting what they have learned in the programs. This can also help to convey the importance of ownership of LoS programming by the whole staff (so programming is not simply regarded as "what someone else does to certain students"). It also reinforces an important principle: nurturing students' strengths and talents calls for methods, techniques, or strategies that can and should be employed in the regular classroom, not just in a separate setting.

Implementation and Management

The second set of continuing tasks involves the actions that are important for successful implementation of the Master Plan and Building Action Plans as well as tasks relating to effective management of programming.

Diagnostic Assessment of Student Characteristics and Needs

The building planning committee, or a subcommittee of it, can also perform a valuable service by functioning as a diagnostic or child study team, supporting the school's efforts to look closely at the unique characteristics, strengths, talents, and sustained interests of students. They may conduct detailed case studies in certain cases, or facilitate planning and use of student profiles, to best determine students' needs and to define appropriate responses. Many schools already have child study teams or screening procedures in one form or another, but these are usually occupied almost completely with cases in which the main emphasis is on remediation, deficiencies, or learning problems. The building committee's role in talent development programming is to ensure that there are also specific efforts made to recognize and plan for students' strengths, talents, and sustained interests. This task involves studying carefully any students whose history and status suggests difficulty in understanding the child's needs or special conditions, such as great variations in performance in different subject areas or difficult circumstances at home or in school. In such cases, the student's learning may best be promoted through input and discussion by several staff members. The district committee's efforts can stimulate discussion of options or alternatives, as well as sharing of successful practices, among the buildings, and can also address the issues of time and resources needed for diagnostic assessment to be undertaken at the building level.

Sustaining Programming Positives

In the initial planning at the building level, one task was to identify a variety of activities and services already being used in the school to extend, enhance, or enrich learning opportunities for students. The items on this list have been described as the school's *programming positives.* That is, these are activities that contribute to the goals and purposes of talent development programming *and* are already in place in the school. Sustaining and supporting these activities is an important ongoing task for each building. Sharing successful practices and seeking support for the buildings' initiatives are related tasks for the district committee.

Extending Enrichment Opportunities for Many Students

Effective programming at the building level incorporates many opportunities for students to explore ideas, topics, and issues that are independent of the regular curriculum. It also includes systematic efforts to guide students in learning and applying methodological skills (e.g., technology, presentation, or research skills) and process skills (e.g., creative and critical thinking, problem solving, or decision making). The planning committee can assist in efforts to identify topics and to plan and conduct such activities, to pool resources from several buildings to bring in outside programs, or to coordinate scheduling of community resources so that schools need not compete separately for the time and services of individuals who may be in high demand.

Solving Problems and Stimulating Innovation

The planning committee can also examine carefully the wish lists that were created in the initial planning stages to identify priorities for future efforts. These lists include activities and services that will help the school to expand and diversify the services it offers to students. The committee should work together to identify the highest priorities among these items and to plan ways to accomplish them. This will call on the committee to put their problem solving and decision making skills to use! Some items in the wish list may be readily attainable, not having been created before only because they were not previously identified as a need or concern. These can probably be implemented quite easily through the committee's efforts. Others may represent much more complex or challenging long-term goals that will require much more extensive time and effort to accomplish.

As work begins on any elements of a wish list, some new projects are likely to emerge for which a particular group within the school is particularly enthusiastic. The planning committee should also be prepared to engage in problem solving and innovation development, providing opportunities for building representatives to bring forward concerns that should be addressed at the district level and encouraging the staff to plan and conduct cooperative or experimental projects at more than one site.

Monitoring and Coordinating Implementation

The balance between autonomy at the school level and continuity or consistency among units within the district can be complex to establish and maintain. Each building may design and conduct programming efforts in its own unique ways. However, it is valid for the district to ensure that policies and procedures do not differ so widely from one school to another that articulation and communication problems are created. For example, students who may move from one school to another should not find that they are denied appropriate opportunities by virtue of their enrollment in a particular school. Nor should students' prior activities and accomplishments be disregarded as they move from one level to another through the school years. Through ongoing sharing and discussion of successes, accomplishments, difficulties, concerns, and new opportunities, the planning committee can serve as a system through which the needed balance and continuity are maintained and fine-tuned.

Continuing Evaluation and Long-Range Planning

The third general area of ongoing work for the district committee and the building committees involves the need for careful continuing evaluation, long-range planning, and revision of programming policies and practices.

Designing Regular Updates or Revisions

Effective programming is dynamic, not static, and education for talent development is a dynamic, rapidly changing area in which new developments in theory and research occur frequently. On the plus side, this stimulates many opportunities for school improvement and program refinement; the minus side, of course, is that it can be very difficult to keep up-to-date without ongoing effort and study. For this reason, the committees must recognize that policies and procedures for talent development programming must be reviewed regularly. Both the Master Plan and each of the Building Action Plans should be viewed as flexible and open to continuous efforts at improvement, rather than fixed and permanent in the form in which they were originally created. This calls for ongoing investigation of new trends and direction in the field, discussion of many alternatives for program growth, and time and effort devoted to long-range planning and the establishment of both districtwide and building level priorities and goals.

Continuing Evaluation Efforts

The evaluation process, which we have already described as an ongoing process, not a one-time action, also requires continuing planning, coordination, and support at both the district and school levels.

Long-Range Planning

The challenges of change and continuous improvement suggest that the planning committees should give serious consideration to planning over a three- to five-year period. These efforts should be ongoing, so that planning will be deliberate and systematic rather than haphazard. When program development or change represents a hurried set of decisions, made under the pressure of crises (real or imaginary), the results are not likely to be very satisfactory to anyone for very long.

Communication and School-Community Relations

The fourth general area of continuing responsibility for the committees involves efforts to inform, educate, and communicate with the public and to disseminate the accomplishments and successes of the district's or school's programming efforts.

Answering Questions

There will always be many, varied, and unusual questions from community members and parents, as well as from staff members who were not directly involved in the initial program planning efforts. There will be some, for example, who will want to know more about policies and procedures in general, or to compare them with other programs they may have heard or read about elsewhere. These questions may arise from a general curiosity or interest, from concerns about proceeding in the best possible manner, or by virtue of people's concern for and interest in their own children's educational services or programs.

Such questions are important and valid and deserve honest and informed responses. When there are concerns about one school's or district's policies and procedures compared to what someone has heard from other places, or when there are discussions of differences in specific activities from one school to another within a district, be certain that the planning committee members have a common base of information to work with, and that staff and administrators know how to get information, to prevent incorrect information from being given out inadvertently.

Disseminating Program Accomplishments and Promoting Good Public Relations

All schools should be alert to any opportunities to document their accomplishments and success for members of their community and to promote positive, cooperative relations within the community. Community members often read, hear, or see only a very small sample of the school's activities and accomplishments—on the positive side, the attainments of winning athletic teams or an annual school dramatic performance, or perhaps the honor roll or features about scholarship or award winners, for example. Too often the publicity is neutral, controversial, or even negative—such as budget, construction, or contract issues; publication of achievement test scores and comparisons among districts (whether or not appropriate); board election campaigns; or special issues that arise. The planning committee can seek opportunities to promote activities and accomplishments throughout the year to build awareness of their efforts to recognize and develop the talents and strengths of many students.

CONCLUSION: PLANNING CONTEMPORARY, INCLUSIVE PROGRAMMING FOR TALENT DEVELOPMENT

Through the use of a Six-Stage Systematic Planning Model, this handbook has provided a comprehensive set of guidelines, procedures, and resources for planning, implementing, and evaluating a contemporary, inclusive approach to programming for talent development. We have drawn upon more than two decades of research, development, and field experience with contemporary, inclusive programming in many states and school districts. Although we have used examples from our experience with the Levels of Service (LoS) approach, the Six-Stage Systematic Planning model and other resources in the handbook can readily be applied to a broad range of other approaches. The CD accompanying this handbook provides copies of many practical resources that you can use or readily adapt (provided that you acknowledge their source appropriately) for your own setting. We welcome feedback and samples of applications of any of these resources in schools or school districts.

Appendix A

Constructing the Master Plan

1.Philosophy statement

Do you have an explicit philosophy statement, vision statement, and/or mission statement?

If so, does it explicitly make a commitment to recognizing and nurturing the strengths, talents, and sustained interests of students? Which statements show that commitment?

If the commitment is not explicit but is implied by other statements, what are they, and how do they relate to the goals of talent development programming?

If there is no statement that addresses, either directly or indirectly, the areas of talent development, how might you best proceed?

- Initiate efforts to revise any existing statement?
- Create a new statement to augment the existing statement?
- Initiate efforts to create a new, more comprehensive statement?

If there is an explicit statement, is it known and understood by: administrators? board members? faculty and staff? parents and community members? students? (If not, how might that be accomplished?)

2. Establish "fit" between programming for talent development and other key areas of concern in your school or district.

Consider any of the following areas of concern that might be of current interest within your school or district. For each relevant area in the left column, note in the right column possible connections with (and implications for) your talent development programming.

Area of Concern:	Connections/Implications for Talent Development:
Restructuring and site-based decision making	
School improvement or strategic planning	
Learning styles	
Thinking skills	
Cooperative learning	
Education of at-risk and special needs students	
Differentiation	
Interdisciplinary studies	
Authentic assessment	
Multiple intelligences	
Standards/state assessment	
Other:	

3. Definitions of key terms in the Master Plan

What definitions will you use for:
TALENT

EXCELLENCE

EXPERTISE

Explain how your definitions are consistent with contemporary theory and research on the nature of human abilities and talents.

How might you best explain these definitions to your staff, to your students, and to your community and parents?

4. What are your principal goals and objectives relating to programming for talent development?

Goal: **Related Objective(s):**

5. How will you assess or recognize students' strengths and talents?

In what ways might you encourage all staff members to search deliberately for students' strengths, talents, and sustained interests? (What do they already do? What new steps are needed?)

How might each school staff expand or increase its ability to recognize and respond to students' unique characteristics and needs?

To what extent does each school take steps to study students individually, to recognize their unique learning styles, and to identify their talents and sustained interests? How will you encourage each school to move beyond "selecting and labeling" a small, fixed group?

What kinds of support will each school require to plan and implement a diagnostic, flexible, and inclusive approach to identifying students' strengths and talents?

6. How will you ensure that each school's programming challenges students, recognizes diversity, and offers opportunities for student productivity?

How might you encourage and help all schools to seek and recognize students' strengths and talents in a variety of specific talent areas or domains?

How might you help schools to assess their present strengths and needs in six programming areas (differentiated basics, appropriate enrichment, effective acceleration, independence and self-direction, personal growth and social development, and career perspectives and futuristic orientation)?

How might you help schools to identify significant efforts that are already taking place at varied Levels of Service (for all, many, some, or few students) at several levels (school-wide, grade level, subject level, team, individual), with a focus on the particular needs and interests of individuals?

How might you stimulate efforts in each school to link pupil assessment and instruction as closely as possible?

7. How will your school(s) determine the need to extend, enhance, or expand their programming efforts for giftedness and talent development?

How might you help schools to create a wish list, toward which they are committed to making new or expanded efforts for talent development?

How might you support and encourage new efforts, at least on an exploratory or "pilot" basis?

What initial steps might you help schools to plan and initiate in order to address some of the more difficult areas of their wish list?

What are some of the long-range changes, expanded services, increased activities, or innovations you will help schools to try in relation to programming for talent development?

How and when might the district best support efforts by staff to work together to solve problems and address long-range goals and priorities?

How will you link these efforts to other components of your ongoing commitment to quality instruction and school improvement?

8. What implementation guidelines will you provide for schools?

What expectations will you establish for planning and implementation in each school?

What support will you provide to help schools meet those expectations?

	At the planning stage:	At the implementation stage:
People		
Materials		
Training		
Time		
Funding		
Other		

What will be the administrator's role at the building level?

How will expectations for each building address:

- "Fit" with the district Master Plan?
- The individual needs, culture, and climate of the school?

- Procedures for review, approval, monitoring, and revision of the Building Action Plan?
- Support and resources?

Will there be an expectation that planning and implementation will be initiated in each school?

9. What inservice or professional development efforts will you need to support the talent development Master Plan?

What *existing* skills and talents within your staff and/or administration will support your efforts to create and carry out your Master Plan?

What *new* skills, resources, or methods and techniques will teachers, administrators, and others need to acquire to support creating and carrying out the Master Plan?

How will you ensure that the necessary resources (and people) will be available and will be carried effectively to the entire staff?

What training opportunities will you need to offer to ensure the staff's commitment and effectiveness, and how will you provide those opportunities?

How will you ensure that training experiences are relevant and rewarding?

How will you document and evaluate the impact or outcomes of training?

10. What resource and budget implications are involved?

What *existing resources* will be involved in carrying out the Master Plan and in supporting the schools' Action Plans? (At the district level? From each school's resources?)

What *new resources* will be required?

From what outside sources might you obtain additional resources (financial, people, materials)? How will you obtain them?

What are the long-range resource implications? If you begin to implement talent development programming, what resources will you need to ensure its successful continuation?

Whose support will you need to ensure coordination, action, and success? How much of their time will you need for successful implementation? How will you ensure their support?

11. What is your time line for implementation?

How many meetings will you need to create the Master Plan? How long will each last? When and where will they occur? How will you ensure that all participants can attend?

With whom will you share the resulting plan? (In draft or final form?) By what decision process will it be approved or adopted? When will the Master Plan be reviewed and evaluated? By whom?

When and how will modifications be considered?

How long will you provide for each school to create its own Action Plan? To begin implementation?

12. What aspects of the plan are developmental, and what aspects are exploratory?

In the Master Plan, what proposals are developmental—that is, helping the schools to do things better by working within the existing system? Will "developers" be heard?

What proposals are extensions or refinements of existing activities or services? How will the Master Plan contribute to the schools' overall progress or forward motion toward continuous instructional improvement?

What will be new and different for the schools? Will "explorers" be heard?

How might you help both developers and explorers to work together more effectively?

13. What is the proposed evaluation plan?

What specific plans and commitments have you made to evaluate the Master Plan and your implementation of contemporary talent development programming?

What criteria will you use to document the effectiveness and impact of the Master Plan and its key components or activities?

How will your evaluation data help you to refine or modify the Master Plan?

Appendix B

Constructing the Building Action Plan

1. Rationale and expected benefits of the proposed talent development programming

What is your school's rationale for adopting and implementing a contemporary approach to programming for talent development?

What benefits do you hope to attain by implementing that approach?

2. Your philosophy and definitions

Explain your philosophy for talent development programming.

What key terms need to be defined in order to build understanding and acceptance of your plan for talent development programming? State your definitions of those terms.

3. Programming goals and objectives

Describe your specific goals and objectives for talent development programming in your school.

How might you best explain and communicate those goals and objectives to your staff, to parents, and to students?

4. Your school's uniqueness in relation to talent development

What are the established methods of operation in your school—the expectations, traditions, rituals, and rewards that everyone knows and expects?

Have you taken deliberate steps to understand and discuss how people in your school feel about the school's climate? (Are you "ready, willing, and able" to carry out talent development programming?) What are your strengths? What areas need more work? How will you do that?

What is *unique* about your school? How do any aspects of your school's uniqueness influence the decisions you will make regarding talent development programming?

Do you have a clear vision of what your school should be like in 5 (or 10) years? Do you discuss how to move toward that vision?

How might your Building Action Plan reflect your best understanding of your school's unique strengths and what you hope to accomplish together?

5. Assessing students' characteristics and needs

In what ways might you search deliberately for students' strengths, talents, and sustained interests? (What do you already do? What new steps are needed?)

How might you increase your ability to recognize and respond to your students' unique characteristics and needs?

To what extent (and how) do you study your students individually, recognize their unique learning styles, and identify their strengths, talents, and sustained interests?

What steps can you take to use identification data for instructional planning, extending beyond labeling or categorizing your students?

6. The regular school program's strengths

How does your school ensure challenge, recognize diversity, and offer opportunities for student productivity?

What programming positives describe the areas in which you are already effectively challenging your students and building on their talents and interests?

How do you maintain a healthy balance between concern for remediation and deficiencies, on the one hand, with efforts to locate and respond to students' strengths, on the other?

In six programming areas (differentiated basics, appropriate enrichment, effective acceleration, independence and self-direction, personal growth and social development, careers and future), which receive the greatest (and least) current emphasis?

Identify significant efforts that already take place in your building to provide appropriate programming at varied Levels of Service (for all, many, some, and few students) at several levels (schoolwide, grade level or subject level, team, individual), with a focus on the particular needs and interests of individuals.

7. Extending, enhancing, or expanding the school program

What are some of the items on your wish list toward which you are already making new or expanded efforts?

What grade levels will be involved initially? In what subject or program areas will students be involved in programming?

What specifically are you now doing to attain your short-term goals for talent development?

What initial steps have you taken, or are you planning specifically to take, to address some of the more difficult areas of your wish list?

What are some of the long-range changes, expanded services, increased activities, or innovations you will attempt to bring about through talent development programming?

How will you link your talent development efforts to other components of your ongoing commitment to quality instruction and school improvement?

8. Identifying active participants and leaders

What will be the role of classroom teachers in implementing your Building Action Plan?

Who are the "champions" of some of the items on your wish list, and how might you encourage and support them in working toward the attainment of those goals?

What will be the administrator's role in talent development programming in your building?

Will one or more staff members be available to work with other staff members and with students to facilitate the development and implementation of new services and activities?

How will you support the faculty and staff in their efforts to plan and carry out programming?

What other people and resources (e.g., volunteers—parents, senior citizens, older students) will be involved? Will area businesses, organizations, or higher education be involved? How?

How and when will your staff work together to solve problems and address long-range goals and priorities?

9. Inservice and staff development needs and commitments

What *existing* skills and talents within your school (staff, administration) will enable you to carry out your Building Action Plan? How will you mobilize and use them?

What *new* skills, resources, or methods and techniques will teachers, administrators, and others need to help them to carry out your Building Action Plan? How will you provide them?

What data from your Needs Assessment, Climate Survey, or other sources document specific needs for staff development?

How will you ensure that the training and resources will be available to promote effective application of new skills and resources?

How will you ensure that training experiences are relevant and rewarding?

How will you determine the impact or outcomes of training?

10. Resource and budget implications

What *existing* school resources will you obtain and use in carrying out your Building Action Plan?

What *new* resources will you require, from what sources, and how will you obtain them?

From what outside sources might you obtain additional resources (financial, people, materials)? How will you seek them?

What are the long-range resource implications? What resources will you require to ensure ongoing support to sustain or expand programming?

11. Your time line for implementation

When will you begin to implement your Building Action Plan?

When will you review, evaluate, and revise your Building Action Plan?

How long will it take for each component of the Building Action Plan to be initiated and fully implemented?

12. Linkages between talent development programming and other initiatives

How might you link your talent development programming to other current areas of concern and involvement (e.g., thinking skills, learning styles, multiple intelligences, standards, school improvement)?

What aspects of your Building Action Plan are extensions or refinements of existing activities or services? How will your Building Action Plan contribute to the school's overall progress or "forward motion" toward continuous instructional improvement? Will "developers'" concerns and needs be heard?

What will be new and different for the school? Will "explorers'" concerns and needs be heard?

13. Your evaluation plan

What specific plans and commitments have you made to evaluate your Building Action Plan and its implementation?

What criteria will you use to document the effectiveness or impact of the components or activities in the Building Action Plan?

How will you use evaluation data to refine or modify talent development programming?

References

Amabile, T. M. (1983). *The social psychology of creativity*. New York: Springer-Verlag.

Betts, G. (1985). *The autonomous learner model for the gifted and talented*. Greeley, CO: ALPS.

Blanchard, K. (1987). *SLII: A situational approach to leadership*. San Diego, CA: Blanchard Training and Development.

Blanchard, K. (2006). *Leading at a higher level*. Upper Saddle River, NJ: Prentice Hall.

Bloom, B. S. (1985). *Developing talent in young people*. New York: Ballantine Books.

Callahan, C. M. (1986). Asking the right questions: The central issue in evaluating programs for the gifted and talented. *Gifted Child Quarterly, 30*(1), 38–42.

Carnevale, A., Gainer, L., & Meltzer, A. (1991). *Workplace basics: The skills employers want*. Alexandria, VA: American Society for Training and Development.

Costa, A. L. (Ed.). (2001). *Developing minds: A resource book for teaching thinking*. Alexandria, VA: Association for Supervision and Curriculum Development.

Dunn, R., Dunn, K., & Treffinger, D. (1992). *Bringing out the giftedness in your child*. New York: Wiley.

Ekvall, G. (1987). The climate metaphor in organizational theory. In B. M. Bass & P. J. D. Drenth (Eds.), *Advances in organizational psychology: An international review* (pp. 177–190). Newbury Park, CA: SAGE.

Ekvall, G. (1997). Organizational conditions and levels of creativity. *Creativity and Innovation Management, 6*, 195–205.

Feldhusen, J. F. (1992). *Talent identification and development in education (TIDE)*. Sarasota, FL: Center for Creative Learning.

Feldhusen, J. F., & Kolloff, M. B. (1986). The Purdue three-stage enrichment model for gifted education at the elementary level. In J. S. Renzulli (Ed.), *Systems and models for developing programs for the gifted and talented*. Mansfield Center, CT: Creative Learning Press.

Feldhusen, J. F., & Kolloff, M. B. (1988). A three-stage model for gifted education. *G/C/T Magazine, 11*(1), 14–20.

Gardner, H. (1983). *Frames of mind: The theory of multiple intelligences*. New York: Basic Books.

Gisi, L., & Forbes, R. (1982). *The information society: Are high school graduates ready?* Denver, CO: Education Commission of the States.

Gould, S. J. (1981). *The mismeasure of man*. New York: W. W. Norton.

Gregory, G. H., & Chapman, C. (2006). *Differentiated instructional strategies: One size doesn't fit all*. Thousand Oaks, CA: Corwin Press.

Guilford, J. P. (1959). Three faces of intellect. *American Psychologist, 14*, 469–479.

Guilford, J. P. (1967). *The nature of human intelligence*. New York: McGraw-Hill.

Guilford, J. P. (1977). *Way beyond the IQ*. Buffalo, NY: Bearly.

Heacox, D. (2001). *Differentiated instruction in the regular classroom: How to reach and teach all learners (Grades 3–12)*. Minneapolis, MN: Free Spirit.

Hersey, P., Blanchard, K., & Johnson, D. (2000). *Management of organizational behavior* (8th ed.). Upper Saddle River, NJ: Prentice Hall.

Isaksen, S. G., Dorval, K. B., & Treffinger, D. J. (1998). *Toolbox for creative problem solving*. Williamsville, NY: Creative Problem Solving Group Buffalo.

Isaksen, S. G., Dorval, K. B., & Treffinger, D. J. (2000). *Creative approaches to problem solving* (2nd ed.). Dubuque, IA: Kendall/Hunt.

Isaksen, S. G., Lauer, K. J., & Ekvall, G. (1999). Situational Outlook Questionnaire: A measure of the climate for creativity and change. *Psychological Reports, 85,* 665–674.

Isaksen, S. G., Lauer, K. J., Ekvall, G., & Britz, A. (2001). Perceptions of the best and worst climates for creativity: Preliminary validation evidence for the Situational Outlook Questionnaire. *Creativity Research Journal, 13*(2), 171–184.

Isaksen, S. G., & Tidd, J. (2006). *Meeting the innovation challenge: Leadership for transformation and growth.* New York: Wiley.

Isaksen, S. G., Treffinger, D. J., & Dorval, K. B. (1996). *Climate for creativity and innovation: Educational implications.* Sarasota, FL: Center for Creative Learning.

Kouzes, J. M., & Posner, B. (2002). *The leadership challenge* (3rd ed). San Francisco: Jossey-Bass.

Marland, S. (1971). *Education of gifted and talented* (2 vols.). Washington, DC: U.S. Government Printing Office.

McClelland, D. C. (1973). Testing for competence rather than for "intelligence." *American Psychologist, 28,* 1–14.

Myers, I., McCaulley, M., Quenk, N., & Hammer, A. (1998). *MBTI manual: A guide to the development and use of the Myers-Briggs Type Indicator* (3rd ed.). Palo Alto, CA: Consulting Psychologists Press.

Parker, M. (1990). *Creating shared vision.* Oslo, Norway: Norwegian Center for Leadership Development.

Purcell, J. H., & Renzulli, J. S. (1998). *Total talent portfolio.* Mansfield Center, CT: Creative Learning Press.

Renzulli, J. S. (1978). What makes giftedness? Reexamining a definition. *Phi Delta Kappan, 59,* 180–184.

Renzulli, J. S. (1981). *The enrichment triad model.* Mansfield Center, CT: Creative Learning Press.

Renzulli, J. S. (Ed.). (1986). *Systems and models for developing programs for the gifted and talented.* Mansfield Center, CT: Creative Learning Press.

Renzulli, J. S. (1994). *Schools for talent development: A practical plan for total school improvement.* Mansfield Center, CT: Creative Learning Press.

Renzulli, J. S., Gentry, M., & Reis, S. (2003). *Enrichment clusters.* Mansfield Center, CT: Creative Learning Press.

Renzulli, J. S., Leppien, J. H., & Hays, T. S. (2000). *The multiple menu model: A practical guide for developing differentiated curriculum.* Mansfield Center, CT: Creative Learning Press.

Renzulli, J. S., & Reis, S. M. (1997). *The schoolwide enrichment model* (2nd ed.). Mansfield Center, CT: Creative Learning Press.

Renzulli, J. S., Reis, S., & Smith, L. (1981). *The revolving door identification model.* Mansfield Center, CT: Creative Learning Press.

Rogers, K. B. (2002). *Re-forming gifted education: Matching the program to the child.* Scottsdale, AZ: Great Potentials Press.

Rundle, S., & Dunn, R. (2005). *Building excellence survey.* Danbury, CT: Performance Concepts International.

Selby, E. C., Treffinger, D. J., & Isaksen, S. G. (2002). *VIEW: An assessment of problem solving style.* Sarasota, FL: Center for Creative Learning.

Selby, E. C., & Young, G. C. (2003). The Levels of Service approach to talent development: Parallels with existing programs. *Gifted Child Today, 26*(4), 44–50, 65.

Sternberg, R. (1986). *Intelligence applied.* New York: Harcourt Brace Jovanovich.

Taylor, C. W. (1978). How many types of giftedness can your program tolerate? *Journal of Creative Behavior, 12*(1), 39–51.

Taylor, C. W. (1985). Cultivating multiple creative talents in students. *Journal for the Education of the Gifted, 8*(3), 187–198.

Taylor, C. W., & Ellison, R. (1983). Searching for student talent resources relevant to all USDE types of giftedness. *Gifted Child Quarterly, 27*(3), 99–106.

Tomlinson, C. A. (2001). *How to differentiate instruction in mixed ability classrooms* (2nd ed.). Alexandria, VA: Association for Supervision and Curriculum Development.

Tomlinson, C. A. (2004). *The differentiated classroom: Responding to the needs of all learners.* Alexandria, VA: Association for Supervision and Curriculum Development.

Torrance, E. P. (1962). *Guiding creative talent.* Englewood Cliffs, NJ: Prentice Hall.

Torrance, E. P. (1987). Teaching for creativity. In S. G. Isaksen (Ed.), *Frontiers of creativity research: Beyond the basics* (pp. 189–215). Buffalo, NY: Bearly.

Torrance, E. P. (1989). *The search for Satori and creativity.* Buffalo, NY: Bearly.

Treffinger, D. J. (1981). *Blending gifted education with the total school program.* Buffalo, NY: DOK.

Treffinger, D. J. (1991). Creative productivity: Understanding its sources and nurture. *Illinois Council for the Gifted Journal, 10,* 6–8.

Treffinger, D. J. (1994, Fall). Productive thinking: Toward authentic instruction and assessment. *Journal for Secondary Education of the Gifted, 6*(1), 30–37.

Treffinger, D. J. (1998). From gifted education to programming for talent development. *Phi Delta Kappan, 79*(10), 752–755.

Treffinger, D. J., Isaksen, S. G., & Stead-Dorval, K. B. (2006). *Creative problem solving: An introduction* (4th ed.). Waco, TX: Prufrock Press.

Treffinger, D. J., & Nassab, C. A. (2005). *Thinking tool guides* (Rev. ed.). Sarasota, FL: Center for Creative Learning.

Treffinger, D. J., Nassab, C., Schoonover, P., Selby, E., Shepardson, C., Wittig, C., & Young, G. (2004a). *Thinking with standards: Preparing for tomorrow (Elementary).* Waco, TX: Prufrock Press.

Treffinger, D. J., Nassab, C., Schoonover, P., Selby, E., Shepardson, C., Wittig, C., & Young, G. (2004b). *Thinking with standards: Preparing for tomorrow (Middle).* Waco, TX: Prufrock Press.

Treffinger, D. J., Nassab, C., Schoonover, P., Selby, E., Shepardson, C., Wittig, C., & Young, G. (2004c). *Thinking with standards: Preparing for tomorrow (Secondary).* Waco, TX: Prufrock Press.

Treffinger, D. J., Nassab, C., Schoonover, P., Selby, E., Shepardson, C., Wittig, C., & Young, G. (2006). *The CPS Kit.* Waco, TX: Prufrock Press.

Treffinger, D. J., Selby, E. C., Isaksen, S. G., & Crumel, J. H. (2007). *An introduction to problem-solving style.* Sarasota, FL: Center for Creative Learning.

Treffinger, D. J., Young, G. C., Nassab, C. A., & Wittig, C. V. (2004a). *Beyond identification: Action planning for talent development.* Sarasota, FL: Center for Creative Learning.

Treffinger, D. J., Young, G. C., Nassab, C. A., & Wittig, C. V. (2004b). *Enhancing and expanding gifted programs: The levels of service approach.* Waco, TX: Prufrock Press.

Treffinger, D. J., Young, G. C., Nassab, C. A., & Wittig, C. V. (2004c). *Giftedness and talent: Nature and definition.* Sarasota, FL: Center for Creative Learning.

Ukens, L. (1996). *Getting together: Icebreakers and group energizers.* San Francisco: Jossey-Bass/Pfeiffer.

United States Department of Labor. (1991). *What work requires of schools: A SCANS report for America 2000.* Washington, DC: Author.

West, E. (1999). *The big book of icebreakers: Quick, fun activities for energizing meetings and workshops.* New York: McGraw-Hill.

Young, G. (1995a). Becoming a talent spotter. *Creative Learning Today, 5*(1), 4–5.

Young, G. (1995b). Celebrating creatively productive outcomes. *Creative Learning Today, 5*(3), 6–7.

Young, G. (1995c). Responding to and nurturing talent. *Creative Learning Today, 5*(2), 4–5.

Young, G. (1995d). Talent spotting: A practical approach. *Creative Learning Today, 5*(4), 6–7.

Index

Academic credit, 147
Acceleration, 32, 69, 147, 151–152f,
    208, 218
    Needs Assessment Inventory and,
        69, 74f, 78f
    wish lists and, 102f
Accomplishments/achievements:
    effective implementation of
        programming and, 155, 157
    evaluations and, 184, 188
    goals and outcomes for students
        and, 34
    identification and, 167
    implications for contemporary
        programming and, 26
    LoS and, 146, 147
    Needs Assessment Inventory
        and, 81
    professional partnership for talent
        development and, 158f
    public relations and, 202
    Student Action Planning and,
        169, 174, 176
    tenets and belief statements and, 31
Accountability, 46
Action planning, 11, 65
    effective implementation of
        programming and, 153, 156
    goals and outcomes for students
        and, 34
    identification and, 167–177, 168f,
        175f, 177f
    Master Plans and, 211
    planning committees and, 198
    tenets and belief statements and,
        32–33
    See also Planning; Student Action
        Planning
Activities:
    Building Action Plans and, 134,
        135, 138, 219
    challenging, 146f
    climate survey and, 92f, 93f
    effective implementation of
        programming and, 153, 154,
        156, 157
    evaluations and, 189, 193
    identification and, 167
    key elements of talent development
        programming and, 143f
    LoS and, 144, 149f
    Master Plans and, 212, 213
    monitoring, 174, 176

Needs Assessment Inventory and,
    70f, 75f
planning committees and, 200
professional partnership for talent
    development and, 158f
programming positives and,
    97, 98, 99, 200
public relations and, 202
Student Action Planning and, 171
student talent profile and, 174f
tenets and belief statements and, 32
Administration:
    Building Action Plans and,
        138, 219, 220
    communicating a vision to, 107
    educational changes and, 7
    evaluations and, 183, 188
    expectations for excellence and, 87
    future-oriented questions and, 108
    implementation of a contemporary
        approach to talent development
        and, 35
    Master Plans and, 205, 209, 210
    planning committees and, 49, 52
    See also Faculty; Staff members
A Nation at Risk, 5
Appreciation, 26, 44f, 54
    See also Recognition
Assessments:
    alternative methods of, 23
    evaluations and, 183
    Master Plans and, 206
    school improvement plans and, 46
    See also Testing
At-risk students, 196, 206
Autonomous Learner Model, 5
Awareness, 4, 10, 16
    Building Action Plans and, 125, 127f
    communities and, 64, 84f,
        128f, 157
    educational changes and, 7
    public relations and, 202
    six-stage systemic planning model
        and, 16

Belief statements, 31, 157
Benchmarks, 157, 169, 170
Best practices, 24, 43, 144
Betts, G., 5
Blanchard, K., 52, 97
Bloom, B. S., 22
Board members, 49–50, 130, 188,
    195f, 205

Budget implications:
    Building Action Plans and, 139,
        140f, 220–221
    Master Plans and, 211
Building Action Plans, 65, 105
    components of, 140
    constructing, 133–140,
        215–222, 217
    flexibility of, 201
    healthy school program and, 150
    six-stage systemic planning model
        and, 15f, 16
    template for, 140, 215–222
    updating, 198
    vision statements and, 116
    See also Planning
Building Excellence Survey, 55
Businesses in partnership programs,
    153, 156

Callahan, C. M., 188
Career perspectives:
    areas of school programs and, 99f
    Building Action Plans and, 138, 218
    effective implementation of
        programming and, 156
    LoS and, 151–152f
    Master Plans and, 208
    Needs Assessment Inventory and,
        69, 77–78f
    tenets and belief statements and,
        32, 33
    wish lists and, 102f
    See also Futuristic orientation
Carnevale, A., 45
Celebrations:
    effective implementation of
        programming and, 157
    expectations for excellence and, 88
    initial assessment form and, 30f
    Needs Assessment Inventory
        and, 81
    See also Recognition; Rewards
Center for Creative Learning, 31, 83
Change, 10
    agents of, 41–42
    challenges of, 37–48
    data and, 12, 17
    dealing with, 40–41
    decision making and, 7
    different styles for, 39–41, 42
    evaluations and, 196
    intelligence/talent and, 23

leadership and, 8, 54. *See also* Leadership
managing, 34
Needs Assessment Inventory and, 70f, 77f
rationale and goals for talent development and, 28
resistance to, 41, 43
responding to, 38–42
six-stage systemic planning model and, 17
tenets and belief statements and, 31
Chapman, C., 9
Child study team, 199
Classroom management, 7, 42–43
Climate, 87–99
Building Action Plans and, 136
effective implementation of programming and, 156
Master Plans and, 209
Climate Survey for Contemporary Programming, 91, 92–95f
Clustering, 145f, 156
Coaches, 139, 146, 169, 171
Coaching, 137, 170
Collaboration/cooperation:
change and, 41, 42
data and, 98
effective implementation of programming and, 157
implementation of a contemporary approach to talent development and, 35
leadership and, 54
planning committees and, 60
professional partnership for talent development and, 158f
Commitment, 10, 11
action and, 87
benefits of effective planning and, 14
Building Action Plans and, 134, 138, 139, 219, 220
change and, 41, 42
communicating a vision of, 107
evaluations and, 182
goals and outcomes for students and, 33
implementation of, 34, 89
LoS and, 146, 147
Master Plans and, 205, 209, 210, 212
Needs Assessment Inventory and, 80, 81
planning committees and, 52, 54
six-stage systemic planning model and, 15f, 16, 19
success and, 9
talent spotting and, 171
tenets and belief statements and, 32, 33
Communication, 10
agents of change and, 42
benefits of effective planning and, 14
evaluations and, 183
expectations for excellence and, 88
initial assessment form and, 30f

Needs Assessment Inventory and, 81
new basics for, 45f
planning committees and, 51, 52, 197
school-community relations and, 197, 202
technology and, 38
Communities:
Building Action Plans and, 135, 198
climate survey and, 93f, 94f
communicating a vision to, 107
contemporary approach to talent development and, 29, 35
effective implementation of programming and, 156, 157
expectations for excellence and, 88
identification and, 165
key elements of talent development programming and, 143f
leadership and, 54
linking school improvement and talent development and, 47
Master Plans and, 205, 207
Needs Assessment Inventory and, 81
new approaches to teaching and learning and, 43
planning committees and, 49, 50, 52, 197, 200
professional partnership for talent development and, 158f
resources and, 29, 43, 44f, 143, 153, 156, 187f, 200
six-stage systemic planning model and, 19
support and, 46
tenets and belief statements and, 32
Competence, 9, 41, 45, 54, 138, 197
Conferences, 81, 85f, 126, 127f, 129, 194, 198
Confidence:
change and, 38–39
goals and outcomes for students and, 33, 34
needs assessment and, 70f, 76f, 78f
professional development and, 130
staff members and, 199
success and, 9
talent spotting checklist and, 173f
Confidentiality, 79, 80–81
Control, 41
Costa, A. L., 153
Council for Exceptional Children (CEC), 5
Counselors, 49, 76f, 176
CPS Kit, 153
Creative/critical thinking, 156
Building Action Plans and, 134, 136
change and, 41, 42
effective programming and, 153, 200
initial assessment form and, 30f
LoS and, 144, 148f
new basics for, 45f
talent spotters and, 170
See also Thinking skills

Creative Problem Solving (CPS), 134, 153, 176, 177f
Crumel, J. H., 39
Culture:
Building Action Plans and, 136
climate and, 89, 94f
goals for contemporary approach to talent development and, 29
initial assessment form and, 30f
Master Plans and, 209
responsibilities of schools and, 29
Curiosity:
activities and, 98
Building Action Plans and, 133
LoS and, 144
tenets and belief statements and, 31
Curriculum:
Building Action Plans and, 133
change and, 7, 38
effective implementation of programming and, 154, 156, 159f
evaluations and, 184
implementation of a contemporary approach to talent development and, 34
key elements of talent development programming and, 143f
Needs Assessment Inventory and, 79
programming positives and, 98
school improvement plans and, 46
Curriculum enhancement teams, 156

Data:
Building Action Plans and, 137, 139, 217, 220, 222
change and, 12
collaboration and, 98
effective implementation of programming and, 155
evaluations and, 183, 188, 189, 192, 193
history and, 90
identification and, 165–167
improvements and, 12
learning styles and, 42
Master Plans and, 213
multiple sources of, 169
Needs Assessment Inventory and, 79, 80
new generations and, 8
planning committees and, 65
policies and, 196
six-stage systemic planning model and, 15f, 17
Student Action Planning and, 168f, 169, 170, 171, 176
student talent profile and, 174f
tenets and belief statements and, 33
views of giftedness and, 26
vision statements and, 116
Data sources, 82–83, 84–85f
Decision making:
activities and, 140
benefits of effective planning and, 14

Building Action Plans and,
135, 217
change and, 7
data and, 12, 83
effective programming and,
153, 156, 157, 200
evaluations and, 179, 182, 184,
188, 189
future actions and, 105
goals and outcomes for students
and, 33
identification and, 164
implementation of a contemporary
approach to talent development
and, 35
initial assessment form and, 30f
intelligence/talent and, 24
linking school improvement and
talent development and, 47
long-range planning and, 202
Master Plans and, 206
new basics for, 45f
new generation of programming
for talent development and, 6
planning committees and, 17, 50,
51, 56, 58, 59, 65, 200
programming at the district wide
level and, 63
six-stage systemic planning model
and, 17
Student Action Planning
and, 171, 174
See also Problem solving
Department of Labor, 45
Differentiated basics:
fundamental tenets and beliefs
and, 32
LoS and, 151–152f
Needs Assessment Inventory and,
69, 70f, 72f, 78f
wish lists and, 102f
District level *See* School districts
Diversity, 6, 21, 25, 28, 38, 63,
137, 208, 217
Dorval, K. B., 56, 88, 89, 91, 176
Dunn, R., 9, 55

Educators *See* Administration; Faculty;
Staff members; Teachers
Ekvall, G., 89, 91
Encouragement, 31, 32, 44f, 127f
Evaluations, 8, 179, 181–183
conducting, 192–193
continuing, 201–202
data and, 12, 17
elements of effective, 183,
188–189
innovations/change and, 196
LoS and, 190–192f, 195f
Master Plans and, 119, 120, 130,
132, 186f
preparing for, 192
reporting findings/follow-ups
and, 193
unique challenges in, 184–185f
Evaluation sources, 186–187f
Executive summary, 64, 132
Experience:
Building Action Plans and, 135
LoS and, 144

Needs Assessment Inventory
and, 72f
new approaches to teaching and
learning and, 43
student talent profile and, 174f
tenets and belief statements and, 32

Faculty:
decision making and, 122
Master Plans and, 205
meetings and, 101
mission statements and, 124
support and, 138, 219. *See also*
Support
wish lists and, 101
See also Administration; Staff
members; Teachers
Families:
challenges of innovation and
change and, 37, 38
identification and, 165
support and, 124
Feedback, 203
evaluations and, 192
identification and, 166
Needs Assessment Inventory and,
79–81
Feldhusen, J. F., 5, 8, 43
Field trips, 44f, 148f, 151f, 154
Fluency, 188
Forbes, R., 45
Fundamental tenets and belief
statements, 31
Funding, 4
Building Action Plans and, 139
creative, 157
data and, 83, 85f
evaluations and, 184, 189
Master Plans and, 209
Future statement worksheet, 115f
Futuristic orientation:
areas of school programs and, 99f
Building Action Plans and, 218
LoS and, 151–152f
Master Plans and, 208
metaphors and, 110, 115
Needs Assessment Inventory and,
69, 77–78f
vision and, 108
wish lists and, 102f
See also Career perspectives; Goals

Gainer, L., 45
Gardner, H., 22, 43
Gentry, M., 8
Giftedness:
contemporary understandings
of, 28
definition of, 21–22, 24
determining who are, 33
Marland report and, 4
tenets and belief statements and, 32
Gisi, L., 45
Goals, 10
assessing needs and, 69
benefits of effective planning and, 13
Building Action Plans and, 134,
136, 139, 140f, 216, 218, 219
change and, 41. *See also* Change
climate and, 89, 93f

contemporary approach to talent
development and, 29, 30f
continuous improvement and,
196–197
data and, 83
effective implementation of
programming and, 155
evaluations and, 182, 183, 188
foundations for a contemporary
programming and, 21
future and, 107–117, 108f
identification and,
163–164, 164, 167
identifying important, 33–34
indicators of quality and, 193
leadership and, 54
Master Plans and, 132f, 207, 209
Needs Assessment Inventory and,
70f, 75f, 79, 80
planning committees and, 87, 200
programming positives and,
105, 200
school improvement plans
and, 46
six-stage systemic planning model
and, 15f, 16, 19
Student Action Planning and, 168f
student talent profile and, 174f
talent development and, 28–29
talent spotting and, 171
tenets and belief statements and, 33
See also Planning
Grades, 169
Grants, 83, 157
See also Funding
Gregory, G. H., 9
Groups:
change and, 41
effective implementation of
programming and, 154, 157
LoS and, 146, 147
Needs Assessment Inventory
and, 82
planning committees and, 51
planning for, 49
school improvement plans and, 46
See also Planning committees; Teams
Guilford, J. P., 22, 43

Hammer, A., 55
Handouts, 10
Hays, T. S., 8
Heacox, D., 9
Healthy conditions, 33, 135, 150, 183
Hersey, P., 52
Home environments:
challenges of innovation and
change and, 27, 38
ecosystem for talent development
and, 44f
new approaches to teaching and
learning and, 43
tenets and belief statements and, 32
Homework, 35, 44f
Human intelligence *See* Intelligence

Identification, 12, 161, 165f
action planning and, 167–177,
168f, 175f, 177f
Building Action Plans and, 135

new challenges and directions
for, 27
principles of, 165–167
shift in approach to, 164f
tenets and belief statements and, 32
Improvement teams, 139
Independence:
areas of school programs and, 99f
Building Action Plans and,
135, 138, 218
climate and, 89, 92f
goals and outcomes for students
and, 33, 34
linking school improvement and
talent development and, 47
LoS and, 144, 151–152f
Master Plans and, 208
Needs Assessment Inventory and,
69, 75f, 78f
tenets and belief statements and, 32
wish lists and, 102f
Individuality, 8, 29, 30f
Individualized Program Planning Model
(IPPM), 5
Initiatives:
Building Action Plans and,
139, 140f, 221
evaluations and, 183
federal support for new, 4
school improvement, 9, 19, 44, 46
Innovation, 10
Building Action Plans and, 138
challenges of, 37–48
evaluations and, 196
implementation of a contemporary
approach to talent development
and, 34
responding to, 38–42
six-stage systemic planning model
and, 15f, 17
Inservice:
Building Action Plans and, 220
data and, 82, 84f, 85f
effective implementation of
programming and, 154
implementation guidelines
and, 125
LoS program evaluation questions
and, 191
Master Plans and, 126, 127f, 128f,
129, 210
Needs Assessment Inventory and,
71f, 83, 84f, 85f
planning committees and, 199
Intelligence:
definitions of, 21–22, 24
expanding views of, 42
new approaches to teaching and
learning and, 42
Intelligence and talent (I/T), 23–24
Interests:
activities and, 98
Building Action Plans and, 133,
135, 136, 137, 217, 218
continuous improvement and, 197
effective implementation of
programming and,
154, 155, 159f
goals and outcomes for students
and, 33

identification and, 164, 165, 166,
167, 176
key elements of talent development
programming and, 143f
LoS and, 146, 147
Master Plans and, 207, 208
Needs Assessment Inventory and, 72f
new approaches to teaching and
learning and, 43
planning committees and, 199
professional partnership for talent
development and, 158f
programming positives and, 97
Student Action Planning and,
168–169, 169, 171
student talent profile and, 174f
talent spotting and, 171
tenets and belief statements
and, 32
wish lists and, 101
Interviews:
data collection and, 192
examples of, 189, 195f
talent spotting and, 169
Isaksen, S. G., 3, 39, 55, 56,
88, 89, 91, 176

Johnson, D., 52

Kolloff, M. B., 5
Kouzes, J. M., 54

Labeling:
Building Action Plans and, 137
evolving tasks and, 48f
identification and, 163–164
Master Plans and, 207
Student Action Planning
and, 176–177
tenets and belief statements
and, 32
Latchkey children, 37
Lauer, K. J., 89, 91
Leadership, 10
benefits of effective planning
and, 14–15
Building Action Plans and,
138, 140f
change and, 8, 41, 54. *See also*
Change
developmental conception of, 49
goals and outcomes for students
and, 33
new approaches to teaching and
learning and, 43
new basics for, 45f
planning committees and,
52, 54–55, 56, 198
research on, 54
responsibilities of schools and, 28
six-stage systemic planning model
and, 19
staff development opportunities
and, 199
tenets and belief statements and, 33
Learning styles:
Building Action Plans and, 137,
217, 221
change and, 38, 42

effective implementation of
programming and, 155, 156
LoS and, 144, 148f
Master Plans and, 206
Needs Assessment Inventory
and, 72f
new basics for, 45f
resources for, 153
tenets and belief statements
and, 31
Legislation, 4, 6, 38, 58f
Leppien, J. H., 8
Levels of Service (LoS), 35–36, 141,
143, 151–152f
Building Action Plans and, 134,
135, 218
effective implementation of
programming and, 158
evaluations and,
189, 190–192f, 195f
examples of, 148f, 195f
Master Plans and, 208
planning committees and, 199
programming for a few students
and, 147, 150
programming for all students
and, 144
programming for many students
and, 144, 146
programming for some students
and, 146
programming for talent
development and, 148f
programming parallels and, 149f
resources and, 194f
talent development programming
and, 143–144
Literacy skills, 138

Mandates, 9, 12, 124, 164, 191f
Marland report, 4, 7
Master Plans, 11, 64, 65, 105
constructing, 119–132,
205–213
effective management of
programming and, 199
finalizing, 140
flexibility of, 201
format of, 132
length of, 132
reviewing, 198
school districts and, 157, 186f
six-stage systemic planning model
and, 15f, 16
vision statements and, 116
See also Planning
McCaulley, M., 55
Meltzer, A., 45
Mentoring:
components of talent and, 26f
effective implementation of
programming and, 153, 156
LoS and, 147, 148f, 149f
Needs Assessment Inventory
and, 82
new approaches to teaching and
learning and, 43
Student Action Planning and, 176
Metacognitive skills, 26f, 156f, 170f
Metaphors, 108, 110, 173f

Mission statements, 108
climate survey and, 92f
examples of, 124
Master Plans and, 205
willingness and, 90
Models, 9
benefits of effective planning
and, 14
data and, 83, 84f
educational changes and, 7
expectations for excellence and, 87
leadership and, 54
new generation and, 8
six-stage systematic planning,
15–17, 15f
Monitoring, 174, 176, 210
Moral principles, 29
Music programs, 147, 149f
Myers, I., 55
Myers-Briggs Type Indicator, 55

Nassab, C. A., 8, 12, 35, 56, 99, 141,
143, 153
National Association for Gifted Children
(NAGC), 5
National/State Leadership Training
Institute on the Gifted/
Talented, 4–5
A Nation at Risk, 5
Needs:
activities and, 98
assessing, 67, 69–85
Building Action Plans and, 134,
137, 140f, 217, 220, 221
change and, 41
continuous improvement and, 197
data and, 83
effective implementation of
programming and, 154, 155,
156, 157–158, 159f
evaluations and, 183
identification and, 164, 166,
167–168, 176
Master Plans and, 207, 208, 209
Needs Assessment Inventory and,
70–78f, 70f, 76f
new approaches to teaching and
learning and, 43
planning committees and,
199–200
professional partnership for talent
development and, 158f
school improvement plans and, 46
Student Action Planning and, 169,
171, 174, 176
willingness and, 90
Needs Assessment Inventory, 69,
70–78f, 79
feedback/discussing results and,
79–81
programming positives and, 99
scores for, 79–82
staff development/training and,
81–82
Neglect, 37
Newsletters, 81, 128f
No Child Left Behind (NCLB), 6

Observation:
Building Action Plans and, 137
LoS and, 146

Student Action Planning and,
168f, 169, 170
talent spotting and, 171
tenets and belief statements and, 33
Organizational climate, 43, 88, 89
Organization skills, 10
effective implementation of
programming and, 156
expectations for excellence and, 87
intelligence/talent and, 24
new basics for, 45f

Parents:
answering questions from, 202
Building Action Plans and,
135, 198, 219
communicating a vision to, 107
effective implementation of
programming and, 156
evaluations and, 188
linking school improvement and
talent development and, 47
Master Plans and, 205, 207
planning committees and, 49, 50, 52
six-stage systemic planning model
and, 19
Student Action Planning and, 176
Parker, M., 107
Partnerships, 43, 157–158
Performance tasks, 33
Personal growth:
areas of school programs and, 99f
Building Action Plans and, 218
LoS and, 151–152f
Master Plans and, 208
Needs Assessment Inventory and,
69, 70–78f
tenets and belief statements and, 32
wish lists and, 102f
Philosophy, 10
Building Action Plans and, 135,
140f, 198, 215–216
data and, 83
expectations for excellence and, 88
Master Plans and, 132f
planning committees and, 52
six-stage systemic planning model
and, 15f, 16, 19
Philosophy statements, 120–121, 123,
157, 205
Planning, 3, 9, 10, 11, 31
assessing needs and, 69
benefits of effective, 13–15
change and, 7, 40, 41
climate and, 96
committees and, 197, 199
data and, 83
definition of talent and, 25
early 1970s and, 4
early 1980s and, 5
evaluations and, 182, 183
expectations for excellence and, 88
ideas and, 101, 103
identification and, 167
implementation of a contemporary
approach to talent development
and, 35
late 1970s, 4–5
learning styles and, 42
linking school improvement and
talent development and, 46–47

logistics of, 49–65
long-range, 44, 201–202
Needs Assessment Inventory and,
79, 80
new generation and, 6, 8
time and, 32
two levels of, 63
vision statements and, 116
See also Action planning; Building
Action Plans; Goals; Master
Plans; Student Action Planning
Planning activities checklist, 17, 18f
Planning committees, 10
Action Plans and, 198
behavior guidelines for, 55, 56
Building Action Plans and, 134
communication and, 51, 52
community and parent
participation in, 50
decision making and, 17, 50, 51, 65
definitions and, 21
diagnostic assessments and,
199–200
extending enrichment
opportunities for many
students and, 200
getting acquainted and, 55
goals and, 87
icebreaker activities for, 55, 63
idea killers for, 57f, 58
leadership and, 52, 54–55, 56
meeting agenda form for, 61f
meeting outcomes record for, 62f
members form for, 53f
philosophy and values of, 52
progressive outlook for, 54, 59–60
public relations and, 202
responsibilities and, 60, 65
role of, 197
school board participation in, 49–50
size of, 51
staff development opportunities
and, 199
start-up questions for, 65
student participation in, 50
successful, 49–50
understanding and applying
generating and focusing tools
for, 55, 56, 58–59
wish lists and, 200
working communities and, 60, 63
Policies:
consistency of, 201
continuous improvement and, 197
data and, 196
evaluations and, 183, 184
planning committees and, 49–50, 51
school improvement plans and, 46
Politics, 6, 37, 43, 63
Portfolios:
data and, 169
evaluations and, 187f, 188
Master Plans and, 123
Student Action Planning and, 174
tenets and belief statements and, 33
Posner, B., 54
Privacy, 79, 80–81
Problem solving, 10
Building Action Plans and,
134, 150, 219
change and, 41, 42

contemporary approach to talent development and, 34, 35
different styles for, 39–41
effective programming and, 153, 154, 156, 157, 200
evaluations and, 188
indicators of quality and, 193
initial assessment form and, 30f
intelligence/talent and, 24
Master Plans and, 209
new approaches to teaching and learning and, 43
new basics for, 45f
planning committees and, 200
rationale and goals for talent development and, 28
resources for, 153
Student Action Planning and, 176
talent spotters and, 170
See also Decision making
Productivity:
adult models and, 87
goals and outcomes for students and, 33
goals for contemporary approach to talent development and, 29
implications for contemporary programming and, 26
tenets and belief statements and, 31
Professional development:
effective implementation of programming and, 157
Master Plans and, 132f
school improvement plans and, 46
tenets and belief statements and, 33
Profiling, 32, 156, 174–176, 199
Programming Climate Survey, 11
Programming positives, 97–100, 100f, 101–103
Building Action Plans and, 133–134
future-oriented questions and, 108
goals and, 105
maintaining, 109f
searching for, 101, 103
sustaining, 200
tips for identifying, 98–99
vision statements and, 116
Psychological climate, 89
Psychologists, 49
Psychology, 4, 31, 42–43
Public relations, 197, 202
expectations for excellence and, 87
professional partnership for talent development and, 158f
See also Communities
Purcell, J. H., 8
Purdue Three-Stage Model, 5
Purpose statements, 108

Quenk, N., 55

Rating scales, 33, 194f
Recognition:
appreciation and, 26, 44f, 54
awards and, 194, 202
change and, 41
effective implementation of programming and, 157
evaluations and, 183

expectations for excellence and, 88
giftedness and, 4
goals for contemporary approach to talent development and, 29
identification and, 165
initial assessment form and, 30f
LoS and, 147
planning committees and, 199
programs for, 81
tenets and belief statements and, 32
See also Celebrations
Reis, S., 8, 163
Renzulli, J. S., 5, 8, 22, 163
Report cards, 169
Resources, 10
Building Action Plans and, 133, 135, 138, 139, 140f, 219, 220–221
challenging, 87
change and, 38–39
climate and, 88–89, 92f, 93f, 94f
data and, 83, 85f
diagnostic assessments and, 200
effective evaluations and, 179
effective implementation of programming and, 153, 154, 156
goals and, 29, 34
identification and, 166
initial assessment form and, 30f
key elements of talent development programming and, 143f
linking school improvement and talent development and, 47
Master Plans and, 132f, 210, 211
Needs Assessment Inventory and, 70f, 75f, 82
new approaches to teaching and learning and, 43
planning committees and, 198
professional partnership for talent development and, 158f
six-stage systemic planning model and, 19
tenets and belief statements and, 32
Web-based, 35, 38
Respect, 51, 93f, 94f, 137
Responsibility:
benefits of effective planning and, 14
change and, 41
climate survey and, 93f
committees and, 202
effective implementation of programming and, 157–158
leadership and, 55
LoS and, 144
planning committees and, 60, 65
rationale and goals for talent development and, 28–29
school districts and, 63
schools and, 32
wish lists and, 110
Rewards:
Building Action Plans and, 136
change and, 41
expectations for excellence and, 88
goals for contemporary approach to talent development and, 29
initial assessment form and, 30f
See also Celebrations; Recognition

Risk taking:
climate and, 90, 96
implementation of a contemporary approach to talent development and, 34, 35
Student Action Planning and, 170
tenets and belief statements and, 31
Rogers, K. B., 8
Role modeling, 156
Rundle, S., 55

Scaffolding, 137
School board associations, 55
School boards, 49–50, 55, 121, 122, 126, 131f, 191f, 195f
School-business partnerships, 43
School districts:
assessing climate of, 67
consistency of policies and, 201
data and, 84f
expectations for excellence and, 87, 88
implementation of a contemporary approach to talent development and, 34
linking school improvement and talent development in, 46–47
Master Plans and, 186f, 209, 211
metaphors and, 110
Needs Assessment Inventory and, 80–81
planning committees and, 49, 199
professional partnership for talent development and, 158f
programming positives and, 200
responsibilities of, 63
support and, 201. *See also* Support
willingness and, 90–91
Schools:
assessing climate of, 67. *See also* Climate
challenges of innovation and change and, 37–48. *See also* Change
data and, 84f
ecosystem for talent development and, 44f
expectations for excellence and, 87, 88
metaphors and, 110
responsibilities and, 28–29, 32
tenets and belief statements and, 32
uniqueness of, 136–137, 140f
willingness and, 90–91
Schoonover, P., 56, 153
Science, 28, 42, 146, 149f, 166, 170
Screening, 48f, 163, 164, 199
See also Identification
Selby, E. C., 39, 55, 56, 153
Self-assessments, 30f, 55, 166, 194f
Self-direction, 69
areas of school programs and, 99f
Building Action Plans and, 138, 218
effective implementation of programming and, 156
goals for contemporary approach to talent development and, 29
identification and, 166

initial assessment form and, 30f
linking school improvement and
    talent development and, 47
LoS and, 151–152f
Master Plans and, 208
Needs Assessment Inventory
    and, 69, 75f, 78f
tenets and belief statements
    and, 32
wish lists and, 102f
Self-esteem, 45f, 135
Self-management, 193
Seminars, 82, 129, 154
Shepardson, C., 56, 153
Skills:
    Building Action Plans and,
        137, 138, 220
    change and, 7, 38–39
    cooperative, 43
    effective programming and,
        155, 200
    goals and outcomes for students
        and, 33
    initial assessment form and, 30f
    Master Plans and, 210
    Needs Assessment Inventory
        and, 72f, 82
    new approaches to teaching and
        learning and, 43
    new basics for, 45f
    school improvement plans and, 46
Smith, L., 163
Social development:
    areas of school programs and, 99f
    Building Action Plans and, 218
    goals and outcomes for students
        and, 33
    LoS and, 151–152f
    Master Plans and, 208
    Needs Assessment Inventory
        and, 69, 76f, 78f
    tenets and belief statements
        and, 32
    wish lists and, 102f
Specialists:
    planning committees and, 49
    professional partnership for talent
        development and, 158f
    Student Action Planning and, 176
Special needs students, 29, 206
Staff development:
    Building Action Plans and,
        138, 140f
    data and, 85f
    intelligence/talent and, 23
    Needs Assessment Inventory
        and, 81–82
    preparation for implementation
        and, 198
    professional partnership for talent
        development and, 158f
    stimulating opportunities for, 199
    time for program development
        and, 64
Staff members:
    answering questions from, 202
    Building Action Plans and, 133,
        134, 135, 138, 219, 220
    communicating a vision to, 107
    continuous learning and, 157

effective implementation of
    programming and, 156
evaluations and, 188
expectations for excellence
    and, 87, 88
implementation of a contemporary
    approach to talent development
    and, 35
linking school improvement and
    talent development and, 47
Master Plans and, 205, 207, 209
planning committees and,
    49, 198, 200
professional development for, 33
programming positives and, 101
recognition of, 157. *See also*
    Recognition
six-stage systemic planning model
    and, 19
tenets and belief statements
    and, 32
See also Administration; Faculty
Standardized achievement tests,
    137, 188, 196
See also Testing
Standards:
    Building Action Plans and, 221
    challenges of innovation and
        change and, 38
    Master Plans and, 206
    NCLB and, 6
    quality and, 193
Stanley, J., 196
Statistics, 24, 26, 69, 107, 164, 169
Stead-Dorval, K. B., 56, 176
Steering committees, 139, 193, 195f
Sternberg, R., 22
Student Action Planning,
    161, 163–177, 168f
    collaborative problem solving
        and, 176
    identification and, 167–177
    monitoring, 174, 176
    profiles and, 174–176, 175f
    talent spotting and, 169–173,
        172f, 173f
    See also Action planning; Planning
Students:
    Building Action Plans and,
        134, 135, 138
    communicating a vision to, 107
    extending enrichment
        opportunities for, 200
    goals and outcomes for, 33–34
    implementation of a contemporary
        approach to talent development
        and, 35
    Master Plans and, 205, 207
    planning committees and, 49, 50
    recognition of, 157. *See also*
        Recognition
    strengths/weaknesses and, 43
    Student Action Planning and, 176
Student talent profile, 171, 174, 174f
Subcommittees, 51, 199
Success, 183
    benefits of effective planning
        and, 14
    Building Action Plans and, 138
    climate survey and, 93f, 94f

continuous improvement and, 197
evaluations and, 189
healthy school program and, 150
history and, 90
implementing contemporary
    programming and, 153
initial assessment form and, 30f
Master Plans and, 211
Needs Assessment Inventory
    and, 81, 82
planning committees and, 50
programming positives and, 200
time for program development
    and, 64
Support:
    benefits of effective planning
        and, 14, 15
    Building Action Plans and,
        138, 139, 219, 221
    change and, 38–39
    climate and, 88–89, 96
    communities and, 46. *See also*
        Communities
    continuing evaluation efforts
        and, 201
    effective evaluations and, 179
    effective implementation of
        programming and,
        155, 156, 157
    evaluations and, 182, 183, 188
    expectations for excellence
        and, 87, 88
    goals for contemporary approach
        to talent development and, 29
    LoS and, 146, 147
    Master Plans and, 208, 209, 210
    Needs Assessment Inventory and,
        70f, 76f, 79, 80
    planning committees and, 54.
        See also Planning committees
    professional partnership for talent
        development and, 158f
    programming positives and, 200.
        See also Programming positives
    six-stage systemic planning model
        and, 15f, 16, 19
    tenets and belief statements
        and, 31, 32
Surveys:
    Building Action Plans and, 135
    climate and, 92–95f
    LoS program evaluation questions
        and, 190–192f

Talent spotting:
    Building Action Plans and,
        135, 137, 139
    professional partnership for talent
        development and, 158f
    six-stage systemic planning model
        and, 17
    Student Action Planning and,
        169–173, 172f, 173f
    tenets and belief statements
        and, 32
Teacher preparation programs, 82
Teachers:
    Building Action Plans and,
        138, 219, 220
    change and, 43

effective implementation of
programming and, 157
future-oriented questions
and, 108
Master Plans and, 210
planning committees and,
49, 52
professional partnership for talent
development and, 158f
responsibilities of, 29
sharing ideas and, 156
Student Action Planning and, 176
talent spotters and, 137. *See also*
Talent spotting
See also Administration; Faculty;
Staff members
Teams:
Building Action Plans and, 134
change and, 40, 41
effective implementation of
programming and, 156, 157
goals and outcomes for students
and, 33
Needs Assessment Inventory
and, 82
new approaches to teaching
and learning and, 43
planning committees and, 51
See also Groups
Teamwork, 35, 45f
Technology:
challenges of innovation and
change and, 38
effective programming and,
156, 200
goals and outcomes for students
and, 34
new approaches to teaching and
learning and, 43
planning committees and, 50
responsibilities of schools and, 28
Tenets and belief statements, 31–33
Testing:
Building Action Plans and, 137
challenges of innovation and
change and, 38
evaluations and, 188
identification and, 166
intelligence/talent and, 23
interpreting results of, 196
NCLB and, 6
tenets and belief statements
and, 33
views of giftedness and, 26
See also Assessments
Test scores:
Building Action Plans and, 136
effective implementation of
programming and, 155
identification and, 167
interpreting results of, 196
public relations and, 202
Thinking skills:
activities and, 140
Building Action Plans and,
137, 139, 221
different ways of, 42
effective implementation of
programming and,
153, 154, 156

goals and outcomes for students
and, 33
goals for contemporary approach
to talent development and, 29
implementation of a contemporary
approach to talent development
and, 34
initial assessment form and, 30f
intelligence/talent and, 24
linking school improvement and
talent development and, 47
Master Plans and, 206
new basics for, 45f
productive, 26f, 123, 135, 153,
156, 170, 193
professional partnership for talent
development and, 158f
school improvement plans and, 46
See also Creative/critical thinking
Tidd, J., 55
Time:
benefits of effective planning
and, 14
change and, 41, 43
climate and, 89, 92f, 93f
continuous improvement
and, 197
definition of talent and, 25
diagnostic assessments and, 200
effective implementation of
programming and, 156, 157
establishing a working community
and, 60
evaluations and, 183
fear/frustration and, 38
implementation of a contemporary
approach to talent development
and, 34, 35
LoS and, 144, 146
Master Plans and, 132f, 209
meetings and, 101
planning and, 32
planning committees and, 51
professional partnership for talent
development and, 158f
program development and, 64
programming positives and, 101
Student Action Planning and,
169, 170
talent spotting and, 171
wish lists and, 110
Time lines:
Building Action Plans and, 139,
140f, 221
Master Plans and, 211–212
program development and, 65
student talent profile and, 174f
Tomlinson, C. A., 9
Torrance, E. P., 22
Training:
Building Action Plans and, 220
data and, 83
effective implementation of
programming and, 157
evaluations and, 183
intelligence/talent and, 23
Master Plans and, 209, 210, 211
Needs Assessment Inventory
and, 81–82
Student Action Planning and, 170

Treffinger, D. J., 5, 8, 9, 12
climate and, 88, 89, 91
CPS and, 176
definition of giftedness and, 22
identification and, 163
LoS and, 35, 141, 143, 153
planning committees and, 55, 56
problem solving and, 39
programming positives and, 99
talent spotters and, 170
tenets and belief statements
and, 32
thinking skills and, 153
Trust, 89, 91

Ukens, L., 63
U.S. Bureau on the Gifted and
Talented, 4
U.S. Department of Labor, 45

Values:
agents of change and, 42
Building Action Plans and, 136
culture and, 89
data and, 83
goals and outcomes for students
and, 34
leadership and, 54
planning committees and, 52
Videoconferencing, 138, 139
VIEW assessment, 55, 153
Vision:
Building Action Plans and, 217
climate and, 89
data and, 83
goals and, 107–108. *See also* Goals
metaphors and, 110
willingness and, 90
Vision statements,
108, 116, 132f, 205
Vision statement worksheet, 117f
Volunteers, 85f, 219

Web sites:
Center for Creative Learning
and, 31, 83
problem solving style and, 39
resources and, 153
West, E., 63
Wish lists, 101–103, 102f
Building Action Plans and, 134,
136, 138, 218
effective implementation of
programming and, 154
future and, 108
identifying, 67
Master Plans and, 208
metaphors and, 110
planning committees and, 200
searching for, 101, 103
six-stage systemic planning model
and, 16
vision statements and, 116
worksheets for, 113f, 114f
Wittig, C. V., 8, 12, 35, 56, 99, 141,
143, 153
Workshops, 98, 198

Young, G. C., 8, 12, 35, 56, 99, 141,
143, 153, 169

**CORWIN
PRESS**

The Corwin Press logo—a raven striding across an open book—represents the union of courage and learning. Corwin Press is committed to improving education for all learners by publishing books and other professional development resources for those serving the field of PreK–12 education. By providing practical, hands-on materials, Corwin Press continues to carry out the promise of its motto: **"Helping Educators Do Their Work Better."**